D1013410

Putting

Amazing

Back into

Grace

Putting
Amazing
Back into

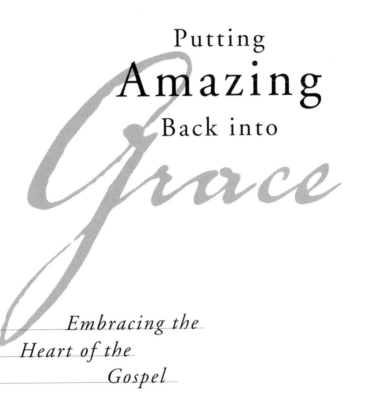

*Embracing the
Heart of the
Gospel*

Second Edition

Michael Horton
Foreword by J. I. Packer

Baker Books
A Division of Baker Book House Co
Grand Rapids, Michigan 49516

© 1991, 1994, 2002 by Michael Scott Horton

Second edition published in 2002.

Previously published in 1994 by Baker Book House Company.

Previously published in 1991 by Thomas Nelson

Published by Baker Books
a division of Baker Book House Company
P.O. Box 6287, Grand Rapids, Michigan 49516-6287

Third printing, January 2005

Printed in the United States of America

All rights reserved. No part of this publication may be reproduced, stored in a retrieval system, or transmitted in any form or by any means—for example, electronic, photocopy, recording—without the prior written permission of the publisher. The only exception is brief quotations in printed reviews.

Library of Congress Cataloging-in-Publication Data

Horton, Michael Scott.
 Putting amazing back into grace : embracing the heart of the Gospel /
Michael Horton ; foreword by J. I. Packer. —[Rev. ed.].
     p.   cm.
 Includes bibliographical references.
 ISBN 0-8010-6400-7
 1. Salvation. 2. Salvation—Biblical teaching. 3. Grace (Theology)
4. Grace (Theology)—Biblical teaching. I. Title.
 BT751.3 .H68 2002
 234—dc21   2002018316

Except where noted otherwise, Scripture quotations are from the HOLY BIBLE, NEW INTERNATIONAL VERSION®. NIV®. Copyright © 1973, 1978, 1984 by International Bible Society. Used by permission of Zondervan. All rights reserved.

Scripture quotations noted NASB are from THE NEW AMERICAN STANDARD BIBLE ®. Copyright © The Lockman Foundation 1960, 1962, 1963, 1968, 1971, 1972, 1973, 1975, 1977, 1995. Used by permission.

Scripture quotations noted NEB are from *The New English Bible.* Copyright © 1961, 1970, 1989 by The Delegates of Oxford University Press and The Syndics of the Cambridge University Press. Reprinted by permission.

Contents

Foreword

Once upon a time, people in the Christian world knew that the most important issues anyone faces are those of eternity. They knew that God the Creator is pure and holy, that we are in his hands, and that one day we must give an account to him. They knew that none of us is naturally fit to do that and that the quest for salvation—not from our pain, misery, poverty, and exploitation, but from the guilt and power of our sins— is life's top priority.

In those days, the study of redemption was everyone's concern, and God's plan of salvation was a matter of general interest. Today, however, it is not so.

Why is that? Not because the problem has ceased to exist. God and people are the same, and the need for salvation remains as acute as it ever was. But we have become distracted by the urgent pace of our culture, preoccupied with the material things we can produce and possess, obsessed with the myth that science has displaced Christianity. We know so many facts about our world, we believe that we are the wisest generation in history, and therefore, we cannot stoop to accept the wisdom of our ancestors. Thus, with all our technological expertise and intellectual arrogance, we have become the cleverest fools in world history.

Mike Horton has seen through all the excuses and appreciates that true and timeless wisdom is found in the paths of the Christian gospel. *Putting Amazing Back into Grace* expresses the thrill of his soul—and mine—as we gaze upon the triumph of God's almighty grace through the life, death, resurrection, present

7

reign, and future return of the Mediator, "God incarnate, man divine," our Lord and Savior Jesus Christ.

Horton says it the way the early Reformers and St. Augustine said it: sin has made us utterly impotent for real godliness in any shape or form, and it takes omnipotent mercy from the Father, Son, and Holy Spirit to save us. I commend most heartily Mike Horton's labor to make it clear, so that God may be praised on earth in the same terms that angels and triumphant saints are already using in heaven.

This book is a breathtaking workout for Protestant laypeople, with a prospect of new health and strength for those who stay the course. Tough, genial, and encouraging (as good trainers learn to be), Horton makes us pump intellectual iron as he puts us through the painful yet healthful discipline of relearning the Reformation's vital message of saving grace. As in current advertisements fit folk tell how well-planned diet and exercise delivered them from a fat and flabby existence, so I predict there will soon be many testimonials about the strengthened grip on grace that Horton's lively pummeling has brought to his readers. Let Horton show you how to lose theological fat and flab! You won't regret it, I promise you. It is a pleasure to commend so businesslike a book on the things that really matter.

Here is the quintessence of the gospel, the new wine of God's kingdom at its purest for us today! Read, mark, learn, and digest *Putting Amazing Back into Grace.*

J. I. Packer
Author of *Knowing God*

Introduction

Welcome to the Reformation

If you are a thinking Christian who is weary of legalism, superficiality, and religious hype, you may be ready for the theology of the Reformation. Many Christians today are experiencing frustrations similar to those which eventually surfaced in the Reformation of the sixteenth century. With a renewed and growing interest among the laity in the doctrines of grace, there is no time like the present for taking this journey.

It's kind of like a plane bound for Honolulu. For some it's a routine business trip (as though any trip to Hawaii could be routine); for others it may be a honeymoon. But whatever experience you have had with that robust, down-to-earth faith, this brief survey can serve as a guide.

In 1517 a stocky Bible professor and monk nailed a set of propositions to a church door (the community bulletin board) for academic debate. Little did he know on that chilly autumn afternoon that it would be the masses rather than the academics who would spread what would be known as the Protestant Reformation. The monk's name, of course, was Martin Luther.

The core of Luther's concern was the selling of indulgences. When the pope got into a bit of a financial bind with the building of Christendom's largest cathedral, St. Peter's in Rome, he offered Christians pardons for sins committed in exchange for a contribution to the construction fund. Nobody in the empire was as clever or as crass in this enterprise as the Dominican preacher, John Tetzel. It is said that his traveling quartet even sang, "When the coin in the coffer rings, a soul from purgatory springs." Others composed their own version: "When the coin rings in the pitcher, the pope gets all the richer." This type of humor should sound familiar to those of us who have been treated with parodies of TV evangelists on *Saturday Night Live* and to lines from such musicians as Huey Lewis, who sings about a fat man selling salvation in his hand, and Ray Stevens, who quips "They sell you salvation while they sing 'Amazing Grace.'"

Those who followed the Reformation were called "evangelicals," taken from the Greek word *evangelion,* meaning "gospel." Believing the gospel had been actually recovered was a radical point of view, but those who used the term believed that to be the case. It was not that there were no Christians and churches, or even bishops and archbishops, who did not believe the *evangel.* There were many throughout the Middle Ages who did their utmost to restore the gospel to its biblical purity. For instance, Luther's own mentor, the head of his monastic order over all of Germany, taught salvation by grace and many of the other truths you will read about in this book. The same is true of the tireless defender of evangelical faith, Archbishop Thomas Bradwardine of Canterbury, during the fourteenth century. A handful of other leading scholars cried out for a recovery of the biblical gospel.

Nevertheless, *preaching* and *teaching* the radical message of a God who does all the saving and leaves nothing for us to claim as our own contribution was considered a threat to holy living and to ecclesiastical regulations. In fact preaching and teaching in general were at a low ebb. For the most part the laity, largely illiterate, had to let their priests do their thinking for them. The people who really mattered in the medieval church were monks and nuns, "the religious," who had given up their worldly stations in life for a better chance at gaining divine favor.

So, what were the revolutionary ideas that disrupted Europe and threw both church and society into turmoil? There were several.

Slogans help us quickly identify someone's point of view. In fact, one can form an opinion of some people just by reading their bumper stickers. The Reformation had slogans, too, which identified its core concerns. The first was *sola scriptura,* which meant "Scripture alone!"

The Scriptures Alone

The study of original texts inspired by the Renaissance led the Reformers back to the Hebrew and Greek manuscripts of the Scriptures. They realized how much mistranslation, misunderstanding, and misinterpretation had accumulated over the centuries, obscuring the biblical text. Can the church legislate doctrines or moral regulations which are not found in the Bible? The Reformers answered, "No, Scripture alone!" Can the church maintain infallibility in interpreting the Bible? No, they responded, absolutely not.

The church was not the pope or the magisterium (the church's teaching body), said the Reformers, but was all Christians gathered together—led, to be sure, by the official teachers and pastors. Doctors (theologians) were desperately needed, but every Christian was responsible to understand the Bible's doctrines. The whole church was to study the Scriptures, learn them, and come to conclusions about the Bible's basic teaching. The people, clergy, and laity were to do these things together, as the body of Christ. Of course, *sola scriptura* did not mean, as it has come to be interpreted in some circles today, that the laity were to use the Bible as a wax nose to be shaped by private, subjective opinion; rather, it meant that all believers had the right and responsibility to read, understand, and obey God's Word—*with* the rest of the church (certainly not without it). While this idea created enormous freedom for the individual to approach God's Word directly, the Reformers insisted that it would not work unless the average Christian was taught enough about its teachings to "rightly divide the Word of truth." In other words, when it came to faith and practice, God wrote the Book. The basic difference between the Reformers and Rome on this point was whether the Bible produced the church or whether the church produced the Bible. The Reformers held the former view. They believed God revealed himself to a people and called that people to himself and gave them his Word. Therefore, the church

11

is always fallible and always liable to correction from God's transcendent, infallible revelation.

Sola scriptura has fallen on hard times again, it seems. Columbia University professor Randall Balmer notes, "In truth, despite all the evangelical rhetoric about *sola scriptura* in the twentieth century, most evangelicals don't trust themselves to interpret the Bible, so they turn to others—local pastors, mendicant preachers and lecturers, authors of thousands of books, commentaries, and reference tools—for interpretive schemes."[1]

Grace Alone

The second slogan, the heart and core of the movement, was *sola gratia* or "Grace alone!" Medieval believers were constantly reminded how much their relationship with God depended on them. The super saints realized it was impossible to live without sin in the world, so they joined the monasteries. Luther was one such monk, but he soon understood the point Christ made to the Pharisees about sin being inherent in each one of us. Jesus told them, paraphrased, "It's not what goes into a man that makes him unclean, but what's already in there!" Sin is not out there, in the world, but in here, in me. It corrupts me regardless of my station or surroundings. Luther reasoned from Scripture that God is no softy. He is just and holy, incapable of overlooking our sins. So the German monk spent hours in confession, hoping God would notice him for his many tears. His fear was, of course, that if he failed to confess, or failed to remember in order to confess, one single sin, that would be enough for God to condemn him.

Luther knew his will was in bondage to sin, so how could he ever break the cycle and be free? Inspirational sermons aimed at motivating hearers to simply use the free will God gave them fell short of comforting him. Luther knew there had to be either another answer, or no answer.

While he was teaching the Psalms, Galatians, and Romans, the gospel began to leap off the pages. As he was reading about God's righteousness, Luther was struck by what felt like a bolt of lightning. All of his life he had hated the righteousness of God, though he appeared outwardly pious. It was that righteousness, after all, which hung above him like the sword of Damocles and reminded him day after day that he was a sinner and must be judged. Now he understood for the first time the righteousness which God not only *is,* but *gives.* "For in the gospel," wrote St. Paul, "a righteousness *from* God is revealed, a righteousness that is by faith from first to last, just as it is written: 'The righteous will live by faith'" (Rom. 1:17, italics added). God not only judges us *by* his righteousness, but *with* his righteousness imputed to our account. The doctrine of justification by grace alone through faith alone was recovered and polished to its New Testament brilliance.

It was at this point that Luther not only understood that salvation was by grace alone, but that the means or method of receiving it was through faith alone; hence, the next slogan, *sola fide,* or "Faith alone." The church had always said we are saved by grace. Some even argued that we were saved by grace *alone,* but that was not safeguard enough for the Reformers. For instance, the official teaching of the church at the time was that grace is *infused* or *imparted* as a boost to help us live a holy life so that eventually we can go to heaven. But we have to make proper use of that grace; all along the way there are opportunities to lose grace, the church taught. Through the rituals, spiritual exercises, pious formulas, and routines of the church, grace lost could be regained. So, in practice, the view was that we are saved by grace transforming us into holy people. To this the Reformers responded that salvation was to be viewed, before anything else, as God's act of declaring righteous those who were, at that very moment, still unrighteous. Thus justification was not something the believer had to wait for until the end of life, but was declared at the beginning of the Christian life—the moment he or she trusts Christ alone for salvation from divine wrath.

In other words, salvation is by grace alone through faith alone. God does not give us the grace to save ourselves with his aid. He declares us righteous the moment we give up our own claims to righteousness and our own struggles for divine approval and recognize the sufficiency of Christ's righteousness as our own. Today once again, this has become a revolutionary idea, it seems, with so many Christians caught up in introspective "navel-gazing" and anxiety because of guilt. Somehow, we reason, something *must* depend on us. Somehow, somewhere, we have to pay something.

Others do not even seem to be bothered by God's justice and wrath, as if he is too nice to judge, or they are too good to deserve a sentence.

The next slogan was *soli Deo gloria,* which means, "To God alone be glory!" In the old section of Heidelberg, Germany, there stands a marvelously preserved hotel and pub, a center of nightlife then and even to the present. At the top of the building, in raised gold letters, one reads this Reformation slogan. Similarly, Johann Sebastian Bach signed all of his compositions, "Soli Deo Gloria" or simply, *S.D.G.* J. I. Packer once told me our view of God is like a pair of old-fashioned scales. When God goes up in our estimation, we go down. Similarly, when we raise our sense of self-importance, our view of God must, to that same degree, be lowered. In the Reformation, the doctrines of election and predestination were recovered and proclaimed from the pulpit. Blacksmiths found delight in discussing these subjects over a pint of ale with friends after a hard day's work. No longer did they have pastors who told them, "Oh, that's for theologians to discuss." God was great, and all were equal before him on their knees.

The Reformation produced an era of great thinkers, artists, and workers because it raised God high and bowed low the human head before his majesty. But today, we have evangelical ditties instead of Bach's or Handel's exuberant and reverent masterpieces. Our services are often celebrations of ourselves more than they are of God, more entertainment than worship. J. B. Phillips has well captured the modern sentiment toward Christianity in the title of one of his popular books: *Your God Is Too Small.* Never before, not even in the medieval church, have Christians been so obsessed with themselves. Never before have people entertained such grandiose notions about humans and such puny views of God. Evangelists talk about God as though he were to be pitied rather than worshiped, as though he were crying his eyes out in heaven, hoping things would go better, that people would "let him have his way." Never before, perhaps, has God been so totally forgotten and lowered in our estimation. Self-esteem, self-image, self-confidence, self-this, and self-that have replaced talk of God's attributes. Ironically, this has created the opposite of its intention. The more time we spend contemplating our own greatness in the mirror, the more clearly we are bound to see the warts.

Without the knowledge of the God in whose image we have been created, and the grace which has made us children of God, narcissism (self-love) quickly evolves into depression (self-hate).

But all of that can change! The pans of that scale can reverse. It happened once, and it can happen again.

Finally, we would be remiss if we failed to mention the Reformation concern over "the priesthood of all believers." Luther and Calvin challenged the monastic way of life, telling carpenters, milkmaids, lawyers, and homemakers that their work in the world was as much a divinely ordained calling, and certainly at least as worthwhile, as being part of the giant bureaucratic network of Christian organizations which characterized medieval religious life. They argued that God takes *this* world and *this* life seriously, as well as the next, and that Christians should, too. Secular work is not merely a means of making money to give to the church or of providing the necessary income in order to have the leisure to volunteer for ministry-related activities. Work is godly, said the Reformers. Christian craftsmen should be the *best* craftsmen. Christian artists should put their hearts and souls into their work. After all, it's not a job; it's a *calling!*

In short, the Reformation liberated believers from the tyranny of the church, but not from its care; from the anxiety of securing divine acceptance; from the preoccupation with self which always winds up driving us to despair; from a low view of God; and from a low view of one's calling and work in the world. The Reformation brought freedom back to the Christian conscience by restoring the focus of the gospel from being us-centered to being God-centered, Christ-centered. We need that sort of shift again today.

Not everyone will agree with the content of this book, but the Reformation tradition is a rich vein. If we ignore it, we shall be the poorer. It is *catholic,* in the best sense of that word. The Reformation sought the reform of the church, not its destruction. It shares with the Roman Catholic and Eastern Orthodox communities a love for the creeds and the early witness to Christ, an appreciation for the wisdom of centuries of insight, and an insistence that Christians learn God's Word *together,* not in an individualistic, subjective way. It is a *biblical* tradition, testing belief and the actions that flow from belief by the Scriptures directly. It is an *evangelistic* tradition, having its roots in the recovery of the *evangel* itself. Many mistakenly criticize the Reformation for a lack of missionary emphasis. Yet what was the recovery of the gospel itself and its spread throughout all of Europe but a singular missionary enterprise? Furthermore, missionaries were sent to far-flung lands. The first Protestant missionaries in the Western hemisphere were sent from Calvin's Geneva. Many of the greatest evangelists and missionaries the world has ever known have been committed to the convictions shared in this volume: David Brainerd, Jonathan Edwards, George Whitefield, C. H. Spurgeon, William Carey, David Livingstone, and many more.

It is a *practical* tradition. The Reformation faith has produced a concern for the physical as well as spiritual welfare of people, convinced that God has called his people to live and work in this world. It is not content to save souls alone, while homeless bodies huddle around a campfire to keep warm. This has been demonstrated in the incredible model Geneva became, as daily thousands of refugees fleeing persecution were cared for, accommodated, and employed. The deacons served as the city's welfare officers and social workers. Under Calvin's personal supervision a hospital was established, industry thrived, refugees were taught simple trades, and the Genevan Reformer himself drew up what were then Europe's most sophisticated and radical sanitation laws. Protestants and Catholics alike recognized the remarkable achievements of Geneva in erecting a center of practical godliness, beyond the individualistic piety often associated with contemporary evangelicalism. The affection the city held for Calvin was portrayed in living color in the last moments of his life, as all of Geneva, with much of Europe, mourned the Reformer's death.

It is a *worshiping* tradition. Because God is great, he ought to be worshiped reverently. Furthermore, many of the Reformers were concerned not to "throw the baby out with the bath water." It was the goal of Luther and Calvin to reform the Mass, not to abolish it. The churches of this tradition produced some of the most impressive hymnody and psalmody in church history, rich and moving musically as well as lyrically. In fact, it was Luther who said, "I am not satisfied with him who despises music, as all fanatics do. I place music next to theology and give it the highest praise."

There are many other contributions this tradition makes, and ought to continue making in the twenty-first century. The world is looking for a church that knows what it's here to accomplish and for Christians who know what they believe and why they believe it. May God use this brief survey in some slight measure toward that end. And let's put *amazing* back into *grace!*

one

Jumping through Hoops
Is for Circus Animals

On numerous occasions I have asked myself, Why am I a Christian? I have never been content with the prefabricated answers we sometimes hear, and I am unwilling to accept with my heart a faith that fails to convince my mind. A compelling faith, and nothing short of it, is required if I am to give myself, heart and soul, to its claims.

There was a time when I thought I would cash in my chips and leave what appeared at times to be a game. Is it *true?* I asked again and again. Can we say that the Bible contains the only reliable revelation from God to humans? I was puzzled that so many people—intelligent people—would think logically and rationally about every other aspect of their lives and then shut their minds when it came to religion. I did it, too. But we all have questions, and my questions grew deeper and deeper until the answer finally stared me in the face.

Reared in a solid Christian home, with the nurture of daily devotions and the simple piety of believing parents, I was offered the warm, supportive, meaningful environment of evangelical Christianity. But during my teenage years, the same clichés, slogans, and experiences that had provided a sense of being "in" and of belonging to a group began to appear shallow and trite, and seemed to embody the contentless trappings of what Francis Schaeffer called the "evangelical ghetto." The rules I had never questioned began to choke me. My Christian schools became prisons. In the seventh grade, I had a Bible instructor who took particular delight in enumerating the things for which we could be damned. If, for instance, we were to die with an unconfessed sin, we could be eternally lost. The implications haunted me, and I could not understand why my schoolmates were relatively calm, especially since the level of actual law-keeping was so unimpressive among them, too. I worried: What if I really messed up some Saturday night and Jesus came back before I could walk down the aisle again on Sunday? What if I couldn't remember a particular sin in order to confess it? There were so many ways I could lose my soul!

Meanwhile, I began reading Paul's epistle to the Romans and couldn't put it down. I would read a passage and then wonder, Why don't I hear this in class or in church? Finally in class one day, when the Bible instructor was haunting us again with doom and gloom, I remembered a passage from Romans. Raising my hand, I interrupted before I could catch myself. "That's not what the Bible says," I retorted—not in a dogmatic way. I just said it. "However, to the man who does not work but trusts God who justifies the wicked, his faith is credited as righteousness," I continued, quoting the apostle Paul (Rom. 4:5). The teacher turned multiple shades of red and shouted, "The Bible also says, 'By their fruits you shall know them'!" "Yes," I replied, "but by their fruits *we* shall know them—God knows them by their faith."

"Blessed are they whose transgressions are forgiven, whose sins are covered. Blessed is the man whose sin the Lord will never count against him" (Rom. 4:7–8)—that's the good news Paul had in mind in Romans. And yet so many Christians I've met have experienced the same doubts and fears that drove me to the brink of despair. Is God for or against me? It doesn't help to soft-pedal sin, as though God is so loving and forgiving that he can just overlook our momentary lapses. Deep down we know that he is holy and just and that we are guilty and must be judged by the letter and spirit of the law.

The "Romans revolution" that day in Bible class gave me a new lease on life, and I began studying the book with obsessive fascination. The towering peaks of Paul's exposition of such themes as the human condition, guilt, justification, union with Christ, sanctification, election and divine sovereignty, and the perseverance of God with his people became the new foundation for my faith. I began meeting other Christians who were on the same trek; we had always heard about grace and sung about grace, but now we felt like we really understood it and experienced it for the first time. God does it all, and we contribute nothing but our sinfulness. What a liberating message! Humbling, to be sure, but liberating just the same.

In his book *The Choice of Truth*, Daniel Thrapp wrote, "The purpose of life is the quest for truth."[1] Christians, of all people, should be committed to that pursuit, regardless of the consequences. Usually we want to control the truth, to decide for ourselves whether it will be helpful, practical, supportive of our general presuppositions. But truth is often unkind to our notions of what is useful knowledge. When Erasmus tried to cool off Martin Luther about the debate over free will and grace, the Reformer responded, "If we are not supposed to know for certain whether God does everything in salvation, then, dear Erasmus, I ask you, what *is* useful to be known?" At a time when Christian cookbooks, dating manuals, and self-help guides are the rage and doctrinal discussions are ignored, there is perhaps no better question we can ask the modern church.

These days the world is often more profound than the church. One frequently hears honest pagans asking really good questions: What is the meaning of life? Does life have purpose? Meanwhile, we evangelicals seem to be making the most trivial queries: Is dancing a sin? Should we immerse, sprinkle, or pour? Is Jesus really coming back in November? Is Iraq "Magog," and if so, is Saddam Hussein the Antichrist? While we're busy organizing ever-greater conferences and conventions so we can talk to ourselves, give each other awards, and dazzle each other with the latest evangelical superstars, the world is taking its business elsewhere, to merchants who care about the big questions. Philosopher Paul C. Payne noted that the world does not take the church seriously today because the church is not serious.

Many Christians are also put off by the term *doctrine,* either because it is perceived as having "for professionals only" written large across it, or because it is regarded as causing unnecessary division in the body of Christ. As for the first objection, it cannot be denied that in our day, as in the period before the Reformation, doctrine is left to the experts, while the laity are simply expected to nod to the essentials. But that is not the biblical way of looking at it. Paul had a soft spot in his heart for the Bereans because they were constantly searching the Scriptures to see if Paul's teaching was true (Acts 17:11). In the apostolic church, according to Acts 2:42, average Christians "devoted themselves to the apostles' teaching [doctrine]" as well as to prayer and the Lord's table. Understanding doctrinal or theological issues was considered the responsibility of every Christian, not just a few select professionals. As for the concern that doctrine always seems to bring strife, I can't disagree more. Actually, doctrine *unites.* How else could the early church hold together those who had come from a variety of ethnic, socioeconomic, and cultural backgrounds? What united them was not a common culture or a common political ideology, nor common experiences, but a common creed. That common doctrinal affirmation transcended any petty divisions and pulled the group together during its most severe trials.

There is, however, a sense in which doctrine does divide. Mormons and Jehovah's Witnesses are not regarded by evangelicals as Christians. Is this due to a lack of charity? Are we being ill-tempered? Not at all. These folks are our neighbors, and we would love to be able to have fellowship with them. But because they deny the Christian creed, we are required to deny them fellowship. Friendship, yes; fellowship, no. If doctrine can do that, it must be important, and if it is that important, it demands our attention.

The message this book explores was the revolutionary force behind the ministries of the apostles and Augustine, the inspiration behind the Protestant Reformation, and the source of the Great Awakening in America. Columbia University historian Eugene F. Rice, Jr., contrasts the Reformation faith with the modern mentality, often pervasive in even Christian circles:

All the more strikingly it [the Reformation] measures the gulf between the secular imagination of the twentieth century and sixteenth-century Protestantism's intoxication with the majesty of God. We can only exercise historical sympathy to try to understand how it was that many of the most sensitive intelligences of a whole epoch found a supreme, a total, liberty in the abandonment of human weakness to the omnipotence of God.[2]

Grace is the gospel. The extent to which we are unclear about who does what in salvation is the degree to which we will obscure the gospel. At a time when moralism, self-righteousness, and self-help religion dominate in much of evangelical preaching, publishing, and broadcasting, we desperately need a return to this message of grace. We need to emphasize once again Paul's inspired commentary, "It does not, therefore, depend on man's desire or effort, but on God's mercy" (Rom. 9:16). Our sense of purpose, as individuals and as a church, depends largely on how clearly we grasp certain truths about who God is, who we are, and what God's plan for history involves. Christians form a new humanity, a new spiritual race. Just as a rib was taken from Adam's side to create Eve, God has taken people "from every tribe and language and people and nation. You have made them to be a kingdom and priests to serve our God" (Rev. 5:9–10). This new race exists for a purpose, a definite reason. It exists to make God's glory felt in a dark and drab world; the new race is to be found in every imaginable ethnic, cultural, social, economic, and national grouping. It is seen dispersed throughout every stratum: in hospitals and schools, in homes and offices, from the coastal beaches to the city skyscrapers.

The message you will find in this book not only has produced the upsurges of Christian faithfulness in past ages. It holds out promise to change the shape of contemporary faith and practice. Speaking for myself, I am confident that I would not be a Christian today were it not for the doctrine of grace. Tired of jumping through hoops? Are you looking for a radical view of God and his saving grace? Then join me on this brief and incomplete tour of the most revolutionary message you will ever encounter.

two

Created with Class

"God saw all that he had made, and it was very good" (Gen. 1:31). Thus the human story began.

Whenever we take up the subject of redemption, that is where we need to begin, at the beginning, with creation. Very often, however, a gospel presentation starts with the fall—the origin of human sin and the need for redemption. But creation is the proper starting point for any consideration of human identity and its recovery through the gospel. Why is this?

When we discuss the fall without having appreciated the majesty of the human creature by virtue of creation, the impression is given that there is something inherent in our humanness that predisposes us to sin, that there is something deeply sinful and unspiritual in being human. This approach presumes the accuracy of Shakespeare's famous words, now become cliché, "To err is human." But the biblical response would be, "To err is the result of human *fallenness*." In other words, there is nothing wrong with the Manufacturer or his product; the problem is with what his creatures decided to do with the freedom he sovereignly gave them.

So creation is not the problem, and it is only when we more fully appreciate the majesty of humanity as God's creation that we can adequately weigh the horror of the fall.

Creation is an important starting point, too, because the better we understand ourselves, the better we will come to know God. As Calvin wrote, "We must now speak of the creation of man: not only because among all God's works here is the noblest and most remarkable example of His justice, wisdom, and goodness; but because . . . we cannot have a clear and complete knowledge of God unless it is accompanied by a corresponding knowledge of ourselves."[1]

Following are some of the important lessons we learn from the biblical doctrine of creation.

Creation Marks Us with God's Image

What makes humans so special? Is it that we have evolved beyond the level of other creatures? We do bear a resemblance to other creatures. For example, wild beasts travel in herds, birds fly in flocks, and humans have often moved in tribes. But we all know that there is something that sets humans apart—something transcendent.

Before his heavenly court, God resolved to "make man in our image, in our likeness." This would entitle this new creature to "'rule over the fish of the sea and the birds of the air, over the livestock, over all the earth, and over all the creatures that move along the ground.' So God created man in his own image, in the image of God he created him; male and female he created them" (Gen. 1:26–27).

Never before had God brought into existence a creature with such intimate ties to his own character. Through ages past the Holy Trinity was entertained at court by angelic hosts—seraphim and cherubim continually crying, "Holy, holy, holy is the Lord God Almighty" and serving him who "makes winds his messengers, flames of fire his servants" (Rev. 4:8; Ps. 104:4). But when he created this new race in his own image, the heavenly hosts must have wondered in silent awe at what this amazing creature would act like, look like, sound like.

A good deal of ink has been used trying to answer the question, "What is the image of God in humanity?" From God's Word, we can discern some of the features.

First, as created, humanity was similar to God in terms of moral perfection. "God saw all that he had made, and it was very good" (Gen. 1:31). God saw no internal defects in his human creature. There was nothing in human nature as God created it that would predispose the race to sin. There was righteousness, holiness, godliness. In short, Adam and Eve were as much like God as a creature can be like its creator. All of life was to be a part of worship. Whether planning the future, naming the animals, raising children, building cities, writing music, playing sports, reflecting on the meaning of it all, everything was God-centered. But while all of creation reflected God's handiwork, only humans could *reflect* on their *reflecting* God's handiwork. In other words, only humans could look back from the clouds, as it were, to contemplate their place in the universe.

We see this even after the fall, with the psalmist as he stargazed from a grassy knoll. Looking at the expanse of the heavens, he wondered,

> When I consider your heavens,
> the work of your fingers,
> the moon and the stars,
> which you have set in place,
> what is man that you are mindful of him,
> the son of man that you care for him?

David concludes his reflection with this answer:

> You made him a little lower than the heavenly beings
> and crowned him with glory and honor.

> You made him ruler over the works of your hands;
> you put everything under his feet:
> all flocks and herds,
> and the beasts of the field,
> the birds of the air,
> and the fish of the sea,
> all that swim the paths of the seas.

This reflection is to lead us, not to some sort of narcissistic self-centeredness, but to raise our eyes toward our Creator: "O LORD, our Lord, how majestic is your name in all the earth!" (Ps. 8:3–9).

Beyond moral perfection, Adam and Eve enjoyed a creative link with their Creator. God imagined a world and brought it into being—and what imagination! Think of the variety in shades and colors of fish and flowers. Even before the microscope and telescope introduced us to the micro- and macrouniverses, the details of shape, size, color, and function were as fascinating and as seemingly infinite as we now know them to be. Of course, God is the Creator, and we are creatures. Nevertheless, humans mimic God in imagination. Think of the technological advances in our own century. Only God has the power to create "out of nothing" *(ex nihilo),* but those he created in his image are able to reflect his creative imagination in singularly impressive imitation.

I once asked a friend who is quite an expert on classical composers what single factor determines a master's genius. He answered, "Most of them would tell you it depended on how well they could imitate the greatest of those masters who had gone before them." That is undoubtedly true of our creativity in relation to our Creator.

The image of God is also reflected in the religious dimension of human existence. In other words, being created in God's image means that we share with God an invincible sense of and concern for the eternal. "For in him we live and move and have our being" (Acts 17:28). We can no more deny spiritual issues than a fish can swim in sand. God shares his world with us, and we cannot pass a single corner of it without being reminded of that fact.

You will notice that I have used the term *perfection* repeatedly. Of course, humanity lost moral, creative, and religious *perfection* in the fall; but the race did not lose moral, creative, and religious *capacity.* God gave us—and expected of us—perfection in all of our likeness to him. Because God created us in his image, we have the *natural* capacity for approaching his perfection, even though we have lost all *moral* capacity for achieving the same.

Creation Is Universal

On the face of it, this is an incredibly obvious point, and yet it is often overlooked. Redemption, of course, is limited to the group of those whom God has moved in history to redeem and call to himself. In other words, only justified believers are saved from God's judgment. But creation is much broader, embracing not only Christians, but non-Christians. James warned the faithful against the hypocrisy of using the same tongue to "praise our Lord and Father" and to "curse men, who have been made in God's likeness" (3:9). Even those outside the household of faith bear the divine image.

In one sense, this universal character of the divine image is a plus, in another sense, a minus. First the good news. The universality of the divine image means that your neighbor, whether the world's most obstinate atheist or a pastor's wife, is an equal in sharing the image of God. This divine imprimatur is the result of creation, not redemption. The image of God which requires us to respect those who bear it, therefore, requires us to recognize the dignity of all human beings, regardless of who they are, what they believe, or what they do.

It is also a positive thing for everybody in the sense that all humans share a capacity for moral, creative, and religious interest. Of course, this does not mean that we can move toward God or even believe in him before he regenerates us, but that all human beings share a common moral, creative, and religious dimension whose indelible stamp cannot be rubbed out even by the most inventive solutions concocted in the rebel laboratory.

Not only has God left his fingerprints all over creation, he has left upon the human heart a yearning that makes human beings dust the creation for them. The majestic imprimatur of God's handiwork that makes us so significant in the universe also holds us responsible for our response to the Creator. Our responsibility is the threat implied in the universality of the image of God. Because the religious dimension is intrinsic to our humanness and because God has so clearly demonstrated his existence in the world around us, there is no such thing as an atheist. There is no such thing as someone who has "never heard."

The apostle Paul explains: "For since the creation of the world God's invisible qualities—his eternal power and divine nature—have been clearly seen, being understood from what has been made, so that men are without excuse" (Rom. 1:20).

People do "suppress the truth by their wickedness" (Rom. 1:18), but one cannot suppress something that one does not believe to exist. The creature will always be the dependent of the Creator, whether the creature recognizes God in this life or is judged by him in the next. And notice the crucial role our conscience plays in all of this: "Indeed, when Gentiles, who do not have the law, do by nature things required by the law, they are a law for themselves, even though they do not have the law, since they show that the requirements of the law are written on their hearts, their consciences also bearing witness, and their thoughts now accusing, now even defending them" (Rom. 2:14–15).

The language Paul uses is legal, courtroom vocabulary. And he enters our conscience, created in God's image and impressed with images of God from years of scanning the creation, as evidence, Exhibit A, against our ignorance plea. On that final day before the bar of judgment, no one will be able to say, "I wasn't given enough information." It is a weighty thing, weighty and dangerous, to be created in the image of God.

Have you ever accepted Jesus Christ as your Creator? We speak of accepting him as Savior and Lord—in other words, as the source of our redemption. But how often do we think of him as the author of our creation? According to John, "In the beginning was the Word, and the Word was with God, and the Word was God. He was with God in the beginning. Through him all things were made; without him nothing was made that has been made. In him was life, and that life was the light of men. The light shines in the darkness, but the darkness has not understood it" (John 1:1–5).

Why Are We Here?

Modern science has promised more than it can deliver. That accounts for much of the cynicism postmoderns seem to have toward finding the answers to their ultimate questions. To be sure, science is better equipped to answer some questions than any other field. For instance, it is science and not theology that will tell us the age of the earth. The Bible does not provide that kind of information, nor does it care to. Nevertheless, it is an important and reasonable question. There are a lot of important and reasonable questions the Bible does not try to answer. If it did, there would be a lot of jobless geologists!

While science will lead the way toward the discovery of *when* we got here and will help us find the reasons for *how* we got here (beyond the revelation we already have in the inspired text of Genesis 1–3), there is a question to which those other questions ultimately lead, a question, nevertheless, which science will never be able to answer any more than theology will be able to determine the age of the earth. That question is "*Why* are we here?"

Sir John Eccles, Nobel laureate and a pioneer in brain research, said, "The law of gravitation was not the final truth," and went on to explain how many modern scientists have turned the discipline into a "superstition" by claiming that "we only have to know more about the brain" to understand ourselves and our significance. Eccles concludes: "Science cannot explain the existence of each of us as a unique self, nor can it answer such fundamental questions as: Who am I? Why am I here? How did I come to be at a certain place and time? What happens after death? These are all mysteries beyond science."

Notice Eccles's indictment: "Science has gone too far in breaking down man's belief in his spiritual greatness and has given him the belief that he is merely an insignificant animal who has arisen by chance and necessity on an insignificant planet lost in the great cosmic immensity."[2]

The rise of modern science in the seventeenth century was largely the self-conscious search for the evidence of harmony and order known to exist in God's universe. Because humanity had a huge place in God's plan, it was assumed that one could know the "whys" from special revelation (the Bible) and go on to piece together the "hows" and "whens" from natural revelation (creation). What, then, does the Bible tell us about the purpose behind our existence?

Every craft points to the skill and character of the artist. And creation speaks eloquently of its Creator. One popular theory seems to suggest that God created us because he was lonely. That notion would surprise many, such as Augustine, who once wrote, not that God had a "human-shaped vacuum," but that man had a God-shaped vacuum that only God could fill. The dictionary defines *lonely* as "the absence of company; destitute of sympathetic companionship." Now, whatever can be said about loneliness, we should find little support in Scripture for the idea that it can be applied to the Holy Trinity, surrounded, supported, and shielded by the presence and choral processions of thousands upon thousands of heavenly hosts in assembly! God is not lonely without the presence of humans; rather, it is we who are lonely without God.

There is yet another theory. Some argue that God created humans because he wanted to have creatures who loved him of their own free will. After all, the angels *had* to do God's bidding. They don't love God freely, but by compulsion. This too, however, seems to give too much to human credit and, more substantially, finds no explicit support in Scripture. Instead, we are told that a great number of heaven's angels freely joined the satanic mutiny (2 Pet. 2:4; Jude 6; Rev. 12:7). So much for compulsion!

This question is not just an exercise in theological "Jeopardy." It is more than semantics; it determines whether we are to view creation from a human-centered or a God-centered point of view. Does God exist for our purpose or do we exist for his?

Once again, the psalmist offers us the biblical answer to that central question:

> How many are your works, O LORD!
> In wisdom you made them all;
> the earth is full of your creatures.
> There is the sea, vast and spacious,
> teeming with creatures beyond number—
> living things both large and small. . . .
> When you give it to them,
> they gather it up;
> when you open your hand,
> they are satisfied with good things.
> When you hide your face,
> they are terrified;
> when you take away their breath,
> they die and return to the dust.
> When you send your Spirit,
> they are created,
> and you renew the face of the earth.
>
> May the glory of the LORD endure forever;
> may the LORD rejoice in his works (Ps. 104:24–25, 28–31).

Notice especially those last two lines: "May the glory of the LORD endure forever; may the LORD rejoice in his works." This is the purpose behind our creation and our daily existence. For the same reason an artist takes pleasure in his masterpiece, God takes pleasure in his works. Thus, the purpose of our creation is the pleasure of God. It is not for our happiness or pleasure that we exist, but for God's. That is a very different orientation from the one we are constantly offered in our popular commercial culture—an orientation that has made vast inroads into our own evangelical subculture.

To the question, "What is the chief end of man?" the *Westminster Shorter Catechism* leads off with its famous answer: "To glorify God and to enjoy him forever." What a loaded sentence! There is a sense, then, in which we were created in order to take pleasure in God as well as his taking pleasure in us. In fact, it is the purpose of earthly pleasures and joys to raise our senses to the enjoyment of God. This means that as long as our pleasure-seeking is calculated to be, in the end, a form of God-seeking, it is an acceptable and, in fact, godly pursuit. Imagine the implications of this sort of thinking! We see it throughout the Old Testament, in the history of a life-loving and world-embracing people who, at their best, squeezed the juice out of life's every grape in order to participate in the fullness of "enjoying God forever." It is the story of a man, God in the flesh, who not only saw fit to bless the union of a husband and a wife, but also provided a miraculous vintage of wine to celebrate the occasion. No one can appreciate the Hebrew/Christian understanding of creation and remain insensitive to its world-affirming character.

I realize this is an especially controversial point of view in circles where we are taught to despise the world and its pleasures. (Of course, we haven't yet come to the chapter on the fall, where we will see in greater detail how the world is, like you and me, both a victim and an active participant in the Adamic rebellion.) Yet, according to Scripture, it is not the world per se that's the problem—just as it is not humanity per se, but rather the world and humanity *set at odds against* their Creator.

An ancient cult, known as Manichaeism (influenced by Gnosticism), attributed evil to matter; the human spirit was pure, but the body, intelligence, and fleshly appetites were inherently demonic. Against this error Calvin countered, "The depravity and malice both of man and of the devil, or the sins that arise therefrom, *do not spring from nature, but rather from the corruption of nature.*"[3] Therefore, "Let us not be ashamed to take pious delight in the works of God open and manifest in this most beautiful theater."[4]

It was Jesus himself who scandalized the Pharisees over their misunderstanding of the nature of sin. Sin, he told them, did not come to them from the world, as though the world carried an infectious disease which, if one got too close, would infect the healthy. Rather, he said, it's the other way around. It is we who, due to the sinfulness of our own hearts, pollute the world. (See Matt. 15:11.) It is we who turn the gifts intended to remind us of God's care and favor toward us into either evils (legalism) or abuses (license).

Thus when we consider the purpose of our creation, it is essential that we appreciate its God-centered justification. God takes pleasure in us and in seeing us take pleasure in him. Only with that perspective as our backdrop can we understand the meaning behind work and leisure, pleasure and restraint, life and death, laughter and tears.

The Doctrine of Creation Has Its Benefits

The practical benefits of this doctrine are obvious. First, we have an incredibly weighty existence which requires that we respect God and our neighbor whether the latter is a Christian or not. It means that we should expect to find common ground with non-Christians as a natural part of human existence. We can build cars together on the assembly line or work together on city councils and school boards without being antagonistic or adversarial. After all, civic life finds its origin in creation rather than in redemption. When George Orwell talks about "Big Brother," or philosophers decry the decline of Western civilization, or our neighbors sit around and discuss the day's news, we are sometimes aloof, unconcerned, and uninformed. Unless the subject is explicitly religious or moral, we don't seem to get all that involved.

Sometimes even when the issue is moral (such as civil rights in the fifties), we have severed our doctrine of creation from our scientific, literal belief in creation. It seems incongruous that those who argue for creation in the classroom so vehemently could, at times, miss its practical relevance for the whole of life.

Abortion is at the top of any list that seeks to apply the doctrine of creation to social issues. Nevertheless, why must a concern for human life end with the birth of a child? Why must non-Christians lead struggles to preserve the environment which we Christians believe God commanded Adam to look after in the beginning? And why must non-Christians often lead the way in defending the civil rights of men and women when they do not even recognize a theological mandate from God? The more we appreciate the exciting truth of the doctrine of creation, the more we will grow in our sense of responsibility to God for our neighbors and our environment.

Another practical benefit is that the doctrine of creation frees us to enjoy work. The rock group Loverboy sings a tune called "Working for the Weekend." There is a real loss in our society of what has been called the Protestant work ethic, a set of values based on the conviction that God has created us for a purpose—to serve our community. *Before* the fall, God instituted work as a holy, God-honoring, noble activity. Adam and Eve were given a calling, a vocation, to tame the lush, wild Garden of Eden. In Eden, everyone had a calling. Even after the fall, all men and women are given a calling by God—again, regardless of whether or not they are believers. According to Scripture, even ungodly rulers are considered "God's servants" (Rom. 13:1–6). Therefore, whether one is a truck driver or a homemaker; a corporate executive or a lawyer; a dishwasher or a doctor, one is pursuing a calling which God has included as part of his image in everyone. Christians especially should be inspired by this doctrine to pursue excellence and diligence in their callings and should recognize it as instituted by God in creation.

Another thing we learn from this biblical doctrine is that God is not interested only in religion. God did not invent Christian music or Christian books. He has never organized a Christian concert or a Christian Yellow Pages. The doctrine of creation teaches us that, while in the realm of redemption (regeneration, justification, sanctification, union with Christ, etc.) we are different from non-Christians, in the realm of what we eat, drink, watch, play, work at, create, and discuss, we share a common humanity. What our convictions require is not that we deny our humanity, but that we be God-centered in the way in which we express our humanity. That is all creation was ever designed to reflect.

The doctrine of creation also convinces us that God is in control. Out of nothing he created order; out of darkness, light; and out of nothing, spectacular variety. Our own limitations make it impossible to understand the purpose behind every event, for often we are too close to a situation. Yet, years go by and finally we see how everything came together into a colorful and orderly pattern. Imagine trying to navigate the globe before there were accurate maps, and compare that to the objectivity we now have due to satellite technology. Information, or a lack of it at the time, accounts for our ability or inability to understand how everything fits together. But we have learned enough through our technological sophistication to convince us of the principle that there *is* purpose, that it *does* all make sense, and that things *do* fit together, even though we might lack the data.

Similarly, we learn from the doctrine of creation that a single Intelligence is responsible for the material universe. The parts are integrated and interdependent, and one random accident could upset the entire balance of nature. To suggest that the present creation is the result of a random, chance event (or, according to nontheistic explanations of evolution, *multiple* random accidents) is more absurd to the human mind and experience than arguing that a fine Swiss watch was the product of a storm that blew through the craftsman's shop and arranged the parts into a working timepiece. This means, therefore, that randomness is excluded from God's universe, since one random accident is all that would be necessary to upset order. This is practical as a reminder that God is in control of every minute detail of our lives.

In his best-seller, *When Bad Things Happen to Good People,* Rabbi Harold Kushner states, "Bad things do happen to good people in this world, but it is not God who wills it. God would like people to get what they deserve in life, but He cannot always arrange it. Even God has a hard time keeping chaos in check and limiting the damage evil can do."[5]

Such a limited view of God is exploded by the biblical notion of creation. It fails to account for a God who "determines the number of the stars" and who "calls them each by name" (Ps. 147:4), who numbers our hairs and sees to it that every robin's breast has a pattern. While sin introduced disorder, destruction, and decay, the same God who created order from chaos is ruling and redeeming his world so that one day "the creation itself will be liberated from its bondage to decay" even though "the whole creation has been groaning as in the pains of childbirth right up to the present time" (Rom. 8:21–22).

Finally, the doctrine of creation leaves us without excuse. In the popular 1990 film *Flatliners,* a group of medical students, through encounters with the "afterlife," realize that everything we do matters. It is only by coming into contact with the eternal that the weight of this life is adequately felt. In the scientific religious ideology that dogmatically presupposes the *a priori* that there is no eternal perspective, we can only conclude with Dostoevsky that everything is permitted. But Scripture teaches us the significance of today's actions in the long run. French philosopher Henri Frederic Amiel said, "I realize with intensity that man, in all that he does that is great and noble, is only the organ of something or someone higher than himself."[6] British philosopher Philip James Bailey added, "Let each man think himself an act of God."[7] Imagine the transforming impact of a thought like that!

Study Questions

1. "To err is human": is that correct? How would you respond in the light of Genesis 1:31?
2. Carrying that a bit further, do you think there was anything inherent in Adam's humanity, as created, that gave him at least a bent toward making a mistake or outright rebelling against God? (See Eccles. 7:29.)
3. What, more than anything else, distinguishes humans from animals?
4. Explain the "image of God" and its implications for the way we treat each other. Are non-Christians also created in God's image? And if they are, how should we view those who are

hostile to our faith? (See Matt. 5:44–45; Rom. 12:14; James 3:9.) How could this affect the way we relate to our neighbors or coworkers? Does it give us more of a sense of having things in common? Does it even mean that ungodly, unchristian rulers are, in a sense, "God's ministers," though in the common (civil) sphere rather than in the church? (See Rom. 13:1–4.)

5. What does it mean to be created *ex nihilo,* "out of nothing," and why is this such an important idea? How does this square with the Greek idea of spirit and matter being eternal?

6. Explain the weight of being created in God's image in terms of both promise and threat. (See Rom. 1:14–20.)

7. Discuss the purpose behind creation. Evaluate each suggested theory in the light of one question: Is that theory God-centered or human-centered? (See also Ps. 8:3–9; 104:24–31.)

8. Define *Gnosticism* and its view of creation. Evaluate it in the light of the creation account (Gen. 1) and Matthew 15:11. Is the body a spiritual, godly, integral aspect of who we are, or should we seek to transcend our human bodies, minds, and passions and concentrate on our spirits? Does God relate to our spirits or to our whole human personalities? Why is this important for a healthy outlook on life?

9. Discuss the implications of the doctrine of creation for enjoyment of working, resting, and playing in the world.

three

Rebels without a Cause

Nearly all of us were involved in the lemonade business at some point during childhood. I can recall my thriving enterprise at the edge of the sidewalk. I spent more time mixing the lemonade than actually selling it. You see, I was not content to simply add the packet and stir. No, no. I was a lemonade connoisseur. Anybody could empty a bit of powder into a jar of water, but my lemonade had to have my own trademark. It had to be *my* product. If the truth were to be known—and I'm man enough today to admit it—that was clearly the worst drink I have ever tasted. Yet even though the lemonade was a culinary assault, I humored myself that it was much improved due to my creativity. And others humored me, my parents especially.

I haven't made lemonade in years, but still I find myself giving in to the irresistible temptation to assume that if something's going to be done right, I have to do it myself. I must contribute something if it is going to be acceptable. And I still humor myself and am humored by others. Advertisers reinforce this humoring process by telling us, "you deserve a break today" and "you can have it your way." They prompt us to demand the very finest hair care "because I'm worth it." We begin thinking, from birth, that we are the center of the universe. But we know better. We know deep down that the lemonade is sour. Just the same we move on, pretending that we can conquer every obstacle ourselves if given half a chance.

This tendency is part of what we inherited from Adam in the fall. The better we understand the tragedy of that event and its results, the better we will appreciate God's amazing grace.

Fallen Stars

You know the story. God created humans in his own image and "took the man and put him in the Garden of Eden to work it and take care of it." Then he gave Adam his instructions: "You are free to eat from any tree in the garden; but you must not eat from the tree of the knowledge of good and evil, for when you eat of it you will surely die" (Gen. 2:15–17).

The process in this fatal decision is instructive. It began with Satan's direct rebellion against God's Word. He declared, "You will *not* surely die" (Gen. 3:4, italics added). There's no beating around the bush here. Satan always downplays the gravity of sin and its consequences. What he really said is, "Look, Eve, you're not looking at this thing with an open mind. God is just intimidating you with all of this talk of 'punishment.' After all, God's bark is worse than his bite." This first strike must have left its mark in Eve's mind, because she began a dialogue with the serpent. The same argument still works on us. God is viewed as a sort of benign George Burns character who looks the other way and lets bygones be bygones. He is not considered quite as holy as the Scriptures make him out to be, nor as just. In fact, he exists for our happiness, not we for his. Mistake number one.

The second stage in Satan's plan was to use the same line on Eve that he had so effectively used on himself in his own rebellion. Eve took the bait, and humans have taken it ever since: "You will be like God" (Gen. 3:5). Adam and Eve decided that day that they would "have it their way." After all, they were worth it. *Invictus,* a nineteenth-century poem by William Ernest Henley, expresses well this sentiment:

> I thank whatever gods that be
> For my unconquerable soul. . . .

> I am the master of my fate:
> I am the captain of my soul.

After all, Satan argued, God was restricting human freedom because he didn't want any competition. "You are obedient," he told Eve, "only because you have never discovered yourself." A quest for enlightenment was what she needed. "Eve, you and Adam deserve a break today." "Sure, it costs a little more, but you're worth it." "Have it your way!" God was trying to take away Adam and Eve's self-esteem and rain on their parade, the serpent reasoned. Satan was arguing that Adam and Eve could transcend their self-identity as creatures and become gods themselves—autonomous individualists who no longer needed the restraints of a creature-Creator relationship.

"Maybe I *do* have an unconquerable soul," Eve began to reason. Satan further undermined God's authority by *adding* to the requirement God had given Adam. "Did God really say, 'You must not eat from any tree in the garden'?" he cunningly inquired (Gen. 3:1). Of course, God did *not* say that they couldn't eat from any tree in the garden, but if Satan can get us to feel oppressed and closed in rather than cared for and liberated by God—if, in other words, he can turn God into a cosmic legalist—he can more easily convince us of the need for mutiny.

In their empirical study of the psychology of religion, Bernard Spilka, Ralph Hood, and Richard Gorsuch point out that numerous studies have concluded that "while Jews show the least abstinence from alcohol . . . ; they possess extremely low rates for pathological drinking." On the other hand, "Methodists express negative attitudes toward drinking, yet a study of a college sample showed that 'more Methodist students drink to get intoxicated than any other group.'" The same irony shows up in Mormon samplings and other legalistic groups. On the other hand, "Judaism considers alcohol a gift of God that must not be abused," and "orthodox and conservative Jews become intoxicated less than their reform or secular coreligionists." Conclusion? "Alcoholism seems to be troublesome among groups that generally take the most negative stance toward unlimited drinking." This is just one example of how legalism can undermine law. Many of the most hardened secularists in society today were raised in repressive, authoritarian religious environments.[1]

Legalism, adding to God's Word, continues to drive people away from God. That is one reason why adding to his commands is condemned equally with subtracting from them. (See Deut. 4:2; Prov. 30:6; Rev. 22:18.) In Satan's strategy, legalism was as useful a tool as lawlessness. And notice Eve's response. She rightly countered that God had said they could eat freely from the trees in the garden. But, she continued, God had also said, "You must not eat fruit from the tree that is in the middle of the garden, *and you must not touch it, or you will die*" (Gen. 3:3). So, on one hand she rejected Satan's addition to God's commandment, but she turned around and added her own—that of not touching the tree. God had given them paradise—"You are free to eat from any tree in the garden," he told them, with the exception of one single tree. Obviously, if Adam and Eve were to eat from *this* tree, it would be out of rebellion, not out of necessity. This is still our way. Although God has given us so much to take pleasure in, we are not content until we have indulged in that which is forbidden.

In his *Confessions,* St. Augustine tells the story of how he and his friends would plunder the neighbor's pear tree. It was not out of necessity, any more than Adam's actions were as he had a pleasant pear tree in his own backyard. Rather, he confessed, the pleasure was in the sin, not in the pear. The neighbor's pears tasted better precisely because they were stolen.

"When the woman saw that the fruit of the tree was good for food and pleasing to the eye, and also desirable for gaining wisdom, she took some and ate it. She also gave some to her husband, who was with her, and he ate it" (Gen. 3:6). Eve was attracted visually by the packaging and was also attracted by the promises the tree was advertised to guarantee.

"Then the eyes of both of them were opened, and they realized they were naked; so they sewed fig leaves together and made coverings for themselves" (Gen. 3:7). This, too, has been part and parcel of the human condition since the fall. We try to cover up our shame. Sometimes we spend hundreds of dollars on seminars or therapists who will tell us how to deny our shame. And yet, we know deep down that we feel ashamed because we have behaved shamefully; we feel guilty because we are guilty. When Adam and Eve took that big risk and "found themselves," they realized they were lost.

Religion is, for the most part, our way of covering ourselves, a means of sewing respectability, morality, and charity into a patchwork garment that can hide our nakedness.

A Declaration of Independence

In a *Time* magazine essay entitled "What Really Matters?" Robert Rosenblatt sought to define "the idea characterizing our age."[2] The essay suggests that the twentieth-century spirit is distinguished by its determination to break away from traditional norms "and eventually from any constraints at all" and that the basis of this determination is the assumption that "what was not free *ought* to be free; that limits were intrinsically evil." This provocative critique of modern culture draws its conclusion about "our age of self-confident autonomy" by noting, "When people are unfettered they are freed, but not yet free." The essayist understood more about freedom of choice than Adam and Eve did that day when they gave in to Satan's grandiose notion of "self-confident autonomy." Yet, it is precisely that notion that has kept God and humans apart since the fall in Eden. Adam and Eve resented God: "How dare God withhold from us the knowledge of good and evil!"

It is curious that the vogue pursuit today is the knowledge—the experience—of good and evil. In fact, we have reached the point where the lines separating the two regions disappear altogether. We moderns talk about sexual liberation and yet, even without AIDS and a host of other sexually transmitted diseases, we know the morning after that "when people are unfettered they are freed, but not yet free." From what does such a sexual liberation free us? From homes where family members care about each other—turning them instead into places where selfish individuals constantly look after their own independence? Or how about the freedom to end the lives of unborn infants? How free is the woman who realizes she has taken her child's life? How free is a jet-set yuppie who finds that he *can't* quit cocaine whenever he wants to? A corporate executive may have made his millions by breaking all the rules, but is he free?

"Your eyes will be opened," Satan promised (Gen. 3:5). But then, he has always been a liar.

I found the following lines written on a painting in one of my favorite cafes:

> I have taken the pill.
> I have hoisted my skirts
>   to my thighs,
> Dropped them to my ankles,
> Rebelled at the University,
> Skied at Aspen,
> Lived with two men,
> married one.
> Earned my keep,
> Kept my identity,
> And frankly . . .
> I'M LOST.

Ours is indeed a generation that has seen it all. And many teens of today are experienced beyond their elders in sex, drugs, and life in general. Many men boast about macho infidelity, while many women, too, make a break with their homes. Individuals we are; no longer fathers and mothers, children, brothers and sisters, but solitary, isolated individuals who happen to live under the same roof and share similar experiences. Yet it's essential to put all of this in perspective.

We should not be shocked by the disintegration of relationships. It is not, as many have argued, the result of a nation's retreat from a supposedly golden era when everybody thought and lived like an episode of *Leave It to Beaver*. It is the result of the fall. Humans have always been sinful, have always been prone to shaking their fist in God's face—and that includes you and me. The Genesis account teaches us that since the fall there never has been an era somewhere in the past known as "the good ol' days."

When we see the fall in contrast to the glory of creation, we have some measuring stick for the tragedy of sin. Suppose a cheap glass vase falls from the top shelf in the kitchen and is broken beyond repair. Into the bin it goes. But suppose a thief breaks into a museum's central vault and makes off with its most prized artifact—a perfectly preserved, one-of-a-kind vase from the ancient Greeks. The police would be called, and the culprits would be hunted down and prosecuted to the full extent of the law.

Similarly, we have made off with God's image. We have distorted and disfigured God's creation. We would have an excuse, perhaps, if we could say that there was a lack or a defect in our nature; yet the problem is not our humanness but what we have *done* with our humanness. We have directed all of our gifts, our religious, moral, creative, and intellectual abilities, toward a declaration of independence from God. We have used the very assets with which he endowed us as weapons against him. Clothed in his very image, we have shaken our fists at God and said, with Adam and Eve, "How dare you!" This is why the threat attached to eating from the forbidden fruit was so severe: "when you eat of it you will surely die" (Gen. 2:17).

Our fall was complete. Every area of human life was affected, and nothing created by God was left untouched. Consequently, the stain of sin corrupts us physically, emotionally, psychologically, mentally, morally, and spiritually. That doesn't mean, of course, that we are all brute savages who always carry out every possible evil; it does mean that each one of us is capable of doing so. Further, it means that there is no hope for human beings to recover themselves or to make amends. God demands a perfection of the qualities with which he endowed us, and we are corrupted in every chamber. No part of us can rescue or heal the rest of us.

When our relationship with God was severed and, in a sense, diplomatic relations were discontinued, all of life went wrong. It was not just our religious or devotional lives that were affected. The sinful condition corrupts our relationships, our health, our happiness, our careers, all of our activities, along with the social, political, and economic effects we see all around us. Those who might want to wish it away with positive thinking simply cannot explain the thick, dark strokes on the canvas. The Bible is a good deal more realistic about the human condition than is popular American culture. The horror of human evil that appeared on September 11, 2001, in New York and the U.S. Capitol comes as no surprise to the reader of Scripture.

Just because humanity *declared* independence does not mean that it *became* independent. We can no more live independently of God than a fish can live independently of water. "For in him we live and move and have our being" (Acts 17:28). Adam and Eve sought a self-identity that did not require God as a reference point; in the bargain, they lost their identity. Experiencing periodical illness now, they became fatigued and frustrated with their work instead of being as fulfilled as they had been before. They grew discontented with each other; the second male, Adam's son Cain, murdered his own brother.

Guilt stained innocence. Adam and Eve were ashamed of themselves and disillusioned; their guilt was more than fig leaves could hide.

We need to stop running from God and from the guilt that we must all own. We cannot find God for the same reason that a thief can't find a police officer. If we find him, or if he catches up to us, he will expose us for who we really are. This is why Paul repeated the psalmist in lamenting, "there is no one who understands, no one who seeks God" (Rom. 3:11).

What fig leaves are we wearing? God is not impressed with our empty offerings of human achievement. We may humor children when they concoct their lemonade, but this business with God is serious. There is nothing we can offer him; nothing we can contribute. So, it would seem that we are in quite a predicament. All have robbed God, and there are no "good" robbers. The thief and the theologian must both come to God on the same terms. Our hope is in God's mercy. "For the Son of Man has come to save that which was lost" (Matt. 18:11 NKJV).

Christ said, "It is not the healthy who need a doctor, but the sick. . . . For I have not come to call the righteous, but sinners" (Matt. 9:12–13). To put it simply, the condition in qualifying for God's grace is to recognize that you can't qualify! After Christ brought his disciples to the place where they despaired of their own efforts before God, they asked, "Who then can be saved?" and he answered, "With man this is impossible, but with God all things are possible" (Matt. 19:26).

Someone to Blame

We're always looking for a scapegoat, much as Adam did. When God confronted Adam after his disobedience, the culprit said, "It's *her* fault—the one *You* gave me made me eat the fruit." And Eve answered, "The devil made me do it." For both, the fault had to be located outside their own will and activity. This should not be too unfamiliar to those of us surrounded by a pampered society that is committed to shifting blame to parents, employers, employees, spouses, children, minorities, majorities, big business, big government, and so on. While sin is institutional as well as individual, the location of our own blame is our own sinful hearts.

If we reconsider Rabbi Kushner's popular alternative to the Hebrew-Christian understanding of an all-good *and* all-powerful God, we can see the same sort of buck-passing that began in Eden. If bad things happen to good people, he suggests, God must not be as powerful as we once thought. But Kushner's argument begins with a most debatable presupposition. When did bad things begin to happen to good people? On the contrary, bad things happen to bad people and good things happen to bad people, but "there is only One who is good" (Matt. 19:17).

According to Scripture, the fall makes us not only victims, but also victimizers. With Adam and Eve, we are all in this thing together, and none of the fall's effects—sin, pain, suffering, tragedy—can be blamed on God. This world as we know it is not normal. It is not as God created it but as humans have shaped it after their own character. God took a look at the world he had created and said, "It is very good." If God were *not* in control of every event and individual, the full force of our sinful hearts would cast off all restraint. While reserving saving grace for believers, God nevertheless gives his common grace to all men and women, and this is responsible for the good we see in bad people like ourselves.

To insist that *we* are the cause of whatever is wrong in this world does not mean, for instance, that we each take personal responsibility for every hostage situation in the Middle East. It does mean, however, that we must realize we are part of the problem and that each day we contribute our sins against God and neighbor. Our pride, arrogance, and rebellion against God are only underscored by blaming God for, say, a bad environment while we continue to release our toxic, unnatural refuse into the air. That is our way: We pollute life and blame God for the results. The fall, in a sense, reverses the act of creation by turning order into chaos. And yet, even the confusion and chaos is controlled and held in check by the Creator.

Although we are entirely responsible for our guilt, the fall did not surprise God; it was part of his plan all along. He had organized a plan of redemption long before that fateful moment in Eden. "For the creation was subjected to frustration, not by its own choice, but by the will of the one who subjected it, in hope that the creation itself will be liberated from its bondage to decay and brought into the glorious freedom of the children of God. We know that the whole creation has been groaning as in the pains of childbirth right up to the present time" (Rom. 8:20–22). Even when bad things happen to bad people, God turns it around for good.

A Lethal Injection

We have all heard tragic stories of people who received blood transfusions donated by those who were unwitting carriers of a deadly disease. When Adam and Eve turned on God, guilt—both the fact and the feeling—rushed into their spiritual veins. However marred and disfigured, the image of God in Adam and Eve remained. Nothing about them changed chemically or biologically; they were not mysteriously changed into a different form of life, but they were guilty for the first time.

Like the victims of a contaminated blood transfusion, we all have inherited Adam's guilt and corruption. This is what theologians call "original sin." Adam included us all in his decision, and that decision was fatal for the entire race.

This concept is often hard to swallow—particularly in America, where we are saturated with the democratic ideal of being able to decide for ourselves what party we will join. But we did not decide whether we would belong to the Adamic party; we were born into it. The same is true, though, in a lot of areas. For instance, when Thomas Jefferson drafted the Declaration of Independence, he spoke for you and me. We were not actually there. We didn't get to help him decide what to write. And yet, this document represents us just the same as if we had been there. We were born American citizens, not British, because of individuals who lived and events that took place long before we came along.

In the same way, Adam was our representative before God and he spoke for us. As Adam's children and heirs, we think his thoughts and imitate his actions—by instinct, without even having met him. That means that while we are capable of incredible artistic, intellectual, and cultural accomplishments (due to creation), we are also capable of unbelievable cruelty and harm (due to the fall).

The psalmist confessed, "Surely I was sinful at birth, sinful from the time my mother conceived me" (Ps. 51:5). And Isaiah recognized that even he was "a rebel from birth" (Isa. 48:8). It doesn't matter whether you are a fifth-generation Christian or a fifth-generation atheist, whether you are a minister or a murderer, whether you sing in the choir or in a topless bar. We are all equally guilty in God's courtroom.

When a corporation dumps toxic chemicals into one end of a stream, it's not just that one area that is affected. Soon the pollution washes all the way down the stream, and the entire river is polluted. Adam's rebellion had just this kind of effect. Our whole race became corrupted—so much so that, viewing us collectively, God concluded, "Together they have become useless" (Rom. 3:12 NASB). Those are strong words, but biblical ones nonetheless. One person is no better than another; we're all in this together.

Another illustration, drawn from the biblical term *testament,* is that of a written will leaving an estate to heirs. We are born heirs of Adam. Everything he has belongs to us: his nature, his condition, his guilt, and his debts. We learn that this patriarch of the human family has left us with a massive estate in debt. His enemies (including God) are ours, and the old rivalries are wounds reopened by us every day. Just as any earthly heir cannot separate his or her personality, character, identity, or resources from the inheritance of ancestors, so none of us comes into the world a blank slate.

When we are born, then, we are born at odds with a God for whose pleasure we were created. There are no "innocent little babies," and the Bible knows of no age of accountability. One can choose to believe, as I do, that all who die in infancy are saved, but one must credit that to God's mercy, not to his justice. God *could* condemn every infant for eternity; there is already enough evidence to make a conviction. "Sin entered the world through one man," said Paul, and "the result of one tresspass was condemnation for all men" (Rom. 5:12–18).

"I Can Quit Whenever I Want To"

All of this means that we are sinners not only by choice, but also by birth. We are not born in a neutral zone but as enemies of God, "by nature children of wrath" (Eph. 2:3 NASB). We do not merely *do* evil; we *are* evil. "The heart is deceitful above all things and beyond cure. Who can understand it?" (Jer. 17:9). We not only fall, we are fallen. We not only get lost, we are lost. We sin because it is our nature to sin; we are most comfortable when we are committing sin in some form or another. In Romans 6:16 the apostle Paul wrote, "Don't you know that when you offer yourselves to someone to obey him as slaves, you are slaves to the one whom you obey—whether you are slaves to sin, which leads to death, or to obedience, which leads to righteousness?" He added that we are, by nature, "slaves to sin," and that "when you were slaves to sin, you were free from the control of righteousness." In other words, righteousness made no demands on us which we, by nature, could fulfill.

Our Lord said that "everyone who sins is a slave to sin" (John 8:34) and infuriated the religious leaders by informing them that, "No one can come to me unless the Father who sent me draws him" (John 6:44).

So desperate is the human predicament because of the fall. So we *can't* "quit whenever we want to." We may be able to stop a certain habit, but we cannot stop sinning. We may be able to curb certain *acts* of sin, but we cannot cease being *sinful.* That is true even of Christians, who will experience freedom from sin only in paradise. When I say we *can't* stop sinning or cease from being sinful, I don't mean "can't" in the sense that an outside force is overpowering us, controlling our actions against our will. Rather, the very sinful disposition of our will determines the unyielding reign of sin in our lives before regeneration. Since the fall, sin is as much human nature as barking is a dog's nature. When Adam sinned, the entire human race died spiritually. Hence, every human birth is, spiritually speaking, a stillbirth. There are no movements toward God. We are, from the very beginning, in bondage to sin, slaves to our selfish wills.

"When you eat of it you will surely die." That was God's warning. Of course, Adam did not die physically on that very day, but he did experience spiritual death then and there. Paul tells Christians they "were dead in . . . transgressions and sins" before God regenerated them (Eph. 2:1). Hence the human will is in bondage to sin. This does not mean that we sin *against* our will (i.e., by force); rather, our will is in bondage to sin, and when we do sin, our sin is in perfect harmony with the will which produced it. Martin Luther put it this way:

> A man who does not have the Spirit of God does not, to be sure, do evil unwillingly, by compulsion, as if grabbed by the neck and forced to do it as a thief or highwayman is dragged to punishment against his will; he does evil spontaneously and with a ready will. But he is unable by his own powers to stop, check, or change this readiness or willingness to do evil; rather he goes on willingly and craves evil. And even if he should be compelled by force to do anything that is outwardly different, yet the will within remains averse to it and rears up in indignation against the power that controls and constrains it.[3]

Dead to God and alive to self, humans are incapable of taking a single step toward God, not because of some internal defect or external pressure, but due to the bondage of the unregenerated will. We really and truly don't *want* to come to terms with God. We want to run from God, like Adam and Eve, and sew fig leaves into a shame-concealing garment. "There is no one righteous, not even one; there is no one who understands, no one who seeks God. . . . there is no one who does good, not even one" (Rom. 3:10–12). We depend entirely on God's mercy if we are going to live again and respond to him. "The man without the Spirit does not accept the things that come from the Spirit of God, for they are foolishness to him, and he cannot understand them, because they are spiritually discerned" (1 Cor. 2:14).

What Can We Do?

Nothing! That's the point: "Salvation comes from the LORD" (Jonah 2:9). "It does not, therefore, depend on man's desire or effort, but on God's mercy" (Rom. 9:16). After all, "No one can come to me unless the Father who sent me draws him" (John 6:44). Here we come back to the lemonade story which began this chapter. We want to get to work and become creative in devising a solution, but we cannot help ourselves out of this one. The saying "God helps those who help themselves" is thought by many Christians to be a biblical reference, but it comes from Ben Franklin's *Almanac*. It is not a biblical quotation, nor is it biblical at all in its content. God does *not* help those who help themselves. In fact, it is people like that against whom God swore in his wrath, "They shall never enter my rest" (Heb. 4:3). Why? "For anyone who enters God's rest also rests from his own work, just as God did from his" (Heb. 4:10). Those whom God accepts are those whom *he* makes acceptable in Christ. When we try to add our own concoctions to God's already perfect remedy, we spoil the whole thing and incur his wrath.

We all know something is wrong, though. And we know that something needs to be resolved. I was deeply impressed with the popular 1990 film *Flatliners,* mentioned earlier, in which some medical students discover a means of inducing death for a brief period in order to probe the afterlife, then resuscitating the body. They relive their sins individually as they encounter threatening apparitions of offended parties. The students realize that one's sins do have consequences and that guilt is real.

That is more than our society—and sometimes even our churches—typically grants. Karl Menninger, the famous secular psychologist, wrote an important book entitled *Whatever Became of Sin?* In it Menninger points out the dangerous psychological implications of denying the reality of sin and guilt. We know they are there and we can't get rid of them ourselves. Yet, the more we admit needs to be done by God because of our own helplessness, the more we feel indebted to God. And nobody likes to be in debt. None of us likes to see ourselves as he or she truly is. Consequently, we will pay pop psychologists,

TV preachers, and entertainers to tell us we are, after all, good people. But if "I'm okay and you're okay," why do we both feel so guilty?

One thing that the Bible makes absolutely clear is that we depend entirely on God, not only for food, air, and shelter, but also for salvation. Remember the confusion that resulted when people began building the tower of Babel, hoping to reach God. He has never been fond of towers. God is out of our reach, but we are never out of his.

God Doesn't Grade on the Curve!

We can merit the favor of other people. For instance, many non-Christians are benevolent. A millionaire can make a large donation to charity, and we are all pleased to see him do so, but as long as that person is "dead in transgressions and sins" and is "in Adam," "a rebel by birth," and "without faith," God actually considers that donation a sinful act. How repugnant to the human mind! Nevertheless, the Bible clearly teaches that whatever does not proceed from faith in Jesus Christ is in fact sinful (Heb. 11:6). We cannot merit God's favor, and he is not impressed with even our best attempts. It's like trying to climb out of a sand pit: The more we climb and struggle, the deeper we get.

The whole point to this is that God must somehow *bestow* on us his own merit, his own righteousness, if we are to be viewed favorably by him. At this point in our study, we don't know how he will do it. In fact, we don't know whether he will do it at all. Just think about it: God would be perfectly just at this point to pull a sheet over the lifeless corpse of humanity. He could have pronounced the judgment about which he clearly warned Adam and Eve without providing a means of redemption. Salvation was never a given and must not be taken for granted by us as though something in God or something in the universe required God to save us. Although God's love moved him to reconcile us to justice, his love would not have been violated if he had condemned all of us to an eternity without that love.

Conclusion

This doctrine has been immensely practical, not only in church history, but in history generally. As one example, it is virtually undisputed that it was this strong, biblical doctrine that figured so prominently in James Madison's mind as he drafted the United States Constitution. The establishment of checks and balances within the power structure of the judicial, legislative, and administrative branches was due to Madison's conviction, gained through years of instruction under the Presbyterian theologian John Witherspoon, that we are all "by nature the children of wrath" (Eph. 2:3 KJV), bent in on ourselves, and that, given half the chance, we will further our own interests at the expense of others. Some might call this a pessimistic view of humanity; however, Madison thought it was a rather realistic view of the human condition. Because he did, the United States is happy to have celebrated the constitution's bicentennial.

This conviction is necessary for churches, too. We have been losing our grip on biblical realism to the point where even in our own churches we often fail to hold leaders accountable, as though somehow they are too good, too holy, to be questioned. But the doctrine of sin reminds us that none of us is excluded from the fall and its effects, that we are all "by nature objects of wrath." No one is exempt from checks and balances on power.

This doctrine also teaches us that there are no good people from God's point of view (Rom. 3:10, 12). Good here is not what we *attempt,* but what we *are.* This, then, deals a deadly blow to self-righteousness. When we think of sin primarily as an action or a behavior, it's easy to think that a "sinner" is the town drunk or the bachelor down the street who's living with so-and-so. But when we see sin as a condition, we begin to realize that we are all sinners, even though we may think our particular sinful actions are pretty tame.

We will never be what Adam was before the fall unless we become perfect, and only Christ's righteousness suffices. But through his obedience, sacrificial death, and triumphant resurrection, we can be clothed with the very righteousness of God himself. This was foreshadowed when, after finding Adam and Eve hiding in shame, God pointed to One who would crush Satan's head (Gen. 3:15), and then God himself changed the homespun fig leaves for the skin of a slaughtered animal, prefiguring Christ, "the Lamb of God, who takes away the sin of the world" (John 1:29).

This means that we have to stop concocting our own lemonade. We must surrender our fig leaves and come to terms with our shame and guilt instead of running from the One with whom we have business. It means that we must stop calling other people sinners and recognize that we ourselves are unacceptable to God apart from Christ alone. I have heard preachers appeal to the goodness of Americans in their calls for a moral revival. "Deep down," I remember hearing one say, "Americans are good people, an honest people, goodhearted people. All they need is to be shown the way back." But this biblical doctrine of sin we have just studied, if you really believe it, takes the wind out of the sails of individuals and movements convinced that moral reform (changing actions) is able to bring about meaningful change in human character. Jesus chastised the Pharisees for focusing on sinful *actions,* without recognizing that the real problem is *affections* and that those affections are ruled by whatever one's master happens to be. The Pharisees reasoned, "If we can just get folks to stop doing this or that, we would have a moral society." And if Jesus had simply offered a new and improved method of moral betterment, the Pharisees would never have disturbed his ministry. But Jesus reminded them again and again that the problem is the heart, not the hands, and that men and women are not just morally handicapped, but spiritually dead.

Finally, this doctrine magnifies God's grace. If we do not know the seriousness of the diagnosis, we can't appreciate the cure. To the degree that moderns feel "stressed out" instead of guilty, they will tailor a gospel that offers a way to relieve stress rather than guilt. But once one faces the real problem, he or she is ready for the real solution. Only with this horrible, unflattering backdrop can we now move on to one of the most exciting acts in the entire play.

Study Questions

1. Go step by step through the process involved in Adam and Eve's fatal decision. Describe the significance of each

successive movement toward rebellion. Can you detect this process in your own rebellion as an heir of Adam?

2. Why is the fall such a tragedy?

3. How extensive was the fall? In other words, how much of our make-up is affected by it? (See Jer. 17:9; Rom. 1:21–32; 3:9–18;1 Cor. 2:14; Eph. 2:1.)

4. Compare/contrast the biblical view of freedom with the world's idea. (See Ps. 119:45; Luke 4:18; John 8:32–36; Rom. 6:16; 8:21.)

5. Define "original sin" and explain how it is communicated to us. (See Ps. 51:5; Isa. 48:8; 64:6–7; Rom. 5:12–19; Eph. 2:3.) Do you think it's fair for us to *inherit* Adam's guilt and corruption even as newborns before we have anything to say about it? Evaluate the illustration that Thomas Jefferson spoke for the whole nation through the Declaration of Independence. (See p. 58.)

6. Can we, apart from God's gift of the new birth and justification, do anything that pleases God or cooperates with him toward our own salvation? Can we stop sinning? (See John 6:44; 8:34.)

7. "Sin is a *condition* before ever it is a matter of individual *acts*." In other words, "We sin because we're sinners," not the other way around. Evaluate. What biblical support would you use?

8. With this picture of the fall in mind, how would you respond to the proverb, "God helps those who help themselves"?

four

Grace before Time

The doctrine of sin has never been a big seller. Just the same, we are encouraged to find that this story has another chapter, for it could very well have ended with God's judgment. Certainly Satan thought he had finally ruined God's plans for the universe. The human race was the showcase of divine creation. Men and women were uniquely designed to have a relationship with God that even the highest ranking angels could never enjoy. Here was the creature in all of the universe that actually bore the divine signature, a priceless integration of body and soul. Now he lay in ruins. But Lucifer forgot to figure in God's love and mercy. Who thought God would set out to recover a race of rebels? Just as the race declared war, God announced peace.

As I mentioned in the last chapter, the fall came as no surprise to God. Nothing does. Things don't just happen—God is always in charge! Just when it looks like the tragic end to a short play, the curtain rises, the orchestra flourishes, and the magnificent drama of redemption begins. The opening act of this redemptive play takes place in the royal court of heaven in eternity past. St. Paul gives us the setting:

> Praise be to the God and Father of our Lord Jesus Christ, who has blessed us in the heavenly realms with every spiritual blessing in Christ.

For he chose us in him before the creation of the world, to be holy and blameless in his sight. In love he predestined us to be adopted as his sons through Jesus Christ, in accordance with his pleasure and will—to the praise of his glorious grace, which he has freely given us in the One he loves. [Eph. 1:3–6]

And Paul explains the wonder of it all. Because we have been chosen in Christ, "in him we have redemption through his blood, the forgiveness of sins, in accordance with the riches of God's grace" (v. 7). By taking us out of Adam's doomed family and placing us in Christ, "we were also chosen, having been predestined according to the plan of him who works out everything in conformity with the purpose of his will, in order that we, who were the first to hope in Christ, might be for the praise of his glory" (vv. 11–12).

We are used to choosing our rulers for ourselves in democratic societies. Every four years we in the U.S. elect a president. But that is not the way it works with redemption. We do not elect our redeemers. Jesus told his disciples, "You did not choose me, but I chose you and appointed you to go and bear fruit—fruit that will last" (John 15:16). We try to choose our leaders on the basis of their track records, but God chooses us *in spite* of ours! "I have chosen you out of the world," Jesus said (John 15:19). Instead of leaving the whole race to perish in a justly deserved eternal sentence, God selected from the rebel race men and women from "every tribe and language and people and nation" (Rev. 5:9). This remnant from all over the world forms a new spiritual race. Certainly those belonging to this new race would still belong to the human race, but would be adopted into God's own family. From the head of the table our heavenly Father reminds us, as Peter put it, "You are a chosen people, a royal priesthood, a holy nation, a people belonging to God" (1 Peter 2:9).

One writer put it this way:

> 'Tis not that I did choose Thee,
> For Lord, that could not be;
> This heart would still refuse Thee,
> Hadst Thou not chosen me.

The person who wrote those lines was convinced of his own inability to achieve salvation. That author knew that one's condition, without God's intervention, is so critical that no one would have chosen God unless God had first chosen him or her. We would all be running from God, trying to cover up our guilt and shame, but God determined to make us his own possession. If we become God's children, it will be only because he "in love . . . predestined us to be adopted as his sons" (Eph. 1:4–5). God is not in the business of helping us save ourselves. "Salvation comes from the LORD" (Jonah 2:9). And yet, this doctrine raises a lot of questions and objections. I have often thought that one good defense for the inspiration of Scripture is the doctrine of election, for no mortal man or woman could have invented an idea that so glorifies God and so humbles the human ego.

Why is the subject of election, or predestination, so divisive? Why is it that whenever the terms are brought up in conversation, people move to other parts of the room? If you ever want to clear a room in a hurry, just announce a discussion of predestination! We can be fairly certain that most of the passages addressed in this chapter are not underlined in most believers' Bibles, yet they deal with one of the most prominent themes running from Genesis to Revelation.

You see, we can talk about grace, sing about grace, preach about grace, just so long as we do not get too close to it. Election is too close. When we give *in* to election, we finally give *up* on ourselves in the matter of salvation. This doctrine takes grace to its logical conclusion: If God saves me without my works, then he must choose me apart from them, too. Martin Luther knew this. We know Luther as the one who turned on the light in the sixteenth century with regard to the centerpiece of the gospel. When he argued for *justification by grace alone through faith alone,* Luther insisted that this doctrine of election was a necessary guardian of justification. When Erasmus wrote to him that such debates were for theologians and "not for common ears," the Reformer responded, "If it is irreverent, if it is inquisitive, if it is unnecessary, as you say, . . . what, then, I ask you, is there that is reverent or serious or useful to know?"[1]

Let's examine some of the questions raised in connection with this teaching.

Free Will

Doesn't election deny free will? If God has already made my decision for me, I really don't have any choice in the matter, do I?

Sometimes in certain areas of life we don't have a choice. A prisoner, for example, has no choice over whether the governor will grant a pardon; the decision is out of the prisoner's hands. But the prisoner was able to choose whether he would commit the crime that merited his sentence. In the same way, Adam was free either to sin or not to sin, and he chose the former. Since Adam's choice, we are all born with a will that is in bondage to sin, able only to choose from among different types and degrees of sin. What sort of choices can a person make who is *dead in transgressions and sins?* Plenty, actually. He can choose whether to wear green socks or red ones. He can choose his house, career, spouse, and so on. But even those choices are determined by personal will, and one's will is determined by one's preference. Suppose the choice is blue socks. It may be because blue is a favorite color, or the person doing the choosing may just be sick of red, or it could be that blue goes best with his suit. Regardless of the reason, at the moment he chooses the blue socks, he *prefers* those socks to all others.

In the same way, we cannot escape our preferences. As Jonathan Edwards pointed out, ultimately no one has a free will, because the will is nothing more than an expression of preferences and preferences are colored entirely by personality and character. So let's move from decisions like socks and discuss the fallen will's relationship to salvation.

If the will is no more than an expression of character, it will never choose something contrary to the character of the chooser. Hence, our Lord's remark to the Pharisees, "You are *unable* to hear what I say. You belong to your father, the devil, and you want to carry out your father's desire" (John 8:43–44, italics added). Because they are *of* their father the devil, it follows that their *desires* are his desires. And notice he said, "*you want to carry out* your father's desire." You really *want* to obey the one to whom you are bound. That is the point. If God left you to yourself to decide whether you would choose or reject him, you would always refuse God as long as you "belong to your father, the devil." As long as you are a child of Adam, Jesus said, "you are unable to hear what I say" (v. 43). Your will always follows your character, your heart, your affections.

We often practice our evangelism as though gimmicks and techniques could get people to raise a hand or walk an aisle or pray a prayer. The problem, we reason, is not that they are in bondage to a sinful *nature* and require supernatural intervention, but that they are merely ill-informed and require a moving testimony or chorus. Sometimes such methods do get people to do these things, but that is not regeneration or conversion. We have simply gotten them to jump through our hoops. Essentially, election is God's making the decision for us that we would never have made for him. "This is love: not that we loved [or chose] God, but that he loved [and chose] us" (1 John 4:10). When we choose God, it costs us nothing compared to the cost of his choosing us. His choice of us signed his Son's death warrant.

Whosoever will, let him come!—that is the unqualified call of Scripture. The Lord Jesus Christ does not say, *Whosoever is white, let him come!* or *Whosoever is American, let him come!* He does not restrict the offer of the gospel to any socioeconomic, political, or ethnic group. Jew and Gentile—all are welcome at God's table! But when a person does *will* to come, it is because he or she has been chosen and converted by God's grace alone. Hence, when a person does come it is, as far as that person is concerned, a free choice, because no one externally coerced the choice. God changes our natural, self-oriented disposition and frees us for the first time from bondage to our sinful will, and then we make the decision that is in harmony with our new, regenerated nature. As freely as we hated God, now just as freely we love him. He decided to regenerate us and did it while we were resisting, but who's going to argue with that, especially when all we ever said before was *no?* I thank God every day that Jesus is *not* "a gentleman" who lets me have my own way.

And yet, it is not by a raw power forcing us against our will. Instead, the Holy Spirit persuades the enemy of God to become his friend by awakening him to his misery apart from God through the law, and overwhelming him with a sense of the absolute freeness of God's gracious provision in the gospel. The gift is never refused when the Spirit effectually calls because when he opens one's eyes, that person immediately (effectually) sees; when the

Spirit softens the hardened heart, those hostile to God are now suddenly made friends; those who were dead are made alive. In all of these metaphors, there is little question of a person causing these things by an act of will: the blind person restoring her sight by an act of will; a hardened enemy becoming a friend of God simply by making a decision; a dead person being made alive by self-resurrection. And once the spiritually dead are raised, there is no question but that this is the best condition in which to be. No one whom God raises chooses to return to spiritual death and alienation from God—not because God's power has turned him or her into an automaton, but because God's love has turned the person into a friend. It is infallible and certain, but is so because God conquers us by loving persuasion and gracious liberation.

The Westminster Confession of Faith states,

> Those whom God had predestined unto life, he is pleased in his appointed and accepted time effectually to call by his Word and Spirit, out of that state of sin and death, in which they are by nature, to grace and salvation by Jesus Christ; enlightening their minds, spiritually and savingly, to understand the things of God taking away their heart of stone, and giving unto them an heart of flesh; renewing their wills [not taking them away or forcing them] and by his almighty power determining them to that which is good, and effectually drawing them to Jesus Christ; *yet so, as they come most freely, being made willing by his grace.* [Chapter X]

The apostle Paul announced that salvation is "not of him who wills, nor of him who runs, but of God who shows mercy" (Rom. 9:16 NKJV). Paul does not mean that we do not will or that we do not run, but he says that salvation ultimately depends upon the will, decision, running, and working *of God*. Perhaps at first that is insulting, but it sure beats living with the alternative. It is a measure of our self-centeredness that we would even resent God for loving us before we loved him.

Determinism

If election is deterministic, isn't it a salvation of fate rather than love?
Obviously, if there is any order in the universe and in our lives, some one or some thing has determined history—from the des-

tiny of earthworms to humans. For the ancient Greeks and Romans it was an impersonal force known as Fate; the Persian and Eastern mystery religions believed history to be a toss-up between the good god and bad god. For Christians history has been determined by a person, and that person has a name— *Yahweh,* our Lord God. He is a good God, a loving God, a just and holy God. And in both Testaments believers knew that God had chosen for himself a people. According to the New Testament, the texts that once referred to the nation of Israel are now applied to the church (see, for instance, 1 Peter 2:9–10), and the prophecies of Hosea and Isaiah are fulfilled in the church:

> "I will call them 'my people' who are not my people;
> and I will call her 'my loved one' who is not my loved one,"
> and,
> "It will happen that in the very place where it was said to
>   them,
> 'You are not my people,'
> they will be called 'sons of the living God.'" [Rom. 9:25–26]

God is gathering a people to worship him and to celebrate his majesty, a "called out" group, chosen out of the world. The point we need to see in all of this is that it is a Person who is electing people, not an impersonal force. And the decision is not arbitrary but is caused by the love and mercy of a kind Creator who has gone to incredible lengths in order to save so many people. Thus we are "predestined according to the plan of him who works out everything in conformity with the purpose of his will" (Eph. 1:11).

Even though election means that salvation is determined by God, it is the antithesis of fatalism. Had God merely provided salvation for everybody and then stepped back to let the chips fall where they may, then you would have fatalism. In other words, if *God* does not determine the success of salvation, we are back to the meadows with Doris Day singing, *Que sera, sera— Whatever will be, will be.* But precisely because God has determined what will be, we have a salvation based on God and not on fatalism.

Christ said, "I know my sheep" (John 10:14). Our salvation is in the hands of a loving Savior who not only chose us, but offered his body as a human sacrifice for our sins! That is why it is so important to frame any discussion of election within the scope of Christ's person and his work. Throughout Ephesians 1, prepositional phrases such as "in Christ," "in him," and "in the One he loves," occur frequently. God did not just choose us; he chose us *in Christ.* Christ, then, is the center of our election. That means we do not discover our election by looking anywhere but to Christ. Do we trust in him? Is he alone our Savior? Are we *in him* through faith in his finished work? This is the only infallible test we have of whether "he chose us in him before the creation of the world" (Eph. 1:4). We must not look to our works or to our success or failure, or to anything or anyone outside of Christ for confirmation of our election. Any discussion that places anything at the center of the discussion—even very good and holy things— is bound to be distorted and unbiblical.

In this connection, it is important to raise a word of caution to some of my Reformed brothers and sisters. Sometimes, when one learns about election for the first time, the new discovery swallows everything in sight. The sovereignty of God is sometimes so emphasized that other attributes responsible for our election—God's mercy, his love, his kindness—are neglected. This creates a doctrine that is less tender, less compassionate, and less biblical. Furthermore, because our knowledge of God the Father is so scant these days, having our eyes opened to his majesty in election is almost overwhelming. And yet, election is Christ-centered, and we must never use such a magnificent doctrine as a vehicle for understanding God the Father without locating its reference point in God the Son. Apart from Christ, any concept of election or predestination is bound to lead to despair rather than joy.

Fairness

Election is unfair. How can God tell people, "Sorry, folks, but you're just not on the list"?

I believe that the accusation of God's injustice in choosing one person and not another is rooted in the fact that we have really lost our doctrine of grace. We no longer really believe that nobody deserves salvation. We no longer really believe that God *could* send us all to hell without giving us time to think about it, and that this would be perfectly just. If we did believe that people were saved in spite of the fact that they really do deserve the very opposite, election would appear to us to be a very logical as well as biblical conclusion. Even if the Bible didn't explicitly teach the doctrine of election from cover to cover, one would be able to infer it clearly from the Bible's doctrine of grace. Paul could not separate election and grace in his own mind. In fact he called it "the election of grace" (Rom. 11:5 NKJV). So what's fair? Getting what we deserve, right? Do you *deserve* to be saved? Does anyone?

This was the biggest question I had, too, when I began to see that this doctrine was taught in Scripture. The crux of my problem was that I could not understand why God would have chosen me. Why not my next-door neighbor? She was a much better person. I struggled at length with the concept of a God who really is big enough and free enough to do whatever he wants. After all, I began to reason, I guess it *is* his universe. I remember reading a section of Romans one morning while listening to the Rolling Stones' tune "Get Off of My Cloud" and thinking that this is exactly what God was telling me in the pages of Scripture: to stop thinking I was his business partner. If you think this is a bit overstated, just think of some of our bumper stickers, such as "God is my copilot"!

My misgivings about election were based on two misunderstandings. The first was my misunderstanding of election itself. It is not a matter of God capriciously racing through the phone book, putting a check by the names of all the people he would send to hell. Election does not exclude anybody from the kingdom of God who wants in. Rather, it *includes* in God's kingdom those whose direction is away from the kingdom of God and those who would otherwise remain forever in the kingdom of sin and death.

My second misunderstanding was related to the gravity of my sin—and that of my neighbor. None of us has the faintest idea of what life would be like if God gave us what we deserve. For example, we don't even deserve the air we breathe, having declared independence from the God who supplies it every day.

We don't ask a philanthropic millionaire why he or she helps one person and not another. After all, it's that person's money. That is our Lord's point in the parable of the laborers. At the end of the day the owner of the vineyard ends up paying the same wages to people who started work later than the others. The workers who had labored all day got a bit irritated that the owner paid those who worked less than they more than they deserved. "But [the owner] answered one of them, 'Friend, I am not being unfair to you. Didn't you agree to work for a denarius? Take your pay and go. I want to give the man who was hired last the same as I gave you.'" And then Jesus gives the owner's rationale: "'Don't I have the right to do what I want with my own money?' . . . So the last will be first, and the first will be last" (Matt. 20:13–16). The point of the parable, then, is to say that God can do whatever he wishes with his mercy. Since everybody deserves his wrath, how can we argue with that? The Scriptures give many examples of God's freedom in selective grace. Near a pool in Jerusalem gathered "a great number of disabled people . . . the blind, the lame, the paralyzed" (John 5:3). Yet, Christ pushed through the crowd and moved toward one man—just one person—and healed him from his paralysis. Now, you have to understand that this was a regular spot for a lot of people who hoped each new day was their day for the miracle. One would think that there would be some sort of healing line, but apparently Jesus only intended to heal one man that day. Why didn't he heal everybody? He could have; he had the power. But he did not choose to do so. Nevertheless, I have yet to hear a sermon on how unfair it was for Jesus to heal the man at the pool that day. Why should election be any different in the realm of our salvation?

William Shakespeare wrote, "That word *grace* on the lips of an ungrateful person is profane." While it is probably unlikely that Shakespeare was thinking of divine election when he penned those words, he nevertheless got to the heart of this issue. It is profane to speak of God's grace while despising him for exercising his gracious privilege to elect those who would otherwise be damned and leave the rest to themselves.

Britain's famous Baptist evangelist, Charles Spurgeon, once said, "What amazes me is not that God does not choose everybody, but rather that he chose *me.*" The apostle Paul wrote:

Therefore God has mercy on whom he wants to have mercy, and he hardens whom he wants to harden. One of you will say to me: "Then why does God still blame us? For who resists his will?" But who are you, O man, to talk back to God? "Shall what is formed say to him who formed it, 'Why did you make me like this?'" Does not the potter have the right to make out of the same lump of clay some pottery for noble purposes and some for common use? [Rom. 9:18–21]

In other words, God's election of sinners is based on mercy. At the cross, God reconciled his mercy and his justice, but the point this doctrine is anxious to make is that believers are saved by God's gracious choice in spite of the fact that they, like all fallen men and women, justly deserve God's eternal contempt. No convicted and condemned criminal ought to plead for the judge's justice, but for his mercy. Election, therefore, is God's choice to not only acquit but to adopt children who contributed only sin and resistance to their liberation.

Foreknowledge

Isn't election conditional? Didn't God elect me because he knew all along I would choose him?

Everyone believes in election and predestination. The terms are found throughout Scripture, and to deny any and every notion of election or predestination is to flatly contradict God's Word. The real question is whether one believes it is, as Paul affirmed, an "election of grace" (Rom. 11:5 NKJV) or of foreseen works. If grace *means* "unmerited favor," then the Bible clearly teaches that nothing, absolutely nothing at all—including our response—can be the one thing that merited God's favor. If God chose you based on his having foreseen your response to him, it would not be an election—or a salvation of unmerited favor.

The natural tendency of the human heart is to expect to get what we deserve. In *The Sound of Music,* when Maria (Julie Andrews) realizes the Captain (Christopher Plummer) is in love with her, she breaks into song: "Nothing comes from nothing, nothing ever could. So, somewhere in my youth or childhood, I must have done something good." Surely to a greater degree we feel overwhelmed by the idea that a holy, just, and glorious God could love the likes of us. That is a sanctified sense of our own moral distance. And yet, nothing comes from nothing, we reason. Somewhere, at some point, we must have done something that got God's attention. But, in fact, creating things *ex nihilo* (out of nothing) is just the kind of business God has been in for a very long time. He loves us because of his own disposition, not because of ours. He can love the unlovely because he is God and he does not need a worthy object; unlike us, he can simply choose to love as he pleases. And if there is anything standing in the way of his love, he is powerful enough to remove any obstacle. The cross, of course, demonstrates the lengths he was willing to go for those he loved.

The apostle Paul zealously defended the unconditional nature of election by reminding us that God chose Jacob and rejected Esau, "before the twins were born or had done anything good or bad—in order that God's purpose in election might stand: not by works, but by him who calls" (Rom. 9:11–12). One might reply, "Yes, but Paul said nothing about God's not having *foreseen* their works or their response." But notice the apostle's line of argument. His whole point is that God's choice had nothing to do with the nature of the twins at all (foreseen or otherwise), but depended solely on the freedom of God to love whomever he chooses to love. In the same text he adds, "Therefore God has mercy on whom he wants to have mercy, and he hardens whom he wants to harden" (Rom. 9:18).

In 2 Timothy 1:9 Paul labors to make clear that God's purpose, not our response, governs the universe. Ephesians 1:4–14 clearly teaches election based exclusively on "the plan of him who works out everything in conformity with the purpose of his will" (v. 11). God is not a reactor, but an actor. He designs the stage, writes the script, and directs the play. Saying this is nothing more than saying that God is indeed God.

Suppose you order a steak in a restaurant. How do you know in advance that you are going to be served a steak and not a hot dog? You know, because that is what you ordered! Of course, God knows beforehand what will happen because he has ordered the end from the beginning. Since "no one can come" to Christ "unless the Father . . . draws him" (John 6:44), what would God have foreseen apart from his own work? He would have foreseen unresponsive, lifeless, spiritual corpses who do "not accept the things that come from the Spirit of God" (1 Cor. 2:14) and are "dead in . . . transgressions and sins" (Eph. 2:1). Hence, election could not have been based on foreseen responses which, apart from regeneration by God's Spirit, we were entirely incapable of making.

The text often offered in support of election based on foresight is Romans 8:29: "For those God foreknew, he also predestined to be conformed to the likeness of his Son." Does this say that God merely knew beforehand who would believe and then predestined them? Not when we look a bit closer. First, the apostle's statement does not say anything about God knowing *information* beforehand, but rather his knowing *people* beforehand; in other words, it is not *what* he foreknew, but *whom* he foreknew. Before time, God knew certain individuals. Our Lord told the Pharisees concerning judgment day, "Many will say to me on that day, 'Lord, Lord, did we not prophesy in your name, and in your name drive out demons and perform many miracles?' Then I will tell them plainly, 'I never *knew* you. Away from me, you evildoers!'" (Matt. 7:22–23, italics added).

That brings us to the definition of *foreknow.* We commonly use it in reference to knowing about something before it happens. Your son or daughter continues pulling at the dog's tail, and finally the pet strikes back with a little snap. You respond, "I knew that would happen." You meant that you could have made an educated guess, based on your previous experiences. But when we are talking about God, we mean more than an educated guess based on past experience. It is a certain, fixed foreknowledge that we apply to God. He knows the future absolutely, certainly, and perfectly. In other words, he cannot be wrong about what he knows will come to pass. Even if God only foreknows the future in all its details, that means that those events are predetermined; otherwise, God could have incorrect knowledge about the future. But this, too, comes short of what the Bible means when it talks about foreknowledge. *Knowledge* is a stronger, more relational term. For instance, Adam "knew" Eve (Gen. 4:1 NKJV); he had sexual relations with her. God "knew" Jeremiah while the prophet was still in his mother's womb (Jer. 1:5). Jesus "knew no sin" (2 Cor. 5:21 NKJV). "The world did not know" Christ (John 1:10

NKJV). When *foreknew* is used, it is always in a different sense than mere pre-awareness. In Amos 3:2, God instructs Israel, "You only have I known [foreknown] of all the families of the earth" (NKJV), and in 1 Peter 1:20, Jesus is spoken of as "foreordained [known] before the foundation of the world" (NKJV).

Surely God *knew* Jeremiah before his birth beyond mere pre-awareness of Jeremiah's existence. Jesus did not *know* sin in the sense that he did not experience it. The world did not *know* Christ in the sense that the people did not embrace him. After all Jesus was well known in his day. God *foreknew* Israel and, surely, his only-begotten Son in a sense that exceeded mere pre-awareness. To say Jesus was "foreordained from before the foundation of the world" means he was intimately, personally, experientially *known* by anticipation by the Father even before his incarnation. Similarly, when it is said, "For those God foreknew he also predestined" (Rom. 8:29), *foreknew* must be seen as synonymous with "being intimately acquainted"—not with facts *about* the person (i.e., his response), but with the person himself or herself. This is why the New American Standard version translates "known" in Amos 3:2 as "chosen." That this explanation of Romans 8:29 is the most natural gains support from the New English Bible, which translates Romans 8:29, "For God knew his own before ever they were, and also ordained that they should be shaped to the likeness of his Son. . . ." And the Good News for Modern Man renders the verse, "those whom God *had already chosen* he had also set apart" (italics added).

In the next chapter we will discuss the practical benefits of this amazing truth. As we shall see, this doctrine, which has been placed on the shelf of theological speculation and obscurity, has vast and rich deposits. Without it we are bound to lose the God-centered, Christ-centered focus of our salvation. With it, grace is quite amazing indeed.

Study Questions

1. Define *election* and *predestination* within the context of Ephesians 1:4–11. Why do you think we try to avoid this subject?

2. Doesn't election deny free will? If God has already made my decision for me, some say, I really don't have any choice in the matter. Respond to this objection, appealing to relevant texts.

3. Respond to this objection: Election is deterministic—a salvation of fate rather than love. (See John 10:14–18; Rom. 9:25; Eph. 1:4.)

4. Is election unfair? Fairness is based on merit. If fairness demands that God cannot choose one and reject another even before they have made a choice, isn't salvation based on merit? (See Rom. 9:10–21; 11:5.)

5. Some explain this doctrine in terms of God's foreknowing our decision. What is "foreknown" in Romans 8:29—people or their decisions? What point is Paul making in relation to this question when he says, "Yet, before the twins were born or had done anything good or bad—in order that God's purpose in election might stand: not by works but by him who calls" (Rom. 9:11–12)? (See Acts 13:48; Eph. 1:11; 2 Tim. 1:9.) What would God foresee apart from his own grace? (See John 6:44; Eph. 2:1.) What does the Bible mean by "foreknow" or "know"? (See Gen. 4:1; Jer. 1:5; 2 Cor. 5:21; 1 Peter 1:20.)

five

So What?

Okay, so maybe all of this is in the Bible, you say, but you just don't see how it relates to your life. You may think this doctrine is more trouble than it's worth. The purpose of this chapter is to convince you that this truth can revolutionize your relationship with God at a most relevant and practical level.

Professor James Daane writes, "Sermons on election are so rare that even a regular churchgoer may never hear one. . . . No other doctrine has been so central in theology and so ignored in the pulpit."[1] Why would a doctrine that has generated so much discussion and fascination in the past have been essentially banished from the average pulpit? At least one reason is that this doctrine is unsettling to our feelings, impressions, and presuppositions about who God is and who we are, and about what God can do without our permission.

Once we leave the war room of theological debate and enter into a vital, honest, and receptive dialogue with the Word of God, we find ourselves falling in love all over again with the One who first loved us. Too often, however, theology is divorced from life. A doctrine like election is discussed by one group, for example, and every phrase is rigorously checked for its doctrinal accuracy. Insults are then hurled at those who are "too blind" to see the truth as clearly. A doctrine calculated to produce humility instead creates pride; a ruby is squandered, the people impoverished, because the object was to win an argument rather than to share the wealth. Another group insists that, based on what they have heard from group number one, they "just want to love Jesus" and forget about theology. These people say they just want to know what will help them live for the Lord, not what will stuff their minds. But when we come to a major truth—and election is a major truth—we begin to understand how wrong both groups can be. After all, theology is the *basis* for loving God and living for Christ. How can one love or serve someone about whom he or she knows very little? While it is impossible to love and serve God correctly without knowing him correctly, it is possible to understand theology without making the connection between theory and practice. Election is one of those doctrines with which we simply cannot afford to do that. It must be understood, and then it must be applied. In fact, we understand it more fully *as* it is applied.

Humility

No other truth will put us in our place quite like this one. The apostle Paul used it both to comfort the lowly and to humble the mighty:

> But God chose the foolish things of the world to shame the wise; God chose the weak things of the world to shame the strong. He chose the lowly things of this world and the despised things—and the things that are not—to nullify the things that are, so that no one may boast before him. It is because of him that you are in Christ Jesus. . . . Therefore, as it is written: "Let him who boasts boast in the Lord." [1 Cor. 1:27–31]

A team of all-stars we are not! At first, that is incredibly humiliating—until we realize that we can stop trying to impress now. We all remember the schoolyard games, when the most popular kids, serving as team captains, would pick the other popular kids. Everyone hoped for at least a third- or fourth-round pick. Being chosen last could be so humiliating that the poor kid who was often just gave up and stood by himself on the sidelines rather than suffer repeat performances. That happens in church too. Choices are made concerning people based on their performance or popularity. But the doctrine of election puts folks in their place. On this playground, Christ is the team captain of the "foolish," the "weak," the "base and despised," the "nothings," in order to show the wise, the strong, the popular, and the "somebodies" of the world that we all come to him on equal terms, empty-handed (1 Cor. 1:18–19). God has chosen a team that any "loser" can join: not an entirely unattainable qualification for many of us.

Knowing that God has chosen us reminds us that we are loved, though not lovely; chosen, even though we're not necessarily choice in the eyes of the boss, the spouse, the parents, or the folks at church. We are accepted—not because we are acceptable ourselves, but because "he hath made us accepted in the beloved" (Eph. 1:6 KJV).

When I'm talking to someone who has a problem with "I will have mercy on whom I have mercy" (Rom. 9:15), one of the first questions I ask is whether that person believes in salvation by *grace alone*. Among evangelicals, the usual response is, "Of course—nothing we do can save us." But then the same person will say, "But I'm saved because I said *yes* to Christ." Election turns to our proud hearts and replies, "You are saved because *Christ* said yes to *you!*"

If at any point we can attribute our salvation to anything we have done—whether it's "willing or running," as Paul described it—we lose our evangelical affirmation of salvation by grace alone. Nevertheless, we always want to step in and say, "I'm saved because *I.* . . ." That is human nature. It goes back to the lemonade-stand illustration in chapter 3. We all want to sing, "I did it my way." This is the sort of language we have even used in sharing the faith. "Give Jesus a chance" sports one popular bumper sticker in California. Wait a second. Give *who* a chance? The second person of the Holy Trinity? Poor Jesus, just waiting for men and women to give him a chance! Is God really my copilot? I'm sure he is happy to hear that he is now given the opportunity to share the spotlight with us, even if it is in a secondary role.

This language is absolutely foreign to Scripture. Nebuchadnezzar was a proud pagan emperor who was humiliated by God. He was a ruined man until he realized that "the Most High is sovereign over the kingdoms of men and gives them to anyone he wishes." Once Nebuchadnezzar finally acknowledged the sovereignty of God, earthly power was put in perspective as he confessed, "All the peoples of the earth are regarded as nothing. He does as he pleases with the powers of heaven and the peoples of the earth. No one can hold back his hand or say to him: 'What have you done?'" (Dan. 4:32, 35).

Religion can be a source of godly humility or of immeasurable pride. *Religious* pride is the most insidious, unholy form of that vice. It is one thing to set oneself above one's coworkers; but self-righteousness ultimately pushes us to the point where we exalt ourselves in heaven, making the kinds of boasts that some popular evangelical slogans and literature actually put in print. In election we come to the God of Abraham, Isaac, and Jacob; the God of the wilderness; the God of the incarnation, death, and resurrection of Christ; the God who is anything but a frustrated deity who "has no hands but our hands" and must pace heaven's floors, ringing his hands, hoping people will "let him have his way." This is the God who is everything *but* a copilot. "God is opposed to the proud, but gives grace to the humble" (James 4:6 NASB).

Appreciation of God's Grace

We have made a great deal out of the importance of election in maintaining a doctrine of grace, but how does it affect our lives? Jesus said, "You did not choose me, but I chose you and appointed you to go and bear fruit—fruit that will last" (John 15:16). That is one notion that really puts *amazing* back into *grace* for me. I am a Christian because God wanted me to be a Christian and saw to it that his will would be realized in spite of the odds.

I remember a movie I saw a long time ago, starring David Niven and Racquel Welch. Determined to win the affection of Welch's character, Niven persists in making overtures toward her. But here's the twist: Welch had gotten close to Niven, a wealthy aristocrat, only to steal his money and valuable collections. In one of the most dramatic scenes of the film, Niven presses Welch to the point where she feels ashamed and confronts her charade. The aristocrat informs her that he has known about her theft all along; nevertheless he insists that his intentions are unmoved. Overwhelmed by Niven's charm, Welch gives in and now falls in love with a man she had previously seen as nothing more than her heist. This is how I felt when I began to understand the doctrine of election. It seemed as though God's sovereignty in his grace, which at first intimidated me, now drew me. It was a compelling sweetness to discover that there was nothing I could do. I couldn't push a button or flip a switch that would get God to love me. I had stolen from him—and he knew it all along. Still, he had chosen me.

One of the church's greatest problems today is that it has come to the place where it takes God's grace for granted. Dietrich Bonhoeffer called it "cheap grace" and said, "Cheap grace is the grace we bestow on ourselves." Isn't that an interesting comment? Well, if in fact grace is something we *can't* bestow on ourselves—if only God can grant grace—his is the most valuable grade on the market! That's what Paul meant when he wrote that when a person *does* something in order to get something in return, he will demand the payment. In this kind of a situation, the payment he or she receives is not a gift, but a paycheck. Grace expected or demanded is a contradiction of terms.

Worship

Martin Luther had a lot to say about the importance of this doctrine in maintaining a proper worship of God. Without it, God is not rightly known, and where he is not rightly known, he cannot be rightly worshiped. Luther said that the chief reason this truth ought to be shouted from the rooftops is because of "the knowledge of the grace of God." He took this matter one step further with his explanation of why this doctrine is essential if we are to worship God properly:

> Therefore, it is not irreverent, inquisitive, or trivial, but helpful and necessary for a Christian, to find out whether the will does anything or nothing in matters pertaining to eternal salvation. . . . If we do not know these things, we shall know nothing at all of things Christian and shall be worse than any heathen. . . . Therefore, let anyone who does not feel this confess that he is no Christian. For if I am ignorant of what, how far, and how much I can and may do in relation to God, it will be equally uncertain and unknown to me what, how far, and how much God can and may do in me. . . . But when the works and

power of God are unknown in this way, I cannot worship, praise, thank, and serve God, since I do not know how much I ought to attribute to myself and how much to God. It therefore behooves us to be very certain about the distinction between God's power and our own, God's work and our own, if we want to live a godly life.[2]

When Paul had finished explaining this marvelous insight to the Roman Christians, he couldn't hold himself back from bursting into worship and praise: "Oh, the depth of the riches of the wisdom and knowledge of God! How unsearchable his judgments, and his paths beyond tracing out! 'Who has known the mind of the Lord? Or who has been his counselor?' 'Who has ever given to God, that God should repay him?' For from him and through him and to him are all things. To him be the glory forever! Amen" (Rom. 11:33–36). One can almost picture the apostle concluding his theological passage through the "Alps" of the previous chapters, now all flooding his mind in one intoxicating image. Up his soul flies in praise and adoration of the God who is God!

Often our services are attempts at entertainment rather than worship. When the preaching centers on our own happiness rather than the attributes and achievements of God, we attend church to passively enjoy and receive from the professionals— the preacher, the choir, the soloist, the occasional drama troupe. But I believe this way of coming to public worship is indicative of a human-centered theological orientation. If Jesus Christ entered at the back of our church on Sunday morning, would we all clap our hands and dance and sing, "Happy Days Are Here Again"? Would we show him our "God is rad, he's my dad" sweatshirt? Or would the room be suddenly filled with awe-stricken silence? Of course, there are different styles of worship, and I am not for one moment suggesting a style better suited to a funeral than to a worship service. Nevertheless, what we believe about God and salvation ultimately determines the object, focus, fervor, and direction of our worship. If we really rediscovered this biblical portrait of God, we would not need entertainment gimmicks; enthusiasm would not be artificially generated. And because our minds would be connected to it all, there would be a lasting impact even when we were not surrounded by choirs, musicians, and a cast of players.

Preaching determines the focus and depth of worship. If the preaching is human-centered, the worship will become entertainment. If the preaching is shallow, the worship will reflect that. If the people expect to hear how God thinks they are the best things since hot dogs and how he happens to lay out in the Bible the same self-help techniques as pop psychology, there is no reason why the congregation should be moved to worship him in a simple, but meaningful, way. No doctrine will drive out the self-help narcissism from our churches and our pulpits as well as this one. No doctrine is better suited to making God's justifying grace in Christ more central. No doctrine is more successful in putting man in his place, and in seeing God in his.

Cold orthodoxy is the result of absorbing doctrine without gratitude. Emotionalism is the result of gratitude without doctrine. We need both doctrine and response. The former tendency leads to an obsession with intellectual data without expression in love, humility, charity, good works, and genuine worship. The latter is like saying, "thank you," 142 times, without exactly knowing why. As we will see, the Protestant doctrine of faith involves three elements: knowledge, assent, and trust. So-called dead orthodoxy is not really orthodox, since *ortho* means "correct" and *doxa* means "worship." People of this persuasion may know the doctrine and give their assent, but if it does not command their trust, Christ is not truly believed. On the other hand, this definition of faith also rules out the opposite tendency to so emphasize the element of trust in terms of a personal relationship with Christ that the doctrinal knowledge and necessary assent to those particular doctrines are viewed as unnecessary or secondary. Both fall short of the biblical concept of faith. All of this is to say that the doctrine of election is liberating. Let it liberate you in worship!

Holiness and Service

You will remember Luther's remark, "But when the works and power of God are unknown in this way, I cannot worship, praise, thank, and serve God, since I do not know how much I ought to attribute to myself and how much to God."[3] Only when we know that it is God who saves us, not we who save ourselves with his help, can genuine worship lead to genuine holiness and service.

John Wesley used to argue that he could not accept the doctrine of election because it undermined the main supports of holiness: fear of punishment and hope of reward. If the motivation for holiness is fear of punishment and hope of reward, then this doctrine does indeed undermine it. In fact, it marks this sort of guilt-and-reward holiness as a gospel-obstructing target which must be shattered. Paul instructed, "For you did not receive a spirit that makes you a slave again to fear, but you received the Spirit of sonship. And by him we cry, '*Abba,* Father'" (Rom. 8:15). In other words, fear is what you had *before* you were a Christian. But, "he predestined us to be adopted as his sons" (Eph. 1:5), and God's generosity is mocked if he can smell either fear or pride in our service to him. Armed with doctrines like election, the believer can face the future unafraid, fearing nothing but God's name, expecting nothing but God's will.

Some time ago I addressed the student body of a Christian preparatory school on the East Coast. This doctrine was part of the extended chapel lecture, and I encouraged the students to ask questions at any point. Writing "fear of punishment and hope of rewards" on the board, I took a vote on whether this was a sound motivation for Christian holiness. Nearly all voted *yes.* Then I asked them what was, on the face of it, likely to be wrong about such a motivation. Immediately, hands began shooting up: "It's self-centered," said one, explaining "—I mean, being concerned about what you get, or don't get, out of something." "Then why," I asked, "did most of you agree that this is a valid, scriptural motivation for holiness?" One cynical student answered, without raising his hand, "What else is there?"

That response continues to echo in my memory, and each time I hear a group repeat similar responses, I am reminded how important it is that we rid our churches, schools, homes, and Christian organizations of this disastrous pattern of thinking. It produces the sort of hopelessness of the kid on the playground who, always being picked last and reluctantly, decides he will just give up trying to play the games at all.

Election is one of those doctrines that entirely reorients our motives at their deepest level. Since we have stated negatively what the motivation for holiness is *not* and why this truth undermines it, what does a doctrine like election put in its place?

The apostle Paul answered "adoption!" So did the early church father Clement of Alexandria of the second century: "It is not becoming that one whom God has predestined before the foundation of the world to be put in high adoption of children should fall into pleasures or fears, and be unemployed in repressing the passions."

When it hits us that we have been predestined to a high and holy calling, we discover a higher and holier motivation for pursuing God's revealed will. When we realize we are part of "a chosen race, a royal priesthood, a holy nation, a people for God's own possession" (1 Peter 2:9 NASB), we begin to reflect that awareness in our daily living.

Why should we walk in works of love and charity toward our neighbor? Because God "prepared in advance for us to" walk in them (Eph. 2:10). Why should we persevere toward the goal of being conformed to Christ? Because we are afraid of losing something or hope to gain something by it? No, but because we have been "predestined to be conformed to the likeness of his [God's] Son" (Rom. 8:29). In 2 Thessalonians 2:13, Paul reminds the congregation, "We ought always to thank God for you, brothers loved by the Lord, because from the beginning God chose you to be saved through the sanctifying work of the Spirit and through belief in the truth." It's important that we understand that God's election was not made in a vacuum. God did not merely *choose* us; he chose us *to be saved*. And, further, he chose us to be saved *through sanctification by the Spirit and belief in the truth.*

When I signed the contract with the publisher for this book, the agreement was that I would deliver an acceptable, completed manuscript. However, the publisher contracted not only for the manuscript, but also for the final product. Therefore, I didn't get up every morning to work feverishly on the draft, hoping each new day that the publisher would eventually accept my efforts. I could spend the day focusing on the work that needed to be done to deliver a completed manuscript instead of worrying about whether I would get a contract. Similarly, God has contracted for the long haul in our salvation. Furthermore, he has contracted, not with us, but between the members of the

Trinity. The Father, Son, and Holy Spirit have committed each other to the joint project of presenting to themselves a redeemed and a holy people. So we can spend our days serving the Lord out of gratitude instead of fear. We have been promised that those whom he has predestined will surely be conformed to Christ's image. "For he chose us in Him . . . to be holy and blameless in his sight" (Eph. 1:4). This holiness is already ours by virtue of our union with Christ, but what is ours by *imputation* will become ours increasingly every day by *imitation* as well as we become what God says we already are. Colossians 3:12 suggests election as something vital for a holy life: "As those who have been chosen of God, holy and beloved, put on a heart of compassion, kindness, humility, gentleness and patience" (NASB).

There's one more thing I have to say on this score. Because an understanding of and an appreciation for our election in Christ changes our bedrock motives, our whole understanding of holiness itself undergoes a revolution of sorts. Once we were among those on the playground hoping to be picked in the early rounds. We put on pious masks and pretended we were okay; no problems here. Daily victory was what we were experiencing, for that was what we were expected to be experiencing. But with this doctrine, we don't have to *get* ourselves elected; we already are! And God has already chosen the weak and foolish from the outset, so what does he expect from us? Now, does that mean that we sit back and forget about the pursuit of holiness? Not if we believe that our election sets us apart unto God as his special possession. If fear of punishment and hope of reward rule our motives for holiness, the character of that "holiness" will look more like penance, on the one hand, and self-righteous ladder-climbing, on the other.

Evangelism and Missions

You may be thinking, "Election and evangelism—in the same breath? I've been told they're mutually exclusive!" I was told that, too. But I can honestly say that evangelism never really meant as much before this truth made its imprint. Sharing the faith with nonbelievers has become a nagging burden to many, and it was to me, until this truth changed my thinking. Election changes our evangelism on three levels: our message, our methods, and our motivation.

First, how does election affect the *message?* Election does not allow us, in good conscience, to tell unbelievers, "God loves you and has a wonderful plan for your life." It reminds us that only *after* one trusts Christ can one rest at night. Furthermore, the gospel does not center on whether God has some exciting plans for our lives, but on whether we will be alienated from him for eternity. Nor can we tell them, "You can make it, with God's help!" The bottom line is that, as related as sin's effects certainly are, what we need salvation from is not drugs, alcoholism, depression, or sexual lifestyles that leave our lives in ruin. Ultimately, salvation must be understood vertically—in terms of being reconciled to an offended God. Election brings the focus back to God, for whom *we* exist, rather than the other way around.

It is often suggested that a doctrine like this one will drive sinners to despair; that they will simply give up. But this is what is required in gospel evangelism! We *must* despair of our own efforts; we *must* give up on ourselves before we can place all of our hope and confidence in someone outside of us. If we *don't* drive sinners to despair, we have not properly preached the law: They are not yet at the end of their rope. When we announce to people, "*I* found it!" we give the impression that God was lost. In fact, some clever non-Christians made a killing during the evangelistic campaign that used that slogan by printing counterstickers which seem to have been more Christian in content, if not in motivation: "I didn't know he was lost." I see the lapel pin "Try God" in many places, as if God were just another "kick" or another way out—the "Jesus Trip," as it was called in the seventies. For people who have tried every other self-help cure from est to eastern meditation, we now bring the biblical God out for a test drive. This creates a terribly human-centered message.

We need to turn from our bargain-basement, human-centered slogans and tell people the truth again. *We* don't find God— "There is . . . no one who seeks God" (Rom. 3:11 NEB). *We* don't "give Jesus a chance." For the life of me, I can't see the apostles preaching those themes—even on a bad day! No matter what sinful men and women choose, they must be assured that their destiny is in God's hands. This is a terribly unsettling thought for those who do not know the Lord. Usually, we make it sound as though "God casts his vote for your soul; Satan casts his. But you must cast the deciding ballot." Will we "let" God be our Lord? But the Bible makes it clear that God is the Lord of all, even of non-Christians. We all remember occasions when an unbeliever, in response to our presentation of the gospel, said, "Maybe later." But election reminds us—and the unbeliever— that "later" is *God's* "later" and that all earthly and eternal circumstances are already marked out by his design. Instead of making unbelievers apathetic, this doctrine ought to make them nervous; they begin to realize that their destiny is not in their own hands. They must accept Christ if they are to find themselves accepted in him from before the foundation of the world.

The apostle Paul did not consider election "strong meat," but the "milk of the Word." He was always reminding his new believers, "But by *His* doing you are in Christ Jesus" (1 Cor. 1:30 NASB, italics added). And Jesus wanted to make absolutely certain that his followers knew who saved whom: "Apart from me you can do nothing. . . . You did not choose me, but I chose you" (John 15:5, 16).

Today we are trying to reconcile God to humanity instead of reconciling humanity to God. Our converts are weak because they depend on their own will and their own ability to trust and keep the thing going. Their faith is weak because they are constantly looking at themselves. God is pleased with the chosen because he is pleased with the Beloved in whom they are chosen, but this emphasis is missing today. With election as the backdrop, the Lord Jesus Christ becomes the focus of attention. After all, he has "the whole world in his hands." Thus, he thunders from heaven, "I am the Living One. . . . And I hold the keys of Death and Hades" (Rev. 1:18). He who holds the keys holds the future. With our destiny under his command, Christ, rather than our own willpower and effort, becomes the object of our trust.

Then there is the matter of *methods*. Sometimes as I have gone witnessing with a group of people, I have wondered whether I'm sharing Christ or selling a line of products. It is interesting to see how some of the airport cults have picked up on some of our successful formulas and patterns of communicating. These cult members are so predictable we can see them coming a mile away. Like us, they tend to offer simplistic pitches.

Because of election, we realize that we as Christians do not have to resort to such packages of last-chance tactics. We know that, in the final analysis, only God's electing, redeeming grace, and not Madison Avenue or the latest fads of pop psychology, will bring lasting reconciliation between humans and God. With this knowledge we can be more comfortable with the biblical message and biblical methods. We can approach unbelievers as human beings rather than targets, consumers, numbers, and converts. I am tired of evangelical conferences where more time is given to the hype than to the hope, where more energy is given to the methods than to the message, and where more effort is devoted to techniques than to truth.

Two thousand years ago our Lord told the woman at the well that his Father was *seeking* people to worship him. The good news is that God is still engaged in this work.

Finally, election affects evangelism at the level of *motivation*. The greatest missionary in church history wrote, "I endure everything for the sake of the elect, that they too may obtain the salvation that is in Christ Jesus, with eternal glory" (2 Tim. 2:10). Election certainly did not dampen this missionary's zeal. The apostle pushed tirelessly from city to city, motivated by God's message to him: "I have many people in this city" (Acts 18:10).

William Carey, commonly called the father of the modern missionary movement, considered election and its related doctrines the undergirding of his whole enterprise. David Livingstone, John Patton, and many others agreed.

Have you ever felt despondent over all there is to do for Christ in terms of spreading the gospel? A missionary was flying over Bombay, India, and saw the massive crowds crawling like ants beneath him. At first he wanted to turn back. "Look at all those people!" he gasped. "I won't even make a dent." Then he remembered that God had not called him to save India, nor to save anyone *in* India, but that he had called him to preach the gospel of Christ in India to all who would listen; God would do the saving. That thought, the missionary said, got him through the frustration and despair so he could be an unencumbered divine instrument.

Charles Spurgeon, the great Baptist evangelist of the last century, packed giant halls with people who needed to hear his message, and he was so inspired by God's electing grace in Christ that he concluded, "This is the gospel, nothing less." Thousands responded all over England. George Whitefield, John Newton, Jonathan Edwards, and a host of great evangelists and missionaries have delighted in God's electing grace. In fact, when Edwards and Whitefield began preaching these neglected doctrines, revival broke out in what came to be called the Great Awakening.

When I tell a group of people about Christ, I know that what I'm doing is important and that it really counts in history as well as in eternity. It counts because, while I am preaching or teaching, God is at work sovereignly bringing people to Christ. He is filling the heavenly table with prodigals whom he calls through his Word and Spirit. I do not know those whom he has chosen and is drawing—it's none of my business! But I do realize that in that moment I am an essential part of God's plan to bring his elect into his kingdom. While election, then, is liberating in the sense that I don't do the saving, it is also a source of tremendous strength in realizing the importance of sharing the gospel with as many as I possibly can.

Why does God need us to evangelize when he has already chosen who will be saved? That's similar to asking why one needs to buy a ticket, pack, and take an airplane to London when one has already decided to go to London. When one decides to go somewhere or do something, it is necessary to determine also *how* that end is to be achieved. God has not only determined *that* we will be saved, but *how* we will be saved: through faith in Christ which comes through the proclamation of the Word. A. W. Pink once wrote, "God is not working at random; the gospel has been sent forth on no uncertain mission." Because salvation *is* determined, because it does have a plan and a goal, we can be certain that we are sent out on a mission that will be accomplished.

Blessed Assurance

Nothing builds our spiritual muscles quite like the assurance we have in being singled out as an heir of salvation. While the biblical message of election is threatening to those who reject the gospel, it is a source of great hope and certainty to those who are trusting in Christ.

Martin Luther, once again, underscored the importance of election for our assurance of salvation:

> And if God be robbed of His power to elect, what will there be remaining but that idol, Fortune, under the name of which all things take place at random! Nay, we shall eventually come to this: That God has not determined by certain and glorious election who should be saved, but has left them to choose for themselves whether they shall be saved, while He, in the meantime, should be gone to an Ethiopian feast!
>
> If therefore we are taught, and if we believe, that we do not need to know these things, Christian faith is utterly destroyed and the promises of God and the whole Gospel entirely fall to the ground; for the greatest and only consolation and assurance for Christians in their adversity is that . . . God does all things immutably and that His will cannot be resisted, changed, or hindered.[4]

In other words, when God sets out to initiate someone's salvation, he inevitably finishes it!

If you're anything like me, a lot of things are "up in the air." But even in a world of overwhelming complexities and insecurities, we can know at the very core of our being that God has fixed his eternal gaze on us, controls our destiny, and will not let anything get in the way. Thus, instead of being the withdrawn kid on the playground, we can be active participants in life, confident that our acceptance is already secured on the team that really matters in the long run.

Prayer with Power

Election reminds us who's boss. It reminds us that God is the One to whom we must go for our petitions as well as for our praise. Just as God has determined to use our words and actions to bring people to his Son, so he has determined to use our prayers to send to us and to those for whom we pray the great gifts he has prepared beforehand to give us.

I'm always puzzled by the question "Why pray for somebody's salvation if election is true?" After all, if election is not true and

God is waiting on pins and needles hoping along with us that folks will use their free will properly, then surely *that* is reason enough to leave prayer out of it. We might expect God to say, "Look, I appreciate the attention, but there's nothing I can do. It's out of my hands. I gave the person a free will, and now we'll just have to see what happens." If God does not overrule our hearts and invade our lives until we invite him to do so, what's the use in *asking* God to overrule hearts and to bring people to Christ?

Prayer is enhanced by this truth. We can pray with hope and expectancy because God has complete charge over whatever it is for which we are praying. He may not choose to answer the prayer the way we would like, but he is the only one who can ultimately change things, and he always "works for the good of those who love him, who have been called according to his purpose" (Rom. 8:28).

Election and the Bible

This doctrine affects us in many other positive ways. But the most significant reason we are to believe something is not how it affects us, but whether it is, in fact, a *biblical* truth. Martin Luther said election is a theme as clearly revealed in Scripture "as the very notion of a Supreme Being." Dr. John Stott wrote, "The doctrine of election is the product of divine revelation, not of human speculation. It was not invented by Calvin of Geneva or Augustine of Hippo. It is above all else a Biblical doctrine and no Biblical Christian can ignore it."[5]

Wherever election appears in Scripture, it is taken for granted as a truth. It forms the background of so much of the Bible's story. Only in a few places is election argued or defended. Normally, it simply "appears" as a premise. It undergirds the entire redemptive story. Without it, it is impossible to clearly understand redemptive history. Again and again we read, "Blessed is the nation whose God is the LORD, the people he chose for his inheritance" (Ps. 33:12). "Every plant that my heavenly Father has not planted will be pulled up by the roots" (Matt. 15:13). "All who were appointed for eternal life believed" (Acts 13:48).

Election can be dangerous when we seek to answer questions the Bible does not answer. But where the Bible does speak on the subject, it speaks clearly. While mystery remains, there is much of this doctrine which is revealed. "The secret things belong to the LORD our God, but the things revealed belong to us and to our children forever" (Deut. 29:29).

Knowledge of One's Election

Not only are we told, "make your calling and election sure" (2 Peter 1:10), we are also told how to do it. In 1 Thessalonians 1:4 Paul wrote, "For we know, brothers loved by God, that he has chosen you." Then he tells us why he knew they were "chosen": "because our gospel came to you not simply with words, but also with power, with the Holy Spirit and with deep conviction. . . . You became imitators of us and of the Lord." Christ said, "My sheep listen to my voice; I know them, and they follow me" (John 10:27). And Romans 8:30 reads: "And those he predestined, he also called." Have you been called? Have you heard Christ's voice and joined his fold? Has the gospel come to you, not only in word but in power, in the Holy Spirit, and in much assurance? Did you become a disciple of the apostles and of the Lord? In other words, do you trust Christ alone for your salvation? Then you are one of the elect. He has given you faith to trust his Son in whom you were chosen before the creation of the world.

If you have not yet made your calling and election sure, respond to the invitation of Christ in his Word: "Come to me, all you who are weary and burdened, and I will give you rest" (Matt. 11:28). Then you, too, will have made your calling and election sure.

Study Questions

1. How does this idea of election teach us humility? (See 1 Cor. 1:27–31.)
2. What does this doctrine teach us about God? (See Dan. 4:32–35.)

3. Explain how this truth would help us appreciate God's grace.
4. Evaluate the worship in your own church. Is it God-centered or human-centered, worship-oriented or entertainment-oriented? How might the doctrine of election influence your worship? Notice the effect on the apostle Paul whenever he brought it up: Romans 8:31–33; 11:33–36; Ephesians 1:3–4.
5. Would this doctrine tend to make people lax in their pursuit of godliness and service? What motive drives a holiness informed by this doctrine? (See Rom. 8:29; Eph. 2:10; Col. 3:12; 2 Thess. 2:13; 1 Peter 2:9.)
6. How do you think this teaching would touch upon the subject of evangelism and missions? Is it too strong to use in some cases with non-Christians or new believers? (See John 6:44; John 15:5, 16; Rev. 1:18.) (Remember, too, that most of the New Testament was written to an audience of new believers.) How might this doctrine affect (1) the evangelistic message and (2) the evangelistic methods? (See Acts 18:10; 2 Tim. 2:10.)
7. Describe how this doctrine would affect your own personal sense of assurance of salvation.
8. How can we be certain that we are among "the elect"? (See Matt. 11:28; John 10:27; Rom. 8:30; 1 Thess. 1:4; 2 Peter 1:10.) If we have not been saved by our own will or effort (Rom. 9:16), can we gauge our assurance of salvation by our progress in willing and running? Should we look for evidence of our election in Christ or in our own growth in holiness? (See 2 Tim. 2:10.)

six

Climbing Jacob's Ladder

I remember the Sunday school stories about Jacob's ladder. In fact, there was a song. It was one of those motion songs. Pretending we were climbing a ladder, we would sing, "I am climbing, climbing, climbing Jacob's ladder, ladder, ladder." We also had other songs: "Jesus loves me when I'm good, when I do the things I should." "Jesus feels so sorry when we're doing wrong; If we're good he's happy all the whole day long. G-double O–D, good, G–double O–D, good, we will try to be like Jesus, G-double O-D, good." Then there was the "O, be careful little hands what you do" chorus, each new verse selecting a part of the body to warn. Not only the songs reinforced the idea that we were climbing the ladder to heaven; so did the merit system in the class itself. I remember those stars by our names. When we brought a friend or memorized a new arsenal of verses or could offer a bit of news to the class on something good we had done the previous week, up would go another star. I always fell short in the star department, and I remember walking up every so often, counting the number, and realizing how short I was compared with everybody else. We begin climbing the merit ladder very early in life indeed.

It was not until seminary that I went back to "Jacob's ladder" as the story is found in Genesis 28. The discovery was startling for someone whose childhood memories had been so profoundly influenced by an entirely different interpretation. In the actual record, Jacob "had a dream in which he saw a stairway resting on the earth, with its top reaching to heaven, and the angels of God were ascending and descending on it" (v. 12). So far, so good. "There above it stood the LORD, and he said: 'I am the LORD, the God of your father Abraham and the God of Isaac. . . . I am with you and will watch over you wherever you go, and I will bring you back to this land. I will not leave you until I have done what I have promised you.'" Immediately, Jacob awoke and said, "Surely the LORD is in this place, and I was not aware of it." Furthermore, "He was afraid and said, 'How awesome is this place! This is none other than the house of God; this is the gate of heaven!'" (vv. 13–17). But, you see, in this dream the point was not the plot of land where Jacob was sleeping. The promise ultimately referred to the point in history when God would actually become human. Our Lord confirmed this by applying Jacob's dream to himself. In Jacob's dream, angels ascended and descended the ladder, and Jacob concluded that the spot where he had the dream was "the house of God . . . the gate of heaven." Jesus declared, "I tell you the truth, you shall see heaven open, and the angels of God ascending and descending on the Son of Man" (John 1:51). Jesus was Jacob's ladder! "The Word became flesh and made his dwelling among us" (John 1:14). Jesus was the "house of God," "the gate of heaven"! You remember our Lord's remark that he was the temple which, being destroyed, would be raised in three days (John 2:19).

This doctrine is absolutely revolutionary and takes us a step further toward putting *amazing* back into our understanding of *grace*. See, the ladder is not something *we* ascend toward heaven. Rather, it is Jesus himself descending from the glory of heaven to become the God-man, the suffering servant, the righteous branch, the Son of God and Son of man. It is not a metaphor of our ascent, but of Christ's descent; not of our coming to Christ, but of Christ's coming to us. This incredible truth will reorient our understanding of Christ's mission.

Cur Deus Homo—Why did God become man? That was the question the theologian Anselm asked in the eleventh century. It is perhaps the most important question any Christian can ask—whether a theologian or an average layperson. On that question hangs our doctrine of Christ, the Trinity, salvation, and man. Historically, the teaching that "the Word became flesh and made his dwelling among us" (John 1:14) has been referred to as the incarnation.

It is clear that election was only the first stage in the progress of redemption. It was the blueprint, but no architect considers his design a success until he sees the finished product. The incarnation is the next stage we shall consider in this unfolding drama.

Having chosen us and devised his strategy, God was now faced with the matter of somehow working out in time and space everything that he had chosen to do in eternity. God needed to come to us, since "There is . . . no one who seeks God" (Rom. 3:11 NEB). Someone once said that Christianity is not a religion because religion consists in humans trying to reach God, while Christianity is a matter of God reaching humans. The story of the tower of Babel (Genesis 11) demonstrates the human longing to reach God through one's own strength and opinions; but in reaching for him, they grasped confusion and frustration instead.

Every step of salvation is God moving toward us; at no point does he wait for us to take a few steps toward him. He is active; we are acted upon. The incarnation was a serious step, the ultimate step taken by God in human history. The council of the triune Godhead—Father, Son, and Holy Spirit—determined that the second person of the Trinity (the Word) would be the mediator who would satisfy both divine justice and mercy in the same person. God, the eternal Son, would become completely human while retaining his divinity in its entirety as well.

The Veiled God

Where is God when people suffer horrible tragedy? Where was God when six million Jews were massacred in the Holocaust or when our own loved ones were taken in a terminal illness or in an accident that didn't seem to make any sense? It seems to us sometimes that he is so distant, so aloof from our daily routine that he cannot see our pain. But is this true?

Theologians have often referred to the "Deus absconditus"—the veiled God. When Moses beheld the glory of God, he had to cover his face before he returned to the people below. They could not behold his glory and live. Always, it seems, God is "up there," beyond our reach. This emphasis, found throughout the Bible, is usually called "transcendence" because God transcends (goes beyond) us and our temporal existence.

But does this mean that God is too far away to hear our cries? Not at all. When the Egyptian bondage became too great for the children of Israel, "their cry for help because of their slavery went up to God. So God heard their groaning and he remembered his covenant. . . . So God looked on the Israelites, and was concerned about them" (Exod. 2:23–25). "And will not God bring about justice for his chosen ones, who cry out to him day and night? Will he keep putting them off?" (Luke 18:7). No, God is not hiding. He has always been intimately involved with his creation even in its rebellion. God *is* beyond us; he is transcendent, removed, above us. But when God descended Jacob's ladder and was born the God-man in Bethlehem one warm night the transcendent, almighty Ruler of heaven also became the immanent ("up-close-and-personal"), vulnerable, suffering servant and Son of David.

As men and women were laying the kinds of charges against God we often level against him ourselves today, God himself joined the human race. "For we do not have a high priest who is unable to sympathize with our weaknesses, but we have one who has been tempted in every way, just as we are—yet was without sin" (Heb. 4:15). God broke through the silence, humbled himself in the person of the incarnate Son, and rendered useless all our cavils against God's apparent disregard for or ignorance of the human condition.

John Boys, a Puritan divine, said, "The best way to reconcile two disagreeing families is to make some marriage between them: even so, the Word became flesh and dwelt among us in the world that He might hereby make our peace, reconciling man to God. By this happy match the Son of God is become the Son of Man, even flesh of our flesh and bone of our bones."[1]

The Living Word

The epistle to the Hebrews offers a profound insight into the mission for the divine Word, the Son of God: "God, after He spoke long ago to the fathers in the prophets in many portions and in many ways, in these last days has spoken to us in His Son, whom He appointed heir of all things, through whom also He made the world" (1:1–2 NASB). That passage sends chills down my spine: The same Word who created us came to us at a point in history *as* one of us! That is absolutely mind-boggling!

Thus, we compare the opening of Genesis, where God created the world through his Word, to the opening of the Gospel of John: "In the beginning was the Word, and the Word was with God, and the Word was God. He was in the beginning with God. All things came into being by Him; and apart from Him nothing came into being that has come into being. In Him was life; and the life was the light of men. And the light shines in the darkness; and the darkness did not comprehend it" (John 1:1–5 NASB).

The Word came to his own, and they rejected him (John 1:14–15). How arrogant we are when we blame God for not understanding our condition or when we charge him with our own rebellion. He was all too human for us to admit that he was our Savior, the eternal second person of the Holy Trinity. "Isn't this the carpenter's son? Isn't his mother's name Mary, and aren't his brothers James, Joseph, Simon and Judas? Aren't all his sisters with us? Where then did this man get all these things?" Then we read, "And they took offense at him. But Jesus said to them, 'Only in his hometown and in his own house is a prophet without honor'" (Matt. 13:55–57). So the Son came to carry out the will of the Father; divine election has just taken on flesh and blood in the Chosen One. The Son comes to secure the salvation of the Father's new family.

Historically, the church has anxiously maintained the biblical definition of Christ as both fully divine and fully human. He not only possessed eternal equality and divinity with the Father and the Holy Spirit; this God-man was also as human as any other person, yet without sin. This is a difficult concept, especially at a time when many are once again influenced by a super-spiritual type of thinking that downplays the goodness of earthly things. I noticed that when the film *The Last Temptation of Christ* was released, evangelicals were outraged to hear about (for few of the protesters actually saw the film) the treatment of Christ as a weak, morally and psychologically flawed person. Of course, this should be an offensive treatment for those of us who believe that Jesus was indeed God incarnate. Nevertheless, there is an opposite tendency that reaction to that film seemed to bring out: downplaying the humanity of Christ in the interest of his deity. I heard a story of a professor who brought into his seminary class a painting of a nude Christ. While there was nothing obscene about the work, it shocked the class. When the professor asked them why it shocked them, they began to realize that they had never thought of Christ as being that human. While not in favor of images of Jesus (or the Godhead generally), the response of the students suggested some reticence to identify Jesus fully with our humanity.

Remember, it is the *corruption* of human nature caused by Adam's fall, not human nature itself, that is the problem. No more poignantly is this illustrated than in the willingness of the second person of the Trinity to humble himself by taking on our humanity. By "being incarnate by the Holy Ghost of the Virgin Mary" (Nicene Creed), our Lord did not inherit original sin (i.e., the *corruption* of human nature). And yet, he was tempted, he laughed and cried. In fact, he was such a "normal"-looking person that the notion of his being God took his town entirely by surprise when it was finally announced (Matt. 14:55–57).

God with Us

When we say that Christ is the Word of God, among other things we are saying that Christ is the eternal wisdom *(logos)* of the Father. Becoming the translator between God and a fallen race that could not speak his language, Jesus proclaimed, "Anyone who has seen me has seen the Father" (John 14:9). Trying to understand God apart from Christ is like trying to understand a foreign nation without an ambassador. We are finite and limited in our reason and will, and our nature is blinded by selfishness and sin. Therefore, Jesus had to be God so he could tell us the truth about the Father. Yet, he had to be one of us so that truth could be communicated to beings like ourselves. Hence, Christ is the bridge from the infinite to the finite. Jesus was and is God saying, "Here I am—right in front of you! This is what I'm like." John calls him God's "one and only Son" (John 3:16). Isaiah proclaimed him "Mighty God" (Isa. 9:6). The angel heralding his birth called him, "Immanuel . . . God with us" (Matt. 1:23).

During one of my childhood crises—you know, the ones from which you are certain you will never recover—I ran into my room and slammed the door behind me. I just wanted to be alone and wanted to shut the world out. Before long, my dad knocked on the door and said, "Son, mind if I come in?"

"Dad," I answered, "believe me, there's nothing you can do to help me right now."

You see, there was this girl in the seventh grade I happened to like, but she didn't even know I existed—except, of course, when she noticed me tripping over my own shadow watching her every move. How could Dad, of all people, understand what I was going through? This was, after all, my "old man." But he started telling me about a girl in *his* seventh grade class. Come to find out, my father *was* a kid once; he did have teenage frustrations. Suddenly I felt as though it really wasn't the end of the world.

Sometimes we tend to view God as our "old man." We think he's the last person who would understand our very human crises. But he has always been understanding of his children and their frustrations. This is true not only of our Lord, who identified fully and truly with our human struggles by becoming one of us, but of the Father, too, who *sent* his only begotten Son for that very purpose. That's an important point, because very often we tend to make God the Father look like the unrelenting destroyer and view the Son as the loving alternative within the Trinity. But not so. God the Father "so loved the world that he gave his one and only Son" (John 3:16).

The incarnation is the entrance of God into human life at eye level. Because of his own humiliation, the Son can plead our case with compassion and understanding. He has been where we are, yet without sin. He has earned his right to represent his brethren in heaven, just as he represented his Father on earth.

In the person of Christ, God "dropped in" on his rebel creatures. He came into our living rooms, our wedding receptions, our places of business. He ate with us, drank with us, laughed with us, and cried with us. The apostles testified not to having experienced a man who walked with God or who somehow became divine; nor to a god who looked and acted like a human being, but to the man who was God and the God who was man. They did not testify to their own subjective religious experiences, but to that "which we have heard, which we have seen with our eyes, which we have looked at and our hands have touched" (1 John 1:1).

This truth deepens our understanding of God's presence in the everyday world. "Spiritualizing" everything denies the incarnation. It says God is only concerned with our "spiritual" lives, that he considers "worldly" things a distraction from our "Christian walk." If, however, the Christian walk is going to have anything to do with Christ, it is going to require a vision of life which comprehends the totality of human experience. In this doctrine, we see God eating, drinking, conducting business, resting, socializing with us, comforting us, telling us about the Father and his plan of redemption, and giving us a vision for his kingdom that embraces so much more than a narrow strip of life we call "spiritual."

Again, many of us are clear on our understanding of Christ's divinity. But is Jesus now isolated "up there," removed from the mundane, common, daily affairs of average people? No, he is also—along with the Father and the Holy Spirit—still interested in our lives. *Immanuel* means "God with *us*"—not "God with *them*." God is no more interested in heads of state, CEOs of major corporations, or well-known Christian personalities than in the most average, common person in the pew. God does not have a special relationship with professional religious people. Nobody has an "in" with God that others don't have. In fact, if we can judge Christ's interests by the sort of people he liked to hang around with, he has a soft spot for social riffraff—"publicans and sinners."

I've often wondered how I would respond if Jesus lived in my own generation. Would he have been too human for me to notice too? Would I frown on his "witness" because he socialized at parties with immoral people and even befriended prostitutes and adulterers? And what if I saw him actually drinking with them? Would I be any less likely than the Pharisees to miss the point? Probably not. By our standards ruined in his "testimony," our Lord finally earned from the religious leaders the reputation "a glutton and a drunkard, a friend of tax collectors and 'sinners'!" "Friend of sinners"—it is a badge he wore, and wears, with honor (Matt. 9:9–13; 11:19).

Study Questions

1. Discuss your own experiences with "ladders." Can you identify with the "merit system" that shapes us even in our childhood?
2. Relate "Jacob's ladder" in Genesis 28 to the one in John 1:51. What is the significance?
3. Define *incarnation* and apply the term to Christ's nativity.
4. What does the incarnation reaffirm in our understanding about God's activity and involvement in our world? (See Luke 18:7; John 1:1; Heb. 4:14.) Sometimes we feel like God is removed and unconcerned. Define *immanence* and *transcendence* and how both are maintained in the incarnation.
5. Why do you think the incarnation took everybody by surprise? What was it about Christ that made his claim to divinity odd or unbelievable? (See Matt. 13:55–57; John 1:14–15.) Also, explain his name—"Immanuel, God with us"—in the light of Matthew 9:9–13; 11:19.
6. Did Jesus have a body just like ours? Did he laugh, cry, endure temptation, have friends growing up? We sing at Christmastime, "no crying he makes" ("Away in a Manger"), but is this true?
7. Even apart from the cross and the resurrection, why is the incarnation important to us?

seven

Mission Accomplished

"Look, the Lamb of God, who takes away the sin of the world!" (John 1:29). That proclamation celebrates the theme before us: the most obvious and profound demonstration of God's love and grace manifested in the sacrifice of Jesus Christ for our offenses. Frederick W. Norwood said, "The cross is central. It struck into the middle of the world, into the middle of time, into the middle of destiny. The cross is struck into the heart of God."

God's plan is to save this world by taking people from every nation and forming a new body of humanity. Christ proved that God's heart was drawn to all people—not just the religious or the people in high places, but to men, women, and children of every interest, position, color, race, and nationality. God is not a racist. "Red and yellow, black and white; they are precious in his sight" is not just a cute little line from a children's hymn. The words tell of a profound truth illustrated in the cross. All people will be saved.

But wait a moment! Isn't that universalism: the belief that everybody will eventually be saved? Not on your life. But while we who take the Scriptures seriously cannot believe that each and every person in the world will be saved, we must be universalists in the sense that we view God's program as being broader than encompassing only individuals. In a sense, God sees the world as a community of humanity, a unit. Christ came not only "to save sinners" (1 Tim. 1:15). He came also to be the "Savior of the world" (John 4:42).

In John 3:17, we notice the universal side of Christ's mission: "For God did not send his Son into the world to condemn the world, but to save the world through him." The next verse adds, "Whoever believes in him is not condemned, but whoever does not believe stands condemned already because he has not believed in the name of God's one and only Son." Verse 17 focuses on the world as a unit and humanity as a race, while verse 18 views the world on the individual level. So God is concerned about saving individuals. And God is concerned about saving the world he created. Let me explain what I mean.

Eventually, sin will be removed from creation. Christ, by his death, secured the purging not only of persons but of the whole creation. Hence, Christ "takes away the sin of the world." And notice that he does not make the removal of the world's sin possible: He accomplishes it! We can be confident that Christ secured the redemption of individuals (new creatures) as well as of creation (a new heaven and a new earth). The world, fallen in Adam, is restored in Christ.

One of the most shocking and divisive doctrines of early Christianity was the universality of God's plan, that it was not limited to one ethnic group (Israel). The Jews, remember, tended to think of the Messiah's work in terms of restoring the nation Israel, not in terms of reconciling the people in all nations to God. No better can this misunderstanding be outlined than in John 11:50–52: "'It is better for you that one man die for the people than that the whole nation perish.' [Caiaphas] did not say this on his own, but as high priest that year he prophesied that Jesus would die for the Jewish nation, and not only for that nation but also for the scattered children of God, to bring them together and make them one."

Later, in 1 John 2:2, the same disciple would write of Christ, "He is the atoning sacrifice for our sins, and not only for ours but also for the sins of the whole world." The atoning work of our God knows no boundaries set by tradition, nationality, period in time, or economic or political restrictions. God's atoning work is for everyone!

We often assume that the command to preach the gospel to the whole world begins with the Great Commission, but in fact God had given to Israel this same commission to evangelize the world centuries before our Lord reiterated it to his disciples. You will remember God's covenant promise to Abraham, that he would be "the father of many nations" (Gen. 17:4), for "all peoples on earth will be blessed through you" (Gen. 12:3). Abraham was justified by grace alone through faith alone, just as we are. Although he did not have as much understanding of God's redemptive plan as we do after the advent of Christ, he and his descendants were led along through illustrations, revelations, promises, and prophecies to the one who would save all believers in this one true God of Israel from their sins. In fact, not only did Abraham know he was justified by grace alone through faith alone (Gen. 15:6, with Rom. 4:3 and Gal. 3:6), but the very names of God revealed a great deal of theology. For instance, "The LORD Our Righteousness" is one such name in which Israel trusted (Jer. 23:6), revealing God as the one who not only commands us to be holy and righteous, or shows and teaches us how to be so, but as the one who himself *is* our righteousness.

It was Israel's commission, then, to take this gospel to the Gentiles, but again and again Israel became inwardly-focused, proud, self-righteous, and internally divided (this may sound all too familiar to us today). For example, Jonah was sent to Nineveh by God to call that wicked Gentile city to repentance and faith in the one true God, but we have to remember that Nineveh had been tyrannizing and persecuting its neighbors, including Israel, for some time. Nineveh was to Israel in those days what Iraq is to Israel today, and God commanded Jonah to be his emissary of good news to this nation. The last thing Jonah wanted to bring to Nineveh was good news. Had God sent him to proclaim judgment alone, Jonah would have been a bold ambassador, no doubt. But Jonah knew that God was sovereign and merciful and that, if he sent Jonah on this mission, he undoubtedly had plans to convert these enemies of Israel and make them share in the covenant promises along with Israel. In the end, God got his way (as he always does). But it has always been a tendency with God's people to keep the good news for themselves, form a tight inner ring of fellowship, and then judge the world instead of bringing the good news it so desperately needs to hear. We think that we are chosen because of something special about us, but as God warned Israel before it entered the land, so he reminds us,

> Hear, O Israel. . . . After the LORD your God has driven them out before you, do not say to yourself, "The LORD has brought me here to take possession of this land because of my righteousness." . . . It is not because of your righteousness or your integrity . . . ; but . . . to accomplish what he swore to your fathers, to Abraham, Isaac and Jacob. Understand, then, that it is not because of your righteousness that the LORD your God is giving you this good land to possess, for you are a stiff-necked people. [Deut. 9:1–6]

The prophet Isaiah anticipated the day when Israel would recover its missionary role, however. In a line made famous by Handel's *Messiah,* God told him, "And the glory of the LORD will be revealed, and all mankind together will see it" (Isa. 40:5). Israel failed as the "servant of the Lord," and yet God told his people, through Isaiah,

> "Here is my servant, whom I uphold, my chosen one in whom I delight; I will put my Spirit on him and he will bring justice to the nations." . . . "I, the LORD, have called you in righteousness; I will take hold of your hand. I will keep you and will make you to be a covenant for the people and a light for the Gentiles, to open eyes that are blind, to free captives from prison and to release from the dungeon those who sit in darkness." . . . Let them give glory to the LORD and proclaim his praise in the islands. [Isa. 42:1–12]

In fact, "Listen to me, you islands; hear this, you distant nations: . . . the LORD says . . . 'It is too small a thing for you [Israel] to be my servant to restore the tribes of Jacob and bring back those of Israel I have kept. I will also make you a light for the Gentiles, that you may bring my salvation to the ends of the earth.' . . . 'See, they will come from afar—some from the north, some from the west, some from the region of Aswan'" (Isa. 49:1–12). But this will happen, in spite of the nation of Israel's unfaithfulness, because the true servant of the LORD will come and extend the borders of Israel. He will succeed where the nation had failed and will actually fulfill the righteousness which we owe. He will be the faithful servant and then, as described in chapter 53, the suffering servant. It becomes increasingly clear that this is not just poetic language about the nation being personified, but that it is actually looking forward to one true Israel to represent all of the true children of Abraham—that is, all who place their trust in Christ alone, whether Jew or Gentile (Gal. 3:9, 26–29).

In this context, we can see the importance of the universal scope of Christ's mission for shifting the believing Jews from a "for Jews only" gospel to one that is "for the whole world." God has chosen people out of every nation to form a new Israel (Rev. 5:9), and that makes Christ's mission universal in scope. That is not to say that it includes every *individual* in the world, but that it includes every *nation* in the world and that the gospel invitation itself, which we proclaim, knows absolutely no boundaries. There is no such thing as a Christian nation other than the body of Christ, which admits no distinctions of race, culture, class, or sex before God.

Savior of the Body

We often talk about missions and evangelism in terms of "winning the world to Christ." Does that mean that we believe everyone in the world will be won to Christ? No. It simply means that we recognize the universal implications of the gospel. The cross is to be taken to every person everywhere because every person is responsible for accepting or rejecting it.

Salvation, then, is universal in that it crosses all barriers and includes every kind of person, but not in the sense that it includes each and every person.

Perhaps this sounds like a contradiction, but bear with me. I can talk about world peace without every person being at peace with his or her neighbor; or I can speak of world hunger while much of the world eats balanced meals. *World* does not always mean every individual inclusively, but rather the world as a general entity.

Luke records that "all the world" was taxed by Caesar Augustus (2:1 NKJV), but obviously not everybody in the world at that time was taxed by Augustus. The Pharisees said of Christ, "Look how the whole world has gone after him!" (John 12:19), but it is clear from many other statements that not everybody in the world had gone after him.

In the latter part of Romans, Paul wrote that "all Israel will be saved" (11:26). A bit earlier he wrote that only "a remnant chosen by grace" (11:5) will be saved out of Israel. He then proceeds to show us that "all Israel is saved" via an elect remnant. If "all Israel will be saved . . . [via] a remnant chosen by grace," then why can't we say that "all the world will be saved via a remnant chosen by grace"? This, I believe, is the intent of John 3:16—God loved the world so much that he sent his Son to save all believers (not those who will die in unbelief). His mission was to save the world, not condemn it. And because of the elect international remnant, the world is, in fact, saved!

This is the point of Revelation 5:9, where the saints sing to the Lamb, "You are worthy to take the scroll and to open its seals, because you were slain, and with your blood you purchased men for God from every tribe and language and people and nation. You have made them to be a kingdom and priests to serve our God, and they will reign on the earth."

The human family is not lost, but continues its lineage through a new spiritual race: the kingdom of God. As God saved the world through Noah and his family, so he will save the world through Christ and his new family.

When we view the universal implications of the cross, then, we see a planet Christ has come to reclaim: "The creation waits in eager expectation for the sons of God to be revealed. . . . The creation itself will be liberated from its bondage to decay and brought into the glorious freedom of the children of God. We know that the whole creation has been groaning as in the pains of childbirth right up to the present time. Not only so, but we ourselves . . . wait eagerly for our adoption as sons" (Rom. 8:19, 21–23).

Yet when we view the cross in its individual implications, we recognize that Jesus saved "*his people* from their sins" (Matt. 1:21, italics added). Both the world and people in that world are actually saved. Hence, Christ is the Savior of the world and the Savior of the body, that is, the church.

Some years ago the Olympics were held in Los Angeles, California. We were told repeatedly that "the world is at our doorstep." Now, I like to have company, and I like to be with people about as much as the next guy. But I could get really worked up if I thought that statement meant every man, woman, boy, and girl on planet earth would literally be "at my doorstep." But we know what they meant: People from every nation were in our city.

While God's plan involves the salvation of the world, that remnant representing the world forms the bride of Christ. And there is no redemption apart from saying "I do."

For Whom Did Christ Die?

Dr. Robert Lightner, though he disagrees with my conclusion, says, "It is doubtful if a more important question could be asked." In defining the extent of the atonement (how many are included), we can discover the nature, character, and results of the atonement.

Every orthodox Christian places limits on the work of Christ. If Jesus died for every person, but not every person is saved, his death did not actually save anybody. Thus, the work of Christ is limited in its power. If, however, the atonement, though sufficient for each and every person, was made on behalf of the chosen people, the church, that atonement is limited in its scope or purpose. If Christ died for people who will be in hell, his efforts cannot accurately be called a "saving work." Dr. Lewis Sperry Chafer said, "Christ's death does not save either actually or potentially; rather it makes all men saveable."[1] If that is true, there is no real "power in the blood." Rather, the power would seem to be in the will of the creature.

That's why I prefer "definite atonement" to "limited atonement." *Atonement* is defined in the dictionary as "satisfaction made." *Definite* is "a specific intention that is neither vague nor general." That, I believe is the atonement we find in Scripture: "Satisfaction made that has a specific intention that is neither vague nor general."

Christ came with a mission from the Father, and that mission was in fact accomplished at Calvary. All of us as Christians are interested in what was (or was not) accomplished at the cross. For upon that premise our very salvation depends.

These points lie at the heart of the Christian message, for they rest at the foot of the cross. Far from being mere items for scholarly debate, the questions "For whom did Christ die?" and "For what did Christ die?" form the basis of the Christian hope. If we consider "Jesus Paid It All" to be more than a nice song, if our salvation was secured "At the Cross," or if we believe instead that our Savior paved the way for redemption and we make it effective, then we will have to wrestle with this matter.

Was Christ's sacrifice an attempt to save everybody? Or was it a success in saving "his people from their sins" (Matt. 1:21)? The Scriptures declare, "He has . . . *accomplished* redemption *for His people*" (Luke 1:68 NASB, italics added). Nowhere is it said in even the vaguest terms, "He has made all men saveable."

Christians have historically believed in God in terms of a Trinity: three in person, one in essence—Father, Son, and Holy Spirit. The Father elects and designs the program, the Son executes it by securing the destiny of the elect, and the Holy Spirit regenerates, uniting them through faith to Jesus Christ. Let's look at the work of Christ, then, in terms of the purpose of the Father, Son, and Holy Spirit.

Part of the problem we have in coming to this discussion is that we view Christ's work as distinct, and, in fact, detached, from the work of the Father and Spirit. The heavenly Father has designed and is governing the plan of redemption. And Christ was sent by the Father to accomplish the Father's purpose. So what is that purpose?

When did God give his Son as our sacrifice? He was "slain," said John, "from the creation of the world" (Rev. 13:8). The meaning of this statement can be understood only in the light of a corresponding passage, Ephesians 1:4: "For he [the Father] chose us in him [the Son] before the creation of the world to be holy and blameless in his sight." In the mind of the eternal Father, the Lamb without blemish had already been sacrificed when he chose the heirs of redemption and placed them in Christ for eternity. Election signed the death warrant of Jesus Christ.

What Was the Father's Purpose?

Before the world existed, the Scriptures tell us, God selected a large number of people out of the humanity he would create to be his sons and daughters. "For those God foreknew he also predestined" (Rom. 8:29). God set his eternal gaze upon them. This work of Christ is based on the covenant between Father and Son, establishing the Son as the head and trustee of the Father's new people. Shedding blood was always an act of atonement on behalf of "the people" (the covenant community) in the Old Testament. Never was the sacrificial system designed to remit the sins of those outside the covenant. In the New Testament, that same covenant continues. Christ has been made the ultimate sacrifice for the sins of "the people," although now that group includes people in every part of the globe, not just the nation Israel. Because of this particular relationship of the covenant to the will of the Father in salvation, Christ's atonement is called "the blood of the *eternal covenant*" (Heb. 13:20, italics added).

The Father's plan, therefore, is selective; not everyone is chosen. "But we ought always to thank God for you, brothers loved by the Lord, because from the beginning God chose you to be saved" (2 Thess. 2:13). And Peter wrote to believers who were "chosen . . . for obedience to Jesus Christ and sprinkling by his blood" (1 Peter 1:2). "For he *chose* us in him"; it is "in him [that] we have *redemption* through his blood" (Eph. 1:4, 7, italics added). If the Father places some—indeed, many—in Christ to "be holy and blameless in his sight" (Eph. 1:4), then we must agree that the rest are not chosen and not placed in Christ to be holy and blameless in his sight. In fact, Scripture identifies these as "the objects of his wrath—prepared for destruction" (Rom. 9:22).

So we do indeed have a definite election, a particular election. God has decreed in his rich and peculiar grace to save a great number of people from all over the world, from every walk of life. But those who were not placed "in Christ" by the Father were not redeemed "by Christ" at the cross. "Who will bring any charge against those whom God has chosen?" Paul asked (Rom. 8:33). After all, he concluded, "It is Christ who died" to remove all charges from God's chosen people (Rom. 8:34 NKJV). This doctrine has no place for self-condemnation! If we are trusting in Christ, we do not have to wonder whether we will escape judgment: It is certain that we already have.

What Was the Son's Purpose?

First Peter 1:2 says that believers are "chosen . . . for obedience to Jesus Christ and sprinkling by his blood." When you go to the store and select some fruit from the stand, do you end up buying all the fruit, or only the fruit you choose to take home? Is it possible for the Father to have one purpose and the Son to have yet another? Could Christ go beyond the Father's generosity by enlarging the scope of redemption's plan?

According to an orthodox understanding of the doctrine of the Trinity, it is absolutely impossible for the scope, intent, and purpose of the Son to differ in any way from the Father's. I often hear it said, "It's no longer a sin issue, but a Son issue." The intention of this phrase is to suggest that the sinner is not condemned on the basis of the person's many sins (since Christ has atoned for them), but because the person has rejected Christ. Hence, some say, Christ has assumed the debt for every person and cleared everyone of all sins; but if an individual rejects this gracious provision, he or she will be condemned on the basis of that rejection.

We can see how this view fails to take into account the fact that rejecting Christ is itself a sin. I can see no distinction whatsoever between a "sin issue and a Son issue." Rejecting Christ is simply one of many millions of sins for which people will be condemned. "Whoever does not believe stands condemned already," Jesus announced (John 3:18). And Paul lists a number of particular sins: "sexual immorality, impurity, lust, evil desires and greed, which is idolatry." He concludes, "Because of these, the wrath of God is coming" (Col. 3:5–6), not simply because of unbelief.

If Christ's sacrifice then covers each and every person—even those who will never accept it—we are faced with two alternatives: either to say that every person will be saved (since there is no longer any basis for condemnation, all sins being canceled) or that there is one sin (unbelief) for which Christ did not atone.

Here is an important point: Christ said, "I have come down from heaven not to do my will, but to do the will of him who sent me. And this is the will of him who sent me, that I shall lose none of all that he has given me, but raise them up at the last day" (John 6:38–39). This passage either teaches universal salvation or definite atonement. Plainly, whomever it is that the Father has given Christ will receive eternal life. And if Christ has come "not to do my will but to do the will of him who sent me," then the Son's purpose must be just as limited in scope as the Father's.

Our Savior tells us precisely that. On one occasion in particular, Jesus was conversing with a couple of Pharisees. He knew they were not responsive to his teachings, and he told them twice: "I lay down my life for the sheep," and then boldly informed them, "but you do not believe because you are not my sheep" (John 10:15, 26). A few hours before the crucifixion, Jesus prayed to the Father: "For you granted [me] authority over all people that [I] might give eternal life to all those you have given [me]. . . . I am not praying for the world, but for those you have given me" (John 17:2, 9). Though Christ was delegated "authority over all people," he chose to focus his saving atonement on his covenant family: "those you have given me." Scripture says Christ died to "purify for himself a people that are his very own" (Titus 2:14). Hebrews makes clear that "bringing many sons to glory" was Christ's intention (2:10). The Savior said, "Here am I, and the children God has given me" (Heb. 2:13).

What Was the Holy Spirit's Purpose?

In Romans 8:30, it is said that "those he predestined, he also called" effectively by God's Spirit into fellowship and communion with the Trinity, although everyone is invited to come. Furthermore, Christ said his sheep hear his voice, and the Holy Spirit "called us to a holy life . . . because of his own purpose and grace. This grace was given us in Christ Jesus before the beginning of time" (2 Tim. 1:9). In Acts 13:48 we read that "all who were appointed for eternal life believed." The witness of Scripture appears clear and emphatic in its description of a specific design for salvation.

Did Christ buy back more people than the Holy Spirit intends to bring back?

But Doesn't God Love Everyone?

In Romans 9, Jacob is used to illustrate the elect of God, and Esau is used to illustrate the nonelect. Jacob is loved and Esau is hated "that God's purpose in election might stand: not by works but by him who calls" (vv. 11–12). I know this is strong language, but I have found no evidence in Scripture to support the conclusion that God loves every person in the same way. It is often said, "God loves the sinner, but hates his sin." Actually, however, the psalmist says of God, "you hate all who do wrong" (Ps. 5:5). It took the reconciliation of Christ's death to turn away God's hatred.

If I asked you, "Do you love everybody in the world?" you would probably say yes. But I can make a reasonable guess that if you were to describe for me your love for your spouse or closest relative, the meaning of that word *love* would deepen. If you love people you don't even know as much as you love your spouse, I can foresee some problems for your marriage. Only the elect were *known* and loved by God before creation (Rom. 8:29). God "sends rain on the righteous and the unrighteous" (Matt. 5:45), but "bring[s] about justice for His elect" (Luke 18:7 NASB). As Creator, God cares for the temporal lives of his creatures, but as Husband, Jesus Christ favors only his bride with sacrificial, eternal love (Eph. 5:25). A father might care about all the children of the world, but that care does not even compare with his concern and love for his own children. So too, Christ died for "the scattered children of God" (John 11:52).

But doesn't this view limit God's love? On the contrary! This view intensifies God's love, by announcing it as a discriminate, special, saving love that truly reaches its target. That sure beats the indiscriminate, general benevolence we seem to be hearing much about today.

A Useful Distinction

This belief that Christ died specifically for the purpose of *saving* people, not just making the salvation of everybody possible, is not new. It did not originate with John Calvin, nor with the more explicit language of the Synod of Dort or Westminster Assembly. Even during the Middle Ages, theologians spoke of the atonement as being "*sufficient* for the world; *efficient* for the elect only." In fact, Martin Luther and John Calvin simply reiterated this long-standing distinction, as did the Synod of Dort, where the so-called Five Points of Calvinism originated.

In other words, the work of Christ is not deficient. It does not fail to save anyone who trusts in Christ, and it can be freely and sincerely offered to the whole world indiscriminately because it *is* sufficient for the salvation of every person who has ever lived or is yet to come into the world. The question is whether the saving work of Christ, any more than the saving work of the Father or that of the Holy Spirit, is particularly designed to make salvation of everyone possible or to actually "save his people from their sins" (Matt. 1:21).

This leads immediately to the question, If this is true, does that mean we can't tell individuals, "Christ died for *you*"? After all, that might not be true. It is interesting to study the invitation we find again and again in Scripture. It is always very general: Christ came into the world "to save sinners," "to save the world," and so on. If you believe, you can be certain that your sins were covered at the cross and that you are saved from God's everlasting judgment. Never in the Scriptures is an unbeliever given any hope apart from believing in Christ. He is not encouraged to think of himself as the object of God's special fatherhood or redemptive purposes unless and until he is in Christ. We can only assure a person that Christ died for him or her if that person belongs to the visible covenant community. Far from weakening the urgency of the gospel invitation, it heightens the sense that apart from trusting in Christ there is not even a *provision* for salvation. But those who do believe have not only a provision and a potential atonement, but an effective redemption that actually accomplishes its purpose.

Satisfaction Guaranteed

Jesus Christ died to satisfy the just demands of a holy God. The prophet Isaiah said of the coming Messiah, "He shall see His seed [the result of his work] . . . and be satisfied" (Isa. 53:10–11 NKJV). But did our Savior *really* satisfy the wrath of God on behalf of all for whom he died? Can we be certain that our sins will never be brought up in court, especially if so many for whom he died are condemned for their sins?

Now that we have explored the purpose and extent of the work of Christ, it is appropriate to extend our discussion of Christ's mission by viewing the cross from the aspect of *what* he accomplished rather than for whom he accomplished it.

All of us, by nature, know that God is pretty mad at us. As a matter of natural revelation, we learn that all people in every tribe and nation are at odds with God. Even pagan religions have appeasing the gods as the center of their beliefs and practices. Although we as Christians sometimes try to reassure people that "God loves you and Christ died for you," most know that things just are not that simple. Things are not okay, and if we are not reconciled with God, the picture is not quite as bright as we would have people believe.

Many people will pay for their sins in hell. But why, if Christ died for everybody to satisfy the wrath of God? Nineteenth-century Princeton theologian Benjamin B. Warfield said of believers who do not accept definite atonement:

> They necessarily turn away from a substitutionary atonement altogether. Christ did not die in the sinner's stead, it seems, to bear his penalties and purchase for him eternal life; He died rather to make the salvation of sinners possible, to open the way of salvation to sinners, to remove all the obstacles in the way of salvation. But what obstacle stands in the way of salvation besides the sinner's sin? And if this obstacle (their sin) is removed, are they not saved?[2]

To affirm a universal atonement, then, one is left with only two options: either to limit the atonement in its effect—that is, in what it really accomplishes—or to accept at face value the clear statements of Scripture regarding the nature of redemption by embracing universal salvation. In other words, if Christ's death secured redemption, propitiation, and satisfaction of divine justice on behalf of each and every individual, we must either affirm that each and every individual will therefore be saved (since the atonement is effective in nature) or that the work of Christ itself must be limited in its scope. Otherwise, it is limited in its nature.

No less an evangelical theologian and revivalist than Charles Finney recognized this. He knew that to embrace the historic view of the atonement as literal payment for sin would require him to also accept either universal *salvation* (if Christ died for everybody) or an atonement that was limited in its scope. So, Finney, refusing to embrace universal salvation or an atonement limited in its scope, chose to accept an atonement limited in its nature. In fact, the belief that Christ died for the elect alone, he argues, "assumes that the atonement was a literal payment of a debt, which we have seen does not consist with the nature of the atonement." Further, the obedience of Christ cannot be imputed to us as though we possessed it ourselves because, after all, "If He obeyed the law as our substitute, then why should our own return to personal obedience be insisted upon as a *sine qua non* for our salvation?"[3] In other words, if Christ's work was sufficient, and if Jesus had indeed "paid it all," what reason would there be for our working for our own salvation?

Finney, then, was willing to follow his view to its ultimate conclusion. If Jesus Christ actually paid for the sins of all men, all men would be saved—leaving them with nothing to be forgiven. But since all for whom Christ died are in fact not saved, payment of the debt of sin could not be the nature of Christ's work. Tragically, Finney was consistent and was willing to accept a weak view of the atonement rather than to embrace Christ's own statement, "I lay down my life for the sheep" (John 10:15).

You see, if Finney's theory is correct—if, in other words, Christ's death merely made it possible for us to save ourselves by following his example, by making a decision, and by living a holy life, then *everybody* loses. If at first this doctrine, like election and predestination, seems too severe, let us remember that an atonement that doesn't atone, a redemption that doesn't redeem, a propitiation that doesn't propitiate, a satisfaction that doesn't satisfy does not help any one of us! The fact that God would choose, redeem, call, and keep a great number known only to him is amazing grace indeed and of infinitely more comfort than the idea that Christ's death actually secured the salvation of none, merely making salvation possible, depending on the ability of those who are "dead in trespasses and sins" to make the right moves to God.

In fact, one evangelical writer comments in response to those of us who hold the view of definite atonement: "They also believe that the work of Christ on the cross was effective in and of itself."[4]

Indeed, we do believe that. Although it is absolutely essential that we trust Christ and accept his sacrifice for our sins, no one for whom Christ died will reject it. Christ's mission was accomplished!

I have frequently wondered, just for the sake of inquiry, "What if the Bible taught that Christ died for every person?" My conclusion was that I would be driven into the arms of universal salvation, not the Arminian view. That is because the Bible does not say Christ made redemption, reconciliation, propitiation, or anything else possible. He secured it for all for whom he died. Because the Bible allows for only a *saving* atonement, every person would be saved—whether a believer or not—because Christ had removed all charges. Let's look briefly then at the nature of atonement.

The Meaning of Atonement

Redemption means "to buy back," to "return to one's possession by payment of a price." You were kidnapped and held hostage by sin. But if you are a believer, Christ paid the ransom price for you to be freed so you could become his possession. What kind of redemption do we have if most of the captives remain forever in captivity even though the ransom has been paid? The dictionary further defines *redemption* as "purchasing a slave with a view to his freedom." How could Christ purchase every person "with a view to his freedom" if all along he knew that most would not ultimately be freed? This seems to be emphasized in Isaiah 53:10–11, "he will see his offspring [the fruit of his work] . . . and be satisfied." How could Christ see people for whom he died in everlasting torment and "be satisfied"? As Charles Spurgeon noted, "If it was Christ's intention to redeem all men, how deplorably has He been disappointed."

Propitiation refers to the breaking away of the enmity and hostility that keeps God at odds with us. Propitiation removes God's wrath. Yet people will be condemned forever *because* they are still at odds with God. John the Baptist said, "whoever rejects the Son will not see life, for God's wrath remains on him" (John 3:36). God is patiently waiting to unleash his wrath on the "objects of his wrath" (Rom. 9:22). If Christ did not "propitiate" God's wrath for me any more than he did for Judas Iscariot, how can I be sure that God is not going to consume me with his wrath? One might say, "Because you believe." Yes, but that means that we rather than Christ propitiate God's wrath, and that makes us our own saviors.

"To render no longer opposed" is the definition of *reconciliation*. Yet people are assigned to hell for eternity because they are and forever will be opposed by God and to God. People who are reconciled are made friends. And Jesus said he would lay down his life for his friends (John 15:13). But will those who finally reject Christ be friends of God? Does God send his friends to hell? "Depart from me, you who are cursed, into the eternal fire" (Matt. 25:41). That is a far cry from friendship. The Bible says nothing of potential reconciliation, or a mere provision for reconciliation. Rather, it promises: "Having been reconciled, we shall be saved" (Rom. 5:10 NKJV). To be reconciled, then, is to be saved.

The concept of *substitution* is found throughout Scripture as the act of one who suffers vicariously, or in the place of another. We read that Christ's blood is connected to "the covenant, which is poured out for many for the forgiveness of sins" (Matt. 26:28). Suppose a criminal were on death row, awaiting execution. A stranger meets with the judge, and the judge agrees to accept the execution of this stranger (who is himself innocent) in the place of the real criminal. This person becomes the criminal's substitute. Then suppose that, after executing the substitute criminal, the judge then executes the real criminal, too. The judge would be guilty of at least one murder. You were the criminal, but Christ stepped in and took your place. Because he took your place, you will not have to take it. God will not condemn both the Redeemer and the redeemed. This fact is an incentive to be numbered with the redeemed by trusting in Jesus Christ.

Sacrifice and Satisfaction

Did Jesus satisfy God's justice on the cross? Or do we satisfy God's justice when we believe? If your answer is "at the cross," then you believe that everyone for whom Christ died is cleared of all charges before God. If your answer is "when we believe," one wonders who is the real savior in this matter. The Scriptures do not teach this theory of self-satisfaction. We do not appease God's wrath by believing. Then many of us, I'm sure, do not think God needs to be satisfied any more. Although some things may unsettle God a bit at times, God is, overall, nice to us. There's no reason to be afraid of God. But the Bible isn't quite so sentimental.

In the Old Testament, animal sacrifices were offered to pre-figure the anticipation of the ultimate sacrifice of God's Son. Unlike the pagans who sacrificed, and continue in some places to sacrifice, to appease the gods, we have no way of appeasing our God. He must appease himself by giving his own sacrifice. "And where these [sins] have been forgiven, there is no longer any sacrifice for sin" (Heb. 10:18). If you are a believer, your sins have been remitted and sacrificial offering is no longer needed to satisfy God. If, however, you are not a believer and you per-sist in unbelief until death, there is no remission of your sins and the holy God is in need of a sacrifice. That sacrifice involves your spending eternity in hell, outside God's covenant of redemption. His offended justice must be satisfied.

One common response that the world makes to the idea of a sovereign God is "It's not fair for Christ to die for one person and not another." But the same argument answers the atone-ment of the Son as the election of the Father. Have we forgot-ten what grace is all about? Is it wrong for people who don't deserve anything not to get anything? What the fallen, alienated sinner needs to hear is not "God loves everybody, so if you're a 'body' then God loves you." No, the sinner needs more than that. He or she needs that intense love from all eternity that would mark him or her out. The sinner needs a passionate love, a committed love, a compelling love, which only comes in a dis-criminate, particular, selective relationship. Unconditional love is not based on the creature but the Creator.

Ambrose, a church father, said, "If you die in unbelief, Christ did not die for you." Don't think *that* didn't make people think twice about the offer of Christ! We can hold out to the person who is at the end of his or her rope a redemption that *is* com-plete, rather than a redemption that must be completed by believ-ing. What this despairing world needs is not a hypothetical sav-ior, but a real one. It doesn't need a "husband" who lets people with whom he is in love be lost eternally. And those who look to Christ need not worry: "Husbands, love your wives, just as Christ loved the church and gave himself up for her" (Eph. 5:25).

The same Bible that tells us that Christ gave "his life as a ransom for many" (Matt. 20:28; 26:28; Isa. 53:12; Heb. 9:28) also beckons, "Come to me, all you who are weary" (Matt. 11:28), and "If anyone is thirsty, let him come" (John 7:37).

The great Baptist evangelist Charles Spurgeon once said:

> And then I hear another objection—
>
> "How can you, sir, upon that theory, go to preach the Gospel unto every creature?"
>
> I could not go upon any other theory, for I dare not go on that fool's errand of preaching a redemption that might not redeem . . . a salvation that might not save. I could not go to a man and say, "Believe and thou shalt be saved."
>
> He would ask me, "Do you think *you* are going to be in heaven?"
>
> "Yes."
>
> "Why?"
>
> "Because Christ died for me."
>
> "But he died for everybody, so my chances are therefore just as good as yours."
>
> And after he had accepted my declaration, he might reply, "Is there any real reason why I should rejoice? Some for whom Christ died are in hell. What makes me so sure I will not go there? It is rather a faulty piece of good news, because it is nothing positive; it is a grand uncertainty you have proclaimed to me."

Spurgeon concludes with the proper attitude toward this doctrine and the gospel message: "If you believe on the Lord Jesus Christ, you shall be saved; if you do not, you shall be lost, and lost forever. You are not redeemed—you are not saved—there is no salvation or redemption for you."

Why should unbelievers get excited when I tell them, "God loves you; Christ died for you"? Christ could have died for them; God could have loved them. But what good does that do them if they are all condemned anyway?

Those whom the Savior loved and for whom he gave his life *are saved!* That's a love that achieves its objectives.

This doctrine sets before the unbeliever the availability and also the urgency of trusting in Christ. The person to whom we are witnessing is not potentially saved; that person is actually lost. Rejecting Christ places a person outside the boundaries of redemption and God's eternal love.

You may ask, "Is God loving when he chooses not to redeem everyone?" And I reply, "Is God loving when he sends a person to hell—even after Jesus has already paid the price for his release?"

Incidentally, nobody will ever be able to say, "Well, I looked for redemption, but there was nothing for me." Christ obtained salvation for all who would, by the grace of the Holy Spirit, believe. The only people who will have no redemption will be those who never really looked. "Seek and you will find" (Matt. 7:7) is the promise of Scripture. If you are looking for redemption, it is because God is working in you. He is not far from you. Accept the sacrifice of his Son as full satisfaction of God's just and holy demands on you. Having trusted in Christ, you can be confident that "Therefore, there is now no condemnation for those who are in Christ Jesus" (Rom. 8:1). Are you "in him"? (See Eph. 1:4, 7, 13.) You can be certain right now by placing your trust in his sacrificial death in your place.

> Jesus paid it all,
> All to Him I owe;
> Sin had left a crimson stain—
> He washed it white as snow.

Study Questions

1. In what sense can it be said that Christ's atonement was universal? (See John 1:29; 1 John 2:2). Does this mean each and every individual, or is it universal in some other sense? (See Rev. 5:9 for a clue.)
2. How do you interpret verses which clearly teach that Christ gave his life for his sheep, his people, many? Does this imply that the focus of Christ's saving intention was the predestined church? (See Matt. 20:28; 26:28; John 10:15, 26; Eph. 1:6–7; 5:22–23.)
3. Does "all" or "all men" always mean each and every person? (See Luke 2:1; John 12:19; Rom. 11:5, 26.)
4. What was God's intention in the first place with regard to redemption? Did he intend to save every person? Will the

Holy Spirit call every person? If the Father and the Holy Spirit are working on the basis of election, how does Christ's work further the eternal plan?

5. Why is the extent of the atonement so important in our understanding and appreciation of its nature (and vice versa)?

6. Does God limit his sacrificial love to the elect? (See Rom. 9:11; Eph. 5:25.)

7. Does this doctrine hinder the universal proclamation of the gospel?

8. Who is the person who needs to be satisfied in our relationship with God?

9. Define the following terms: a) *redemption* (See Isa. 53:10–11.); b) *propitiation* (See John 3:36; Rom. 9:22.); c) *reconciliation* (See Matt. 25:41; John 15:13; Rom. 5:10.); d) *substitution* (See Matt. 20:28; 26:28.); e) *sacrifice* and *satisfaction.* (See Eph. 5:25; Heb. 10:18.)

10. Explain the relationship between particular redemption (i.e., Christ's death for the elect) and the free, universal offer of the gospel. (See Matt. 11:28; John 7:37.)

eight

Intoxicating Grace

Earlier I mentioned that the reason God always gets his way in the matter of our conversion is not because of his raw power, forcing us against our will, but because he effectually persuades us and, in changing our will, gives us the desire for him that is entirely contrary to our sinful nature. In this chapter, we will take a closer look at this doctrine of the new birth or "effectual calling." It has often been called "irresistible grace," but because of the way *irresistible* is used today, I would prefer the term "*intoxicating* grace." For this is what God does by his Spirit: He overwhelms us with his love and grace, liberating us to freely embrace what we had before just as freely rejected.

Paul said, "Do not get drunk on wine, which leads to debauchery. Instead, be filled with the Spirit" (Eph. 5:18). So we can assume that the influence of the Spirit in our lives can be compared with the way in which alcohol influences us. That being the case, let me use this illustration. When a person pops open a seventh can of beer, that person's decisions are being, to a large extent, influenced by alcohol. If he or she drives "under the influence" and swerves and dodges other cars for excitement (doing things he or she would not normally do sober), that person is responsible for his or her actions because, influenced or not, those actions were his or her decisions.

By nature, sin has intoxicated our whole being, and we cannot please God in any way. Nevertheless, our decision to turn from God is our decision. Sin controls our faculties, but the decisions we make really are our own and God holds us accountable for them. When the Holy Spirit descends and intoxicates us with his new desires and power, we just as naturally turn to God. Both the decision to turn from God and the decision to turn to God are really our decisions. But apart from God's grace (*intoxicating* grace) a decision for Christ is never going to happen.

Redemption Applied

God's grace works! Just as it worked at the cross in sealing and securing your redemption, it works when the Holy Spirit invades your life and transforms you with his powerful love. This is the Holy Spirit's act in this drama of redemption. When he draws people to himself and creates new life within them, not circumstances, the devil, nor even death can keep God's eternal love from conquering us.

Imagine the joy of a husband and wife as they come to the end of an adoption process and can now take their new son or daughter into their home as a member of their family. The process began when the parents selected the child from among other children. Then there was the contract, the financial stage. The fees had to be paid, and outstanding debts had to be handled. And now, finally, the child is notified about his or her new family. After certain steps were taken, the child has a home. The child can feel secure and loved, part of a real family now.

God also takes some steps in securing our adoption into his family, things he has done to give us new life.

Resurrection

Because we are "dead in . . . transgressions and sins" (Eph. 2:1), we have to be given new life. That process requires a resurrection, and it must come from an outside source.

When Jesus told his disciples that Lazarus had "fallen asleep," they responded, "Lord, if he sleeps, he will get better."

"So then [Jesus] told them plainly, 'Lazarus is dead'" (John 11:14). And you know the rest of the story: Jesus went to the tomb and brought Lazarus back from the dead. This act was a preview of things to come. Not long thereafter, Christ was crucified and rose again. And because he lives, we are promised new life.

We are dead and unresponsive to the gospel in our natural condition. "He will get better," we are so often told today. "Just give him time."

But God responds, "Humans are dead." Just as Jesus' words to his disciples were that Lazarus could not and would not recover, he convinces us elsewhere in Scripture that our spiritual condition is just as final; we "are all under sin" (Rom. 3:9).

Jesus told the multitude, "You belong to your father, the devil, and you want to carry out your father's desire" (John 8:44). You can't separate a person's will from the person's nature; and a nature that is opposed to God cannot, will not, make a decision for God. Jesus said, "everyone who sins is a slave to sin" (John 8:34). This, he said, is why "you must be born again" (John 3:7).

We hear a lot about being "born again." The American media refer frequently to the born-again constituency. At a time when even editors of pornographic magazines can claim to be born again, for our own good we must understand what the words mean.

First of all, the word translated "again" should more accurately be rendered "from above." The new birth is *from above,* not from within. We do not cause or initiate regeneration. We are not born again because we believe. We believe because God reaches down from heaven and grants us the new birth.

In our first birth, we entered our world in the family of Adam. Hence, the psalmist lamented, "Surely I was sinful at birth, sinful from the time my mother conceived me" (Ps. 51:5). We are "by nature objects of wrath" (Eph. 2:3). Our natural state is to reject God and do our own thing. This immediately rules out bringing about our own change or even contributing toward this new birth.

Why? "Those controlled by the sinful nature cannot please God" (Rom. 8:8). Jesus said, "a bad tree cannot bear good fruit" (Matt. 7:18). A person's nature must be changed before his or her behavior will change. The old person must be replaced by the new.

We had about as much to do with our new birth as Lazarus had to do with his physical resurrection. Again, our Lord says, "No one can [even] come to me unless the Father who sent me draws him, and I will raise him up at the last day" (John 6:44).

We will never know, I suppose—at least not until we see our Lord—why God did not just turn and walk away from this mess. God had warned Adam, "you will surely die" (Gen. 2:17). Adam refused to believe God, as we still do today. But God's grace and mercy prevail.

Our Calling Decreed

Earlier I referred to this popular illustration: God has cast his vote for your soul; Satan has cast his; now it's up to you to cast the deciding ballot. I am convinced that if our Master was on earth today, he would respond to us as he did to his first disciples: "You did not choose me, but I chose you" (John 15:16). I am afraid that we come perilously close to blasphemy in our exaltation of the human will, setting it over and above (or at least on a par with) the will of God. If our decision determines whether God or Satan wins the great battle for our souls, we are in serious trouble.

Since I have discussed predestination and election elsewhere in this book, I will not dwell on them extensively here. Let me say simply that J. B. Phillips is right: Our "god" today is far too small. One evangelical scholar writes, "Indeed, God would save all men if He could. . . . God will achieve the greatest number in heaven that He possibly can. He does not love just some men; He loves all and will do everything within His loving power to save all He can. . . . God will save the greatest number of people that is actually achievable without violating their free choice."[1]

The marvelous truth is that because God has selected the recipients of his grace and placed them in Christ, God will do all that is necessary, not only to make it *possible* for them to return to him, but to make *sure* of it!

"And those he predestined, he also called." "And all who were appointed for eternal life believed" (Acts 13:48; Rom. 8:30). That is how committed God is to your salvation!

Our Calling Secured

The work of our Savior was the payment of the ransom price that set us free insofar as judgment and condemnation are concerned. When we are born again, we begin to actually experience this freedom secured by the Savior.

We might think of this in terms of the construction of a building. The Father is the architect, the Son purchases the materials and the land, and the Holy Spirit takes the Father's design and the Son's materials and constructs the magnificent cathedral of grace.

Christ's death not only removed the penalty of sin. He endured the penalty of sin in our place. In the mystery of union or identification with Christ, he trampled death by death, and we hung there with Christ on the cross. So, Paul says, "If we have been united with him like this in his death, we will certainly also be united with him in his resurrection. For we know that our old self was crucified with him so that the body of sin might be done away with, that we should no longer be slaves to sin" (Rom. 6:5–6).

Everything we lost in the fall, Jesus Christ purchased back for us by his death. He crucified our old human nature, inherited from Adam; buried our old identity as being "in Adam"; and bought for us a new life, a new identity. When the Holy Spirit comes to us, he renews us (Eph. 4:24; Col. 3:10). We let go of our old identity and affirm the new. Christ spoke of our losing our life and natural identity to discover real life and a supernatural identity.

The same Christ who created the world and then redeemed it now comes to us as re-Creator: "For God, who said, 'Let light shine out of darkness,' made his light shine in our hearts to give us the light of the knowledge of the glory of God in the face of Christ" (2 Cor. 4:6).

The great expositor, A. W. Tozer, took the work of Christ on the cross seriously and pointed out weaknesses in popular contemporary views:

All unannounced and most undetected there has come in modern times a new cross into popular evangelical circles. . . . This new evangelism employs the same language as the old, but its content is not the same and its emphasis is not as before. . . .

The new cross does not slay the sinner; it redirects him. It gears him into a cleaner and holier way of living and saves his self-respect. To the self-assertive it says, "Come and assert yourself for Christ." To the egotist it says, "Come and do your boasting in the Lord." To the thrill-seeker it says, "Come and enjoy the thrill of the abundant Christian life."[2]

Being "bought at a price" (1 Cor. 7:23) means that we have become the property of someone else. At the cross, then, we were freed from slavery to sin—not to become "in control" again, but to become the property of Jesus Christ, who frees us from other allegiances to be entirely his.

Called to Glory

The dictionary defines *glorification* as "to magnify; to treat as more splendid or excellent than would normally be considered; brilliantly beautiful or magnificent." *Glorification* is a state or condition of exaltation. From the term *glory* (*doxa* in Greek) we get our word *doxology.* So then, to glorify someone is to dignify, honor, and esteem that person.

Jesus said, "For everyone who exalts himself will be humbled, and he who humbles himself will be exalted" (Luke 14:11). When we are united with Christ and become identified with his nature by humbling ourselves in recognition of our dependence upon him, we are exalted to the very heavens where Christ is seated in glory. But first we must recant from all the claims we used to hold to esteem, dignity, righteousness, and glory apart from God. Humiliation gives way to glorification.

So the death of Christ corresponds to our redemption. His resurrection corresponds to our spiritual resurrection, as well as the judicial act of justification. And the ascension of Christ to the right hand of the Father corresponds to our glorification. That means that when Jesus died, we died; when he rose from the dead, we were granted a title to a new start, a new identity, and a renewed heart. Then, when the Savior ascended, we too were guaranteed to be exalted and glorified with him in heaven's courts.

Artists used to illustrate this truth by painting a golden halo above the head of a saint. Glorification is the consummation of salvation, the grand finale. And every justified believer is a saint, "holy and blameless" before God (Eph. 1:4).

Hebrews 6:20 says, "Jesus has entered as a forerunner for us, having become a high priest forever according to the order of Melchizedek" (NASB). That means that Jesus pioneered the route we are going to travel. He was not the only one to ascend to the place of honor, just the first! For he has taken us with him. Because Jesus returned in victory to the Father, he has guaranteed our entrance. When the disciple Stephen was being stoned to death, he, being "full of the Holy Spirit, looked up to heaven and saw the glory of God, and Jesus standing at the right hand of God" (Acts 7:55). Stephen could die in peace, knowing that Jesus was standing at his defense, prepared to crown him with the same glory he had seen in the vision.

Among the riches of the psalms is the twenty-fourth: "Who may ascend the hill of the LORD? Who may stand in his holy place? He who has clean hands and a pure heart, who does not lift up his soul to an idol or swear by what is false. He will receive blessing from the LORD and vindication from God his Savior. Such is the generation of those who seek him, who seek your face, O God of Jacob" (vv. 3–6).

For years I had heard this presented as referring to believers, as if to answer the question, "How can we be saved?" We have to have clean hands and a pure heart, so here are the ways to be prepared to meet the Lord when we die. But that is not what this psalm is all about. In fact, the very next verses make it clear that we are not the subject here, but that it is someone else who is singularly qualified to ascend the hill of the Lord and to stand in his holy place: "Lift up your heads, O you gates; be lifted up, you ancient doors, that the King of glory may come in. Who is this King of glory? The LORD strong and mighty, the LORD mighty in battle. Lift up your heads, O you gates; lift them up, you ancient doors, that the King of glory may come in. Who is he, this King of glory? The LORD Almighty—he is the King of glory" (vv. 7–10). The psalmist paints the picture of a castle built on a high mountain and of the triumphant king, who has just vanquished his enemies in battle, as he makes his triumphant procession through the gates. Most likely, this psalm was actually composed for the triumphal entry of the ark of the covenant into Jerusalem, but it is clearly a messianic psalm looking forward to the ascension of Christ. Only he, the King of glory, the Lord strong and mighty, the Lord mighty in battle, is worthy to ascend God's holy hill and stand in his holy place. We know what happened to those who were unqualified to stand in the holy place. Even though Aaron's sons were trying to please God as his high priests by offering an unauthorized service in his holy place, "fire came out from the presence of the LORD and consumed them, and they died before the LORD" (Lev. 10:1–3). As Aaron, dumbstruck, could not even put his thoughts into words, Moses explained, "'This is what the LORD spoke of when he said: "Among those who approach me I will show myself holy; in the sight of all the people I will be honored."' Aaron remained silent."

Most people today, in modern Western democracies, think they can waltz into God's presence without much fear of reprisal. There is hardly anything left of this biblical idea of God's holiness. But the psalmist knew very well how holy God was and, by contrast, how unholy we all are in his presence. To imagine even for one moment that this psalm, requiring "clean hands and a pure heart," could possibly refer to anyone but the spotless Lamb of God is to fail to take God's holiness and human sinfulness seriously.

But this is just one more piece of good news in this redemptive drama. Although we are ourselves unworthy to ascend the hill and stand in the holy place, in Christ's ascension, "God raised us up with Christ and seated us with him in the heavenly realms . . ." (Eph. 2:6). We were with and in Christ as he hung on the cross, dying to ourselves and to the judgment of the law, buried with him, and then raised with him. But then we ascended with him, representatively, and will one day ourselves actually experience our resurrection and ascension where, only in Christ, the King of glory, we are assured a safe and triumphal entrance. For he is our righteousness and, therefore, only as we are, as it were, hidden under his royal robe, can we ascend that heavenly hill and stand in that very holy place where angels fear to tread.

One of my all-time favorite movies is *Eddie and the Cruisers,* a film about a rock-and-roll group. One night Eddie took his girlfriend to a certain junkyard. He hadn't been back to the junkyard since he was a child. While sitting on the steps of the entrance, Eddie told his girlfriend about how he used to watch its elderly owner gradually transform the junkyard into a festival of lights and creative structures. "That old man actually thought he could make a castle out of junk," Eddie reminisced. As I heard those lines, *That old man actually thought he could make a castle out of junk,* I thought, with the exception of age, *that sounds like God.*

One popular poster has a child saying, "I'm somebody, 'cause God don't make no junk." Well, that's true! God doesn't make junk. He makes castles. So let's start seeing ourselves that way! While we retain a humble sense of our own sinfulness, we are "living stones . . . being built up as a spiritual house" (1 Peter 2:5 NASB).

The Holy Spirit and Human Response

One question often asked in discussing God's sovereign activity in our lives is "Does God drag people into heaven kicking and screaming, against their will?" Far from it. God changes their will and their disposition. "No one can come to me unless the Father who sent me draws him" (John 6:44), so his nature must be changed.

Try drinking water from a rusty cup. The water is not rusty; the cup is. No matter what kind of drink one might put in the cup, the rusty taste will still be there. The problem with us is not simply that we cannot make the right decision for Christ; instead the problem is that we possess a nature that is opposed to God. We reject Christ of our own free will. And if we accept Christ, it will be because God changed our nature so our will would respond naturally and freely to God's grace.

We cannot separate a person's will from his or her nature. If it is a coyote's nature to howl, its instincts will lead it every so often to a particular rock where it will unleash its morbid call. But a rabbit will not howl nor will a groundhog, for it is not their nature. The difference is that, with us the problem is not that we were not *created* to glorify and enjoy God, but that we *refuse* to accept that as the goal of our creation and existence. Jeremiah said of humans, "The heart is deceitful above all things and beyond cure. Who can understand it?" (Jer. 17:9). If an unbeliever rejects

Christ, that person is only responding as his or her nature dictates. If a person accepts Christ, the person's nature has been transformed. But in either case, that person's will makes the choice.

The real question, then, is whether our choice is the determining factor in our salvation. I would answer yes and no. Yes, if you do not choose Christ you will be condemned, and if you do choose Christ, you will live. But the answer is also no in the sense that only a move of God's grace can change your nature so you will say yes to him. The human heart, untouched and unrenewed by God's effective grace, will never move a person toward the truth. "Without faith it is impossible to please God" (Heb. 11:6), and faith is God's gift (Eph. 2:8).

Regeneration is irresistible only because the God who regenerates is irresistible. Our natural blindness keeps our eyes from recognizing God's captivating features. So when God heals our sight, what can we say but, "Now I see!"?

God's Part and Our Part

We often speak of salvation in terms of "God's part and our part." However, this approach might suggest that we do, in fact, contribute to our own salvation.

I remember hearing the kind criticism of a man who said, "Be careful; you almost make it sound like we don't have any part in salvation."

"Almost?" I responded. "I didn't go far enough!"

Why do we insist on having something to do with God's gift? Why can't we just say, "To God alone be glory"—and really mean it? Any reference at all to "our part" immediately tends to make for a salvation by works, not grace; hence, salvation would be a product of humans and God, rather than God alone. Not even our decision merits eternal life.

But, you know, that is often the way we look at it. We agree perhaps that various "works" such as being good to one's neighbor and going to church every Sunday will not merit for us eternal life; however, if we "make a decision" and perhaps walk down an aisle or sign a card or pray a "sinner's prayer," we will then attain eternal life.

On the contrary, when we respond in faith, we are only reaching out for something that is already accomplished by God. Our faith does not merit anything at all. Rather, it is our responsibility to embrace what God has done. John R. W. Stott speaks to this: "We must never think of salvation as a kind of transaction between God and us in which He contributes grace and we contribute faith. For we were dead and had to be quickened before we could believe. No, Christ's apostles clearly teach elsewhere that saving faith too is God's gracious gift."[3]

Lutheran theologian Rod Rosenbladt says that, to the question "Don't we contribute anything to our salvation?" Scripture answers "Yes, your *sin!*"

The Role of Faith

An Orthodox priest was asked some time ago, "Father, do you believe we are saved by faith or by works?"

"Neither," the priest replied wisely, "but by the mercy of God."

We talk too much about faith today and not enough about the object of our faith. When we do that, faith becomes something subjective; it becomes an end rather than a means to the end, namely, Jesus Christ. Have you ever found yourself running around in circles, trying to keep the faith going? I know I have. The act of believing is not in itself the central issue. The One in whom the faith is placed is the source of our salvation, not faith itself.

Being justified by grace alone, because of Christ alone, through faith alone means that we are declared righteous because of what Christ has done, not because we have accepted what Christ has done.

Look at the following sentence and form an opinion about its truth or error: "It is mine to be willing to believe; it is the part of God's grace to assist."

This slogan may appear harmless, and is, in fact, in line with what most of us have been taught. But the slogan's author and his teachings in this regard were condemned by more church councils than any other heretic or heresy in the history of the Christian religion. His name was Pelagius. If there is anything we have learned from the principal texts quoted throughout this book, it should be that Jesus Christ is the "author and perfecter of our faith" (Heb. 12:2).

This distinction is important, as Martin Luther noted:

> If I know not the distinction between our working and the power of God, I know not God Himself. Hence, I cannot worship Him, praise Him, or serve Him; for I shall never know how much I ought to ascribe unto myself and unto God. . . . No, the mercy of God alone does all things, and our own will does nothing; it is not active, but rather acted upon. And so it must be; otherwise the whole is not ascribed unto God.[4]

We must, therefore, look to God even for the ability to trust in him. That is, after all, what faith is—depending completely on God as he gives himself to us in the gospel of his Son.

The Whosoever Wills

"Come to me, all you who are weary and burdened, and I will give you rest" (Matt. 11:28). That is an unqualified, bona fide offer from God to you and to every person who will come. There are no exceptions. God's electing, redeeming, calling grace does not exclude people from the invitation. Rather, God's grace includes people who would otherwise exclude themselves. In fact, this sovereign grace makes certain that the invitation will be successful, that people will respond. For "No one can come to me unless the Father who sent me draws him" (John 6:44).

Why does God invite everybody to salvation if he knows that only the elect will come? First of all, it is through that general, universal invitation that the Holy Spirit gets his Word and gospel to the elect. God has included you and me in the plan of missions and evangelism as agents and coworkers with him in bringing people to faith. Thankfully, since you and I do not know who the elect are, we must simply cast our seeds upon the whole field and leave the results to God.

Also, the universal invitation makes sure that when unbelievers stand before God on judgment day, they are without excuse. Nobody will be in heaven who did not choose to be, and nobody will be in hell who did not choose estrangement from God.

Everybody will get whatever he or she chose. It is not as if people want to come to God but can't. They do not want to. The problem is not God's failure to speak, but rather our failure to hear and respond.

D. James Kennedy uses this illustration: He knows five men who are about to rob a bank. He tries to convince them not to commit the crime, but these men, evil-natured as they are, run for their car. Kennedy tackles one of the men and wrestles him to the ground. The others drive off to the bank. In the process, a guard is shot and the four men are sentenced to the electric chair. Can the one man whom Kennedy tackled say, "I didn't go to the electric chair because I am better than the others"? Of course not. He was spared because Kennedy tackled him, not because his heart wasn't in the robbery. Dr. Kennedy concludes, "Those who go to hell have no one to blame but themselves. Those who go to heaven have no one to praise but Jesus Christ."[5]

John Calvin said, "We should be so minded as to wish all people to be saved." I could not agree more. God said, "I take no pleasure in the death of the wicked" (Ezek. 33:11). Neither can we.

When we make the general proclamation, "Jesus Christ saves sinners," the Spirit of God internalizes that and makes it relevant to particular individuals. This assures us that when we preach the gospel, God sees to it that his Word "will not return to me empty, but will accomplish what I desire" (Isa. 55:11). That makes the evangelistic enterprise exciting! It really *is* fishing for people.

We learn from all this that even the application of salvation is God's gift. We look in vain for a rack upon which to hang our hat of conceit. He chose us before we chose him (election), came to us before we came to him (incarnation), made friends with us while we were hostile enemies (redemption). He even accepted us before we accepted him and made us alive while we were dead (calling). The Spirit's calling grace is the "straw that broke the camel's back." And that camel's name is *Pride*.

Is it not marvelous that you can place your faith in someone who makes dead people live, who makes sinners into saints, and who turns caterpillars into butterflies? Isn't it phenomenal that in a world of selfishness and shallow relationships, the Creator of the universe has taken such an interest in *us?*

Will Metzger writes,

Our King is assured of a Kingdom and will neither be frustrated by human resistance nor obligated to save His creatures because of their supposed rights to His favor. . . . The apostles were not preaching salvation by "making Christ your Savior and Lord" in a good works fashion. He is already Lord; and therefore, our evangelistic call must be to come to Him as to the feet of a monarch, in submission to His person and authority.[6]

Jesus Christ is your Lord, your Sovereign to whom you owe full allegiance. Will you do him homage? God's adventure with us has been in process "before the creation of the world" (Eph. 1:4), and ours with him is about to begin. God's love has captured us, and our lives will never be the same.

Study Questions

1. True or false: You were born again after you accepted Christ. Defend your answer with Scripture.
2. Does God force people to accept Christ against their will? Who wants to come to Christ?
3. Discuss the role of faith in this matter. If God does it all, why should we even have to believe?
4. Explain some of the practical implications of this chapter.

nine

Righteous Sinners

Duke George was a man of his times. A fence-straddling German prince during Luther's day, he comforted his dying son, Duke John, with the doctrine of justification. The dying prince was to look to Christ and his merits alone and to renounce all his "works." But, Luther tells us, "When the wife of Duke John subsequently heard this, she said: 'Father, why may not such truths be preached publicly?' Duke George replied, 'It may be told to the dying only, not to those who are well.'" Perhaps it was perceived then, as now, that too much grace can be dangerous.

The medieval church taught that justification—that is, the declaration of acceptance before a holy God, was something that happened at the end of one's life. Grace was always "on tap" to be drawn as necessary. Or, like coffee, it got you going in the morning. It assisted you in living an obedient, godly life to the end that you could finally be accepted before God when you died.

The Protestant Reformers countered by arguing, with the Scriptures, that grace was not an energy boost to assist us in doing what we could do anyway, though less effectively, on our own, but that it was a favorable disposition, an attitude toward us on God's part. Thus, the key question of the Reformation was not, "How can I be a better person?" but "How can I, an evil person, be accepted by a holy and righteous God?" Do I have to get better before I can be well? The Reformation answered, with the New Testament, that we would always be "ill," spiritually and morally, in this world; that we were, even as Christians, still sinners. Nevertheless, God declared us righteous while we were still unrighteous. Grace, then, is not first a power infused to help us become good, but God's acceptance of us *as* good even while we are still evil.

The Reformation way of putting it was, *simul iustus et peccator*—"simultaneously justified and sinful." This was the Reformation debate more than anything else. Rome agreed that the sinner is saved by grace—but by grace *transforming* the unrighteous into righteous, the unholy into the holy, the disobedient into the obedient. Depending on how one appropriates and makes use of this grace, one could eventually be accepted by God. Not so, said Luther and Calvin. Even on a good day, the average Christian is wicked. The believer, however, does not await a verdict in the future; he reminds himself of the verdict already declared: "not guilty." He lives each day as though he had fully satisfied the requirements of the law. And to enjoy this promise, he does not have to meet certain criteria for growth in grace. Before he can be confident in this promise, he need not "clean up his act." More than this, he knows he *can't* clean up his act to the degree that he can make enough progress to be accepted or approved by sanctification.

One wonders at the way the contemporary church approximates the medieval church on this central gospel tenet. Many modern believers have been taught, as one contemporary evangelical theologian teaches, that "we can love God perfectly and that we can be righteous in this world even as Christ is righteous. . . ." Further, the Bible "leaves no place for voluntary and known sin in the life of the believer."[1] Pentecostal theologian Russell P. Spittler writes, "But can it really be true—saint and sinner simultaneously? I wish it were so . . . *Simul iustus et peccator* ['simultaneously justified and sinful']? I hope it's true! I simply fear it's not."[2] William Law, John Wesley's favorite writer, penned these anxious words: "We are to consider that God only knows what shortcomings in holiness He will accept; therefore we can have no security of our salvation but by doing our utmost to deserve it." "We have," said he, "nothing to rely on but the sincerity of our endeavors and God's mercy."[3] John Wesley himself urged his supporters to warn the Calvinists "against making void that solemn decree of God, 'without holiness no man shall see the Lord,' by a *vain imagination of being holy in Christ.* O warn them that if they remain unrighteous, *the righteousness of Christ will profit them nothing!*"[4]

In more recent times, it seems that the evangelical ship has sailed even further from its Reformation harbor. No more poignantly is this illustrated in my own mind than by a recent experience at a nondenominational Christian high school. The Bible teacher, an old college friend, asked me to spend a day defending the Reformation position on grace. In six class periods, with a total of 160 Christian high school students, only one person raised her hand when I asked, "How many here have ever heard the term, *justification?*" Out of 160 Christian young people, only 1 person had even *heard* of, much less understood, the central tenet of the Protestant Reformation and, indeed, of the gospel itself. When I explained the doctrine, hands shot up all over the place, in each period. It was a radically new concept they had never heard before in all of their years of Christian churches, camps, conferences, and youth groups, or in their homes.

As in the medieval church, grace is once again spoken of as the assistance of the Holy Spirit in helping us live the "victorious Christian life." When we fall, he picks us up again and gives us the power to keep going. But before we can ever speak of grace *imparted,* we must speak of grace *imputed.* Let me explain what I mean by that.

Original Sin

Ultimately, our view of grace is rooted in our understanding of sin. Martin Luther the monk hated God. You would have thought, by his feverish activity and pious zeal, that he loved God. He prayed daily, fasted, confessed even to potential sins, and filled his days with spiritual devotions and exercises. Then why did he hate God? For the same reason many Christians today hate him even while they perform empty spiritual exercises: They know he drives a hard bargain—"righteous in this world even as Christ is righteous."[5] And while they know they don't have the goods, they keep on the treadmill. "What other option do I have?" they reason.

It was in his masterful treatment of the work of Christ that Anselm, in the eleventh century, warned those who thought God would overlook their shortcomings if they just tried their best: "You have not yet considered how great your sin is."

It is indeed a piece of irony that those who are constantly telling us what sins to avoid and how to avoid them actually have a *low* view of sin! But it's true. This was the case in Jesus' day. The Pharisees, you will recall, subscribed to a perfectionistic program. And to make their calls to perfection stick, they had to view sin as external—as actions rather than attitudes basic to fallen human nature. If sin consisted in actions, all one had to do in order to become holy was to stop this or that action. The same view of sin abounds today. A problem with lust? It's because of movies and dancing—stop going to them. Are your kids rebellious? It's because of rock music, or perhaps due to their friends. It's always interesting to see the mother of a delinquent teen who just robbed a shop and shot the owner tell the reporters, "It's that bunch he runs around with. Deep down, Danny's a good boy." But the crowd didn't pull the trigger. Danny did.

The Bible teaches *original sin.* That is, we sin because we are sinners. We hate, kill, destroy, slander, rob, lust, and rebel because that is who we are. "Surely I was sinful at birth," David confessed (Ps. 51:5). "Even from birth the wicked go astray; from the womb they are wayward and speak lies" (Ps. 58:3). Jeremiah lamented not that our actions alone are wicked, but that "the *heart* is deceitful above all things and beyond cure" (17:9, italics added). When we sin, it is not simply because we are victims of external influences (as though, like Danny, we were really good people deep down), but because we are of just that sort of character.

This view of sin cautions us against zealous but misguided views of sanctification. "But," one might say, "those verses are talking about the unsaved. Christians are set free from sin." This brings us to the next point.

Justification by Faith Alone

As we noted earlier, Luther's rediscovery of "justification by faith alone" was not radical because Rome believed we were saved by works, but because Rome believed we were saved by grace-empowered works. In other words, we're saved by grace, Rome would argue. After all, we could not even perform these works without grace. But Luther and Calvin insisted that grace was something more than divine assistance and inner transformation. We could never be so inwardly transformed by the Holy Spirit in this life that we would be without sin. So surely justification by inward transformation is no way to salvation, the Reformers said. God demands *his* best, not *ours*.

Well, this is Paul's argument in all of his epistles. Even as an apostle, he recognized, "the law is spiritual; but I am unspiritual, sold as a slave to sin. I do not understand what I do. For what I want to do I do not do, but what I hate I do" (Rom. 7:14–15). In other words, even when we have a "quiet time," we feel proud of ourselves for having done so. Whenever our new affections (grace *imparted*) set out to do something right for a change, our old affections are right there waiting to corrupt them. So grace imparted is not enough to save us—not because the law is flawed or because grace is weak, but because we cannot eradicate our sinful nature.

So, we need what the Reformers called an "alien righteousness," that is, someone else's righteousness, if we are to be saved.

After my junior year in college, I went to Europe with some friends. Having misjudged the expenses by several digits, I phoned home for help. My parents transferred money from their account to cover outstanding bills and included an additional sum from which I could draw until the end of the trip. Now, was this money, which I was going to draw daily as needed, strictly speaking, *my* money? No, it belonged to my parents; nevertheless, because they had transferred it to my account, it was my money. My account was now filled with money I had not earned but was mine to use nonetheless.

In a similar way, we are spiritually bankrupt, broke. Not only don't we have a single penny in our accounts; we are deep in debt. Even if we got a job to put food on the table, it would never begin to pay off the unbelievable debt that has piled to the heavens.

It would be similar to an average daily laborer thinking he can pay off the national debt of the United States. We not only have a *lack* of funds; we have an *abundance* of debts. So we need two things in order to settle the account with God. We need a payment of all the debts. And then we need a full line of credit. God requires both: Negatively, we must be guilty of no sins, but, positively, we must also be just as morally perfect, righteous, and holy as God himself. The glass must not only be *empty* of *un*righteousness; it must be *full* of righteousness. This is where the popular definition of justification—"just as if I'd never sinned"—falls short. Rather, it is just as if I'd never sinned *and* had, instead, loved God and my neighbor perfectly all my life.

So we not only inherited Adam's unrighteous character; we got his bills! Every child born into this world is already guilty. When we discussed the fall, we noted the way in which Thomas Jefferson represented all Americans, even future generations, by his Declaration of Independence. We are Americans, not because we made a decision to become independent of British rule, but because our forebears decided to long ago. Similarly, we are all identified with Adam's sin, even before we commit an actual act of sin. In the same way, those who look to Christ and his righteousness are identified with his obedience. So, just as we are condemned in Adam, even apart from our own actions, so too we are justified in Christ, even apart from our own actions. This is Paul's point in Romans 5: "The judgment followed one sin and brought condemnation, but the gift followed many trespasses and brought justification. . . . For just as through the disobedience of the one man the many were made sinners, so also through the obedience of the one man the many will be made righteous" (vv. 16, 19).

Sin and the Christian Life

Often we make sharp distinctions between our lives before and after conversion. It is sometimes said in testimonies, "Before, I used to want to do . . . , but now I'm free from those desires." Of course, it is true that, because the dominion of sin is toppled by the new birth, we have new desires and affections. This must not be underemphasized. Nevertheless, in our zeal to see "before" and "after" shots of ourselves, we sometimes fail to appreciate the ongoing condition of sin in the Christian life.

First of all, *are* those biblical texts which teach original sin limited in their scope to unbelievers? David's confession in Psalm 51, "Surely I was sinful at birth," is part of a general prayer of confession that is clearly the penitence of a believer. "Have mercy on me, O God, according to your unfailing love," begged the psalmist. "Blot out my transgressions. Wash away all my iniquity and cleanse me from my sin. For," he said, "I know my transgressions [*not,* I *knew* my transgressions] and my sin is *always* before me" (italics added). *Then* he wrote, "Surely I was sinful at birth." Clearly David was confessing individual sins that he attributed to his own fallen nature.

When Jeremiah speaks of the incurable wickedness of the fallen human heart, he includes believers in that observation. After all, it is straying Israelites who are eventually brought back by the watchful Shepherd.

Though the passage is hotly debated, it appears certainly to indicate that the apostle Paul had in mind himself as a believer when he recognized, "We know that the law is spiritual; but I am unspiritual, sold as a slave to sin" (Rom. 7:14). Even though Christ had redeemed him from the law's curse and sin's tyranny, "What I want to do I do not do, but what I hate I do. . . . I know that nothing good lives in me, that is, in my sinful nature" (vv. 15–18). "For," he said, "I have the desire to do what is good, but I cannot carry it out. For what I do is not the good I want to do; no, the evil I do not want to do—this I *keep on doing*" (vv. 18–19, italics added). Clearly the apostle was speaking of his life as a believer, since he stated elsewhere that the natural (unsaved) person cannot even desire the good, that the unbeliever *hates* the law. The unbeliever "does not submit to God's law, nor *can* [he] do so" (Rom. 8:7, italics added). Further identifying his point as sin in the Christian life, the apostle stated, "So I find this law at work: When I want to do good, evil is right there with me. For in my inner being I delight in God's law [this can only be the delight of the believer]; but I see another law at work in the members of my body, waging war against the law of my mind and making me a prisoner of the law of sin at work within my members" (7:21–23). Finally, the apostle concluded in a vein similar to that of the psalmist, "What a wretched man I *am* [not *was*]! Who will rescue me from this body of death? Thanks be to God—through Jesus Christ our Lord!" Nevertheless, a war continues: "So then, I myself in my mind am a slave to God's law, but in the sinful nature a slave to the law of sin" (Rom. 7:24–25, italics added).

Any theory of the Christian life, therefore, which downplays the seriousness of sin even in the ongoing struggle of the Christian, is bound to result in unbiblical and unhealthy programs of sanctification.

Union with Christ

So then, if we are going to be sinful all of our Christian life, but remain justified anyway, what's the use in pursuing a godly life? Paul addressed this after he suspected someone might ask the question, "What shall we say, then? Shall we go on sinning so that grace may increase?" And what was the apostle's answer? "By no means! We died to sin; how can we live in it any longer?" (Rom. 6:1–2). And then he justified his response on the basis of union with Christ:

> Or don't you know that all of us who were baptized into Christ Jesus were baptized into his death? We were therefore buried with him through baptism into death in order that, just as Christ was raised from the dead through the glory of the Father, we too may live a new life.
>
> If we have been united with him like this in his death, we will certainly also be united with him in his resurrection. For we know that our old self was crucified with him so that the body of sin might be done away with, that we should no longer be slaves to sin—because anyone who has died has been freed from sin. . . . In the same way, count yourselves dead to sin but alive to God in Christ Jesus. [Rom. 6:3–7, 11]

When we discussed the incarnation, we briefly addressed the subject of union with Christ. "Immanuel—God with us." Moving beyond the incarnation to union with Christ through faith leads to "God *in* us" and "God *through* us."

This notion of "union with Christ" was, especially for the apostle Paul, the glue that held the gospel together. It is to the degree that this concept is misunderstood or insufficiently grasped that unbalanced views of sanctification emerge.

Here's what "union with Christ" means:

We are born into this world in union with Adam. Everything he had, we have; everything he is we are. He earned God's judgment for himself and for us. Had he kept from eating the forbidden fruit, he would have earned for himself and for all of humanity eternal life. There would have been no sin, no suffering, no sickness, no pain, no guilt, and no death. As it happened, Adam disobeyed and we were identified with him in the likeness of his sin. His guilt was imputed to us, and his sinful, rebellious nature shaped us in the womb, even before we committed actual sin. We were baptized into Adam—into his spiritual death, "dead in . . . trangressions and sins" (Eph. 2:1).

But there came a second Adam who made it to the end without disobeying God. He was sent as a new representative. Instead of being taken to a tree in the middle of the garden, this second Adam was taken to a high mountain peak. "Jesus was led by the Spirit into the desert to be tempted by the devil" (Matt. 4:1). Instead of feeding, he fasted; instead of indulging his flesh by eating, he denied himself. Finally the devil—the same tempter who was in Eden—"took him to a very high mountain and showed him all the kingdoms of the world and their splendor. 'All this I will give you,' he said, 'if you will bow down and worship me'" (Matt. 4:8–9). But instead of easy exaltation ("you shall be like God"), Jesus, who *was* God, nevertheless took the long road of obedience, the slow road of suffering, the rough road of sacrifice that would lead eventually to Calvary. In this obedience, and the other thirty years of consistent, sinless perfection, Jesus Christ earned for us what Adam failed to earn.

Thus, the guilt imputed to us through Adam was charged to Christ, and the righteousness of Christ was imputed to us. This is the difference between a biblical view of the Christian life and so many of the other programs and methods which abound in popular evangelicalism. In this story, there is only one "victorious Christian life." There is only one "sold-out Christian," only one "totally surrendered, completely consecrated" servant of the Lord. The litany in the Book of Common Prayer, a product of the English Reformation, prays to the Lord for deliverance from condemnation "By the mystery of *Thy* holy Incarnation; by *Thy* holy Nativity and Circumcision; by *Thy* Baptism, Fasting, and Temptation, . . . by *Thine* Agony and Bloody Sweat; by *Thy* Cross and Passion; by *Thy* precious Death and Burial; by *Thy* glorious Resurrection and Ascension; and by the Coming of the Holy Ghost." One could imagine the angels, who lack omniscience, peering intently over the edge of heaven, as the second Adam—this time, God incarnate—faces the contest for souls.

This means that Christ's life is much more than a mere example to us for moral living. By faith we are baptized into his obedient life, sacrificial death, and victorious resurrection in such a way that even though we are still sinners, we have an entirely new identity in heaven. Consequently, "God raised us up with Christ and seated us with him in the heavenly realms in Christ Jesus" (Eph. 2:6). This is where we are right now before the throne of God. It is a present reality whose full realization will be experienced at his coming. This is where we live our lives day by day. As in Adam we inherited a sinful nature (which will torment us until we die), so in Christ we inherit a new nature. We participate in his heavenly life; we feed on him (John 6). Because he was chosen and accepted before the Father by his works, we can be chosen and accepted by the Father by the Son's works, too. "For he chose us *in him*" (Eph. 1:4); *in him* the Father has "freely given us" his grace (v. 6). "*In him* we have redemption through his blood" (v. 7). "He made known to us the mystery of his will according to his good pleasure, which he purposed *in Christ*" (v. 9). Finally, we are sealed in Christ forever (v. 13, italics added throughout).

In other words, our righteousness came to us from the outside. You see, Luther's greatest frustration was reading and hearing calls to holy living. It was as though Christ were not even necessary, except perhaps as the leading example. God could command and we could obey. Every time he read about God's holiness or righteousness, he was reminded of how far he was from attaining it. So divine righteousness was always a threat to Luther until he realized that there was not only a righteousness which God *demanded,* but a righteousness which God *gave.* Hence, the law terrorizes our consciences with the righteousness God *requires.* But in the gospel, we learn about the "gift of righteousness" (Rom. 5:17). The force of that revolutionary idea finally hit

Luther: "For in the gospel a righteousness from God is revealed, a righteousness that is by faith from first to last, just as it is written: 'The righteous will live by faith'" (Rom. 1:17). In the law, the righteousness *of* God is revealed; but in the gospel, the righteousness *from* God is set forth. "This righteousness from God comes through faith in Jesus Christ to all who believe" (Rom. 3:22). "God made him who had no sin to be sin for us, so that in him we might become the righteousness of God" (2 Cor. 5:21). Jesus Christ is himself "our righteousness, holiness, and redemption" (1 Cor. 1:30). And this justification comes at the beginning, not at the end of the Christian life. Therefore, "to the man who does not work but trusts God who *justifies* the *wicked,* his faith is credited as righteousness" (Rom. 4:5, italics added).

The same union with Christ that *credits* us with Christ's righteousness also *imparts* to us the fruit of that righteousness. The faith which justifies—that is, faith which trusts Christ alone as Savior—inevitably produces works. Due to Adam, we sin because we're sinners; because of Christ, we do righteous things because we are righteous in Christ. The fruit of the Spirit is just that— the result of the regenerating life of God which, too, is part and parcel of our union with Christ. In him we are justified; in him we are being sanctified; in him we shall be glorified.

Christ Alone

I have noticed for some time now how St. Paul's epistle to the Ephesians puts the theme of union with Christ in a nutshell, leaving all of the many confusing subtheories we've invented over the recent decades out of the picture entirely. In Christ we were chosen before time (1:4), predestined to be adopted into God's family, and predestined to receive an inheritance by virtue of our sharing Christ's sonship (vv. 5, 11). In him we were accepted by God, holy and without blame (vv. 4, 6). "In him we have redemption through his blood, the forgiveness of sins" (v. 7). In Christ we were sealed with the Holy Spirit, guaranteeing our final redemption and inheritance (vv. 13–14). This prepositional phrase, "in him," makes salvation Christ-centered rather than believer-centered. Notice, he "has blessed us *in the heavenly realms* with *every spiritual blessing* in Christ" (v. 3, italics added). There is no need for a second or third blessing. Nor are we to seek blessings beyond what we already enjoy in Christ. Even the Holy Spirit is not, properly speaking, the ground of any blessing.

The temptation, at least for me, is often to *use* Christ for getting blessings, rather than resting in Christ *as* my blessing. This is what the believer is promised: that he or she has been chosen, adopted, accepted, justified, redeemed, forgiven, and sealed. *Every spiritual blessing* is contained in these truths. We really need a blessing "in the heavenly realms" more than anywhere else, because that is where God sits enthroned as judge of the cosmos. It is the royal court where verdicts are rendered for all eternity. In that court we shall all appear on the final day.

The Reformers used to have a way of saying this: *"solus Christus,"* or "Christ alone!" Medieval religion had obscured Christ with techniques and rules, programs for spiritual growth, and monkish rituals. In fact, Luther distinguished much of medieval religion as a superstitious "ladder of glory"; people climbed up into heaven in order to get a peek at the "naked God" *(Deus nudus).* The beatific vision—seeing God in his glory—was the *summum bonum,* or the highest good. But the Reformers noticed that this sort of religion didn't even really need Christ. If monks could steal into God's presence without the mediation of Christ, what use did the Son of God serve? No, said they, Christ alone is our blessing in the heavenly realms. We don't need to see the naked God; we are content to have him come to us in Christ.

Today, again, believers are looking for direct experiences or encounters with God. Mysticism abounds in contemporary evangelical spirituality. Songs about "reaching up and touching the hem of his garment" have replaced the Christ-centered hymnody. In one ditty, worshipers are supposed to hear the brush of angels' wings as evidence that "the presence of the Lord is in this place." This is the sort of thing Spielberg might direct! It has nothing to do with Christ or the cross or union with Christ. It's all about my personal moment with the "naked God." I can well remember waiting, in some worship contexts, for that moment, that spiritual "buzz" for which I was searching, during the fourth or fifth chorus of "Alleluia." There is nothing about Christ in that chorus, just the repetition of the new password. It really is a dangerous shift, brothers and sisters, and we must protest that it is *not* the worship of God as he has come to us in Christ. Many today have made the Holy Spirit so central and the Christian life so central that Christ is no longer the only Mediator.

Furthermore, "Christ alone" in our own day is often replaced with an emphasis on the personal decision to accept him. Most of the sermons I heard as a child preached faith, not Christ. And, of course, that's not even really preaching faith, since faith is nothing without its reference point. One popular evangelist even wrote a tract entitled, "How to Have Faith in Your Faith." This, of course, makes an idol out of faith. But according to the Scriptures, faith is the *instrument* of justification, not the *object*. Let me break this down a bit. Let's say you are a friend and you come running to inform me that you are in love. Nearly breaking into song, you extol the virtues of love. "Love," you muse, "is a many-splendored thing." For twenty minutes, you rhapsodize about the magnificence of love while making only passing references to your girlfriend. Would it not be at least a possibility to surmise from this that you are more enchanted with falling in love than with the girl?

This can easily become the case in our relationship with the Lord. It becomes subjective: Obsession with the *act* of faith replaces the centrality of the *object* of faith, Jesus Christ. We are not justified by faith because of something intrinsic to faith itself. There is nothing magical about believing. It is faith *in Christ,* and not only faith in Christ but faith in the finished work of Christ, that constitutes saving faith. By faith, we take Christ's righteousness as our own; his holiness for our unholiness. I have heard a number of people say, "I just wish I had the faith to believe." To believe what? Or whom? There is no virtue in believing. The only virtue is Christ. As having love can replace one's fascination with his girlfriend, so "having faith" (the act) can push Christ himself (the object) out of the picture. Stop looking to faith and start looking to Christ. That looking to Christ, after all, *is* faith!

One can see how a return to texts, simple texts such as Ephesians 1 and 2, can bring us back to Christ and rid us of the techniques, rituals, second blessings, and numerous other distractions we have invented. Instead of listing steps to victory or tips for Christian living, we ought to be studying the Bible itself more closely, refocusing our gaze on that which *God* considers "spiritual blessings in heavenly realms": election, adoption, redemption, calling, assurance, preservation, justification—and it's all "in Christ." Someone once asked Martin Luther what would be left in Christianity if the Reformer got rid of all the superstitions, rules, techniques, and programs. "What would be left?" "Christ," he answered.

Savior but Not Lord?

Billed the "lordship-salvation debate," the widely held view that Jesus can be one's Savior without being one's Lord is finally getting the criticism it deserves. Nevertheless, there are dangers on both sides of this debate.

On one end, there are those who affirm that one may turn to Christ in faith without ever submitting to his lordship. We are saved, they say, by making Christ Savior, not by making him Lord. The other side counters that this is "devil's faith"—that is, the sort of "faith" of which James spoke when he asked rhetorically, "Can this faith save you?" Saving faith includes not only dependence on Christ for deliverance from judgment, but commitment to Christ and submission to his lordship.

In the case of those who deny the necessity of "making Christ Lord," we should respond, first of all, by agreeing that we are not saved by "making Christ Lord." But then, we are also not saved by "making Christ Savior." We don't make Christ anything! He *is* Savior and he *is* Lord regardless of what we think or make of him. In fact, it is because he is Savior quite apart from our activity that we are saved in the first place. He came to us "when we were dead" (Eph. 2:5). He regenerates us, gives us the gift of faith, and then justifies us through that faith in Christ. The "make him your Savior" school of thought adheres to what has been called "decisional regeneration." It is, for many, the one "little" work we do that merits eternal life.

A second flaw in the "Savior but not Lord" teaching is the recurring Wesleyan error of making justification and sanctification gifts which are separately obtained by separate acts of faith.

According to Scripture, there is one act of faith which unites us with Christ and, once we are united with him by this one act of faith, both justification (a once-and-for-all declaration of righteousness) and sanctification (a gradual, slow, and painful process of growing in righteousness) become ours in Christ. All at once we are justified, but only in gradual progress are we sanctified. Nevertheless, both the declaration and the process are given through the same condition of faith alone in Christ alone (Rom. 8:30; 1 Cor. 1:30; Eph. 2:8–10).

Therefore, to this camp we should insist upon union with Christ as the sovereign work of God in not only making new life possible, but in creating it where no cause but his own will and effort existed. It stands to reason that if *we* "make Jesus Savior," we can also determine whether we will allow him to be our Lord. But the Bible doesn't speak of allowing him to be or do this or that. "For it is God who works in you to will and to act according to his good purpose" (Phil. 2:13). It is, therefore, inevitable that a good tree will produce good fruit. Those whom God regenerates become living trees. "You did not choose me," Jesus said, "but I chose you and appointed you to go and bear fruit—fruit that will last" (John 15:16). When salvation is viewed as man's program, it is left up to man as to whether he will let God do this or that, but when it is viewed as God's program, there is a confidence and a certainty that no one whom God regenerates will be a "carnal Christian." Said Luther, "If works and love do not blossom forth, it is not genuine faith, the gospel has not yet gained a foothold, and Christ is not yet rightly known."[6] Again, if we have Christ, we have his imputed holiness (justification) as well as his imparted holiness (sanctification). Without a sense of one there cannot be a sense of the other.

At the same time, however, there is an equal danger when reacting against this false message: To so emphasize the inevitability of fruit that we downplay the reality of ongoing sinfulness. Again, it is "simultaneously sinful and justified." Calvin cautioned us on this score. There is the visible church, consisting of all professing Christians from all times and places, and then there is the invisible church, consisting of all true believers. To belong to the former, one need only confess Christ, be baptized, and receive Holy Communion. And we accept all in our congregation who belong to the church in this way, whether or not they seem to possess the zeal or degree of commitment we would expect. Since we cannot ultimately know the number of the genuine believers (the invisible church), we ought not to become "fruit police." In Calvin's own words, "To know who are His is a prerogative belonging solely to God (2 Tim. 2:19). . . . For those who seemed utterly lost and quite beyond hope are by His goodness called back to the way; while those who more than others seemed to stand firm often fall."[7]

There is a further and more critical flaw, as I see it, with some versions of "lordship salvation." That is, the tendency to broaden the definition of faith to the point where it actually becomes a work. For instance, the Reformers defined faith as *knowledge* (grasping the facts of the gospel), *assent* (being convinced that they are true), and *trust* (entrusting the soul's safety to Christ on the basis of knowledge and assent). Yet one leading proponent of "lordship salvation" wrote that "faith encompasses obedience" and that *trust* (the third aspect of faith) "is the determination of the will to obey truth." It may well be a case of semantics here, but when we are speaking of the highest and holiest subject in all of the Scriptures, every word is important. Faith does not encompass obedience. That is the apostle Paul's point in Romans 4, and, for that matter, throughout all of his writings: We are justified by grace through faith—*not* through obedience. Therefore, when we make obedience an aspect of faith, we blur faith and works, justification and sanctification. Once justified, faith and works are not at odds—the former produces the latter. Yet faith remains at odds with merit. Never can the fruit we notice or fail to notice be used as a measuring stick; in this case, faith produces *merit* instead of *works,* and this is clearly unscriptural. Works righteousness can easily become confused with "faith" when faith is defined as encompassing obedience. Further, justifying trust is *not* "the determination of the will to obey the truth," but the confidence God gives us that Christ has already fulfilled our obedience. These are indeed important words.

Nevertheless, while faith does not *encompass* obedience, it does *produce* it. And while trust is certainly not "the determination of the will to obey the truth," trusting in Christ by faith alone will inevitably lead to a new willingness to obey the truth. For the

"Savior but not Lord" camp, there ought to be a recognition that faith *inevitably* produces obedience due to God's sovereign initiative (rather than to one's making him Lord). And for the "lordship salvation" school, there should be the recognition that, while faith inevitably produces obedience, faith is nevertheless *not* obedience.

The Reformation really did answer this question in a manner sometimes overlooked by both sides in the present debate. For instance, Luther spoke of our being justified by faith alone, but not by faith that is alone. To those who would add to faith an element of active obedience (other than Christ's), the Reformers would snap, "Faith *alone!*" But to the antinomians (i.e., those who would deny the effect of saving faith), they would insist that true faith is never isolated. This, indeed, is the seed that falls on rocky ground or is choked by the weeds. Another definition of the Reformation position is expressed in the Heidelberg Catechism. Against any perfectionism we are warned, "Even the very best we do in this life is imperfect and stained with sin," rendering all obedience imperfect at best. This, of course, is consistent with Isaiah 64:6, where we are told, "our righteous acts are like filthy rags." And yet, the Catechism hastens to answer the question, "Doesn't this teaching make people indifferent and wicked?" "No. It is impossible for those grafted into Christ by true faith not to produce fruits of gratitude."

So here are the two Reformation guardrails: We are justified solely by knowledge of, assent to, and trust in the person and work of Jesus Christ. And yet, anyone who is justified has been regenerated, grafted into the life of Christ, and fruits of gratitude will inevitably follow. Without an interest in the Savior and his Word and sacraments and the fellowship of his people, there is no life. Christ's lordship is not an option for the first-class Christians, but an inevitability for all who share his life.

Piety versus Pietism

That word *piety* used to really get me. It is often used these days in a derogatory way. Non-Christian friends joke about a particularly stuffy individual as being "pious." We picture an unreal, polyester-clad supersaint grinning ear to ear, with his elaborately decorated Bible tucked under his arm. And yet this has not always been the reaction Christians have had to that very biblical term.

During the seventeenth century, a movement emerged in reaction to the stale, dead orthodoxy of the Reformation countries. Like God's people in biblical times, the children had forgotten what their parents lived and died for in the Reformation struggle. Many churches had gone into a holding pattern. There was not much enthusiasm—in fact, enthusiasm itself was considered dangerous to the social order. One could get excited about a lot of things—sporting events, beer, a new job, a new addition to the family. But to get excited about God, that was a different matter. One should not get too excited about God. The very truths their grandparents had fought to recover—truths which had excited their grandparents more than anything else—had become bare words on a piece of paper.

So, while most of the grandchildren got excited about everything but God and signed the creeds and confessions on the dotted line (without really understanding them), others saw through the hypocrisy and launched what later came to be called the Pietist movement.

The Pietists, however, reacted in the opposite direction. They thought doctrine, theology, liturgy, and Christian liberty had conspired to drive out the thirst for holiness and simple faith. But they were wrong. Many of their contemporaries were hypocrites, to be sure, not because they had "head" knowledge without "heart" knowledge, but because they really didn't grasp the truth they claimed to believe in the first place!

First it must be acknowledged that the Pietists often led the modern missionary movement, built orphanages, and contributed classics to Christian hymnody. Unfortunately, however, this Pietist movement eventually became legalistic, moralistic, and at times cultic. It eventually fostered a low view of the church, of grace, of teaching, of the intellect, and of the sacraments. How quickly they forgot the Reformers' warnings, first issued by our Lord himself, against setting up human standards of righteousness. The Pietists were not as interested in objective proclamation of Christ's person and work as in tempering the outward affections by inspiring inward feelings. They wanted to warm the heart without necessarily feeding the mind.

Most evangelicals or conservative Christians in America today are heirs of the Pietists, since their influence dominated so much of the development of the American church. The founders of Pietism wrote tracts and manuals designed to lead believers into a deeper walk with their Lord. But the human, shallow, numerous, and burdensome methods and techniques became once more the very shackles of human superstition and ritual that had necessitated the Reformation. Today we know more about steps to God than about God himself. We are more likely to hear a sermon next Sunday on getting closer to Christ than on Christ himself. Technique over truth, method over message—these are Pietist legacies, in spite of its positive contributions.

With that historical background, we can see how easily our perception of holiness can be distorted. The Pharisees could well have been good Pietists. They followed their cues, knew the right methods, and at least appeared outwardly spiritual, to the point that they delighted in saying so to others. But their spirituality was selfish. It wasn't a matter of taking care of others, but of taking care of themselves; not of making sure others were fed, but of feeding themselves. It was an inward-looking piety. James countered, "His religion is worthless. Religion that God our Father accepts as pure and faultless is this: to look after orphans and widows in their distress and to keep oneself from being polluted by the world" (James 1:26–27).

Even if we can name the books of the Bible in order, what difference does it make if we do not notice our neighbor who has no groceries? What good does it do for us to be known by the world as people who *don't* do this or that rather than as people who *do* unto others as we would have them do unto us (Matt. 7:12)? Real religion is for real life, and it is larger than our own private piety.

Godliness or piety is, therefore, quite a different matter than Pietism. Godliness is a fruit of the Spirit. Closely related is the term *holy,* meaning "set apart for a purpose." The proper focus of holiness is not on being set apart *from* something (i.e., the world), but on being set apart *for* something. While Pietism would define holiness as being physically set apart from the world and opposed to participating in its forms of entertainment, business, culture, politics, and so on, biblical holiness goes much deeper. It is much more profound and demands much from us. What is the difference?

The ancient nation of Israel had a tendency to lose its distinctiveness. Though in Egyptian captivity, the Hebrews, on the whole, were not treated poorly. Unfortunately many people of Israel began to get settled; they began to lose their identity. When Moses led them out of Egypt into the desert, the Israelites snapped at their leader for having the gall to take them from Egypt into this wasteland. They left their hearts in Cairo.

In his wisdom, God has taken us out of Egypt. With Christ we have passed through the raging torrents of God's wrath. Nevertheless, he has not taken us out of the world. While we are "in Christ," we nevertheless share a common humanity with our unbelieving neighbors. We participate in normal "Egyptian" life insofar as it does not cause us to renounce our faith. Holiness, then, has nothing to do with separating from the world. Rather, it has to do with our being set apart unto God *in* the world. In other words, a Christian who plays a violin should try to perfect his or her skills to the point where he or she can play in the city's symphony to God's glory. A Christian writer should be so good at his or her craft that favorable reviews can be clipped from secular as well as religious publications. A Christian husband and wife should seek the interests of the other and care for poor or elderly family members. A Christian artist may find it a holier pursuit to paint new and creative works for local shows than to produce cover art for the church bulletin.

Christians have a great deal of integrity when they are known as uncommonly devoted to their calling. But it is terribly difficult to get the boss (or, for that matter, the coworkers) to listen to your evangelistic pitch if your work is less than heavenly.

Instead of withdrawing from society, then, holiness embraces the world. Instead of viewing the world as the source of sin, we begin to recognize that the world itself is only a reflection of the brokenness we all cause. Christian cars emit exhaust fumes, too. Once we see that sin is not "out there," but "in here," we begin to lose our self-righteous distance and we can be agents of reconciliation. "For God did not send his Son into the world to condemn the world, but to save the world through him"

(John 3:17). The whole creation—rocks, trees, beasts of the field, and birds of the air—is anxiously awaiting redemption (Rom. 8:22). If God's salvation program embraces the world, why shouldn't we?

Let Go and Let God?

I'm a California native—at least I admit it! That, I suppose, makes me somewhat of an expert on being laid back. Just recently I learned that the state seal, when translated, does *not* read, "Hang loose"! So if anybody has been brought up in an easygoing environment, I have. And I'm sure my theology has been warped to some degree by that philosophy as I, and many other Christians, have translated it into more spiritual terms such as "Let go and let God."

Popular evangelicalism is full of calls to "let Him have His way," to "let the Spirit lead," and so on. We hear that if we just step out of the way, we will get that sudden burst of Christian growth we are looking for. But very often, "let the Spirit lead" is just a baptized version of the world's slogan, "If it feels good, do it." Too often, where we suppose we're letting God lead we are actually doing nothing more than using divine sanction for what we intended to do all along.

As Christians, we are not fatalists. We do not believe—for the Scriptures do not teach us—that "what will be, will be." The Reformation teaching concerning election and divine calling does not mean that we are not active. Rather, it means that our activity does not *merit* anything good from God. One of the biggest potential stumbling blocks in our growth and maturity in Christ is the attitude that suggests we can sit back, let the Spirit have his way with us and, "presto," we are victorious Christians. In the first place, we are not called to passivity. Before God regenerated us, it is true that we were "dead in . . . transgressions and sins" (Eph. 2:1). Therefore, it stands to reason that we would be acted *upon* rather than active in our own new birth. Nevertheless, once we are born again, we are active. Instead of hiding, we seek; instead of hating, we love him; instead of being tyrannized by rebellious self-interest, we are able for the first time to produce the fruit of the Spirit through faith rather than attempting it through self-righteousness. For the first time, our response to God is positive. Therefore, to urge a passive "let go and let God" attitude is to underplay the reality of the new birth as well as sin.

While we do not cooperate in our regeneration, we do cooperate with God in our growth. It is similar to our natural birth in the sense that we are born into this world quite apart from our own will and effort, but once we are born we begin to mature and gradually take on greater responsibilities for our growth, our health, and our future. "Work out your salvation with fear and trembling," Paul commanded, "for it is God who works in you to will and to act according to his good purpose" (Phil. 2:12–13).

The Victorious Christian Life

Earlier in this chapter, reference was made to Luther's quest for freedom from the law's demands. As a monk, he was taught that mystical speculation was one method of gaining the infusion of grace necessary for living above sin. Through contemplation, purgation, and finally union (a sense of losing oneself in the Eternal Spirit), Luther thought he could be free of all known sin.

Similarly, modern Christians are plagued with a mystical spirituality revived in the "Higher Life movement" at the turn of the century. Instead of contemplation, purgation, and union, the "victorious Christian life" uses terms like "full surrender," "yielding," "letting go and letting God." But the new terms merely recast an old error.

It was John Wesley who, enlarging upon the Pietistic view of holiness, argued that there were two stages of salvation. One may be converted, but a "second blessing" was required. At that moment, one was instantly and perfectly sanctified just as instantaneously as he was justified. Thus, Christian perfection was attainable in this life. The believer could be free from any known sin. Eventually, this two-level doctrine of the Christian life flowered into a version of holiness which increasingly confused grace with works. By Charles Spurgeon's day (late nineteenth century), perfectionism had become a popular evangelical movement. The

Baptist evangelist warned, "It will be an ill day when our brethren take to bragging and boasting and call it 'testimony to the victorious Christian life.' We trust that holiness will be more than ever the aim of believers, but not the boastful holiness which has deluded some of the excellent of the earth into vainglory, and under which their firmest friends shudder for them."[8]

In the wake of Moody's campaigns in England, the Keswick movement was born and organized "conventions for holiness," urging "true believers" to separate from secular work and become employed in "full-time Christian service."

It was that movement which invented the terms we now live and breathe in the evangelical world: *surrender, yield, lay all at the altar*. I remember well the anxiety I felt growing up listening to pleas to surrender all. The question was always "Have I surrendered enough?" The nagging doubt was whether I had yielded every corner of my heart to Jesus. Any mention of salvation by grace was obscured by this constant emphasis on salvation by surrender. Looking back on the experience, I can actually say that there would be less anxiety in a setting where I was told I must keep the Ten Commandments in order to be saved. At least there are only ten of them and they are written down; they're right in front of me. None of this guesswork. I know when I have sinned against God with the Ten Commandments, but how can I be sure I have "surrendered all" today?

Once again, this view lacks the seriousness of the biblical doctrine of sin. Here one more view falls victim to Anselm's devastating critique: "You have not yet learned how great sin is." The Westminster Confession defines sin as, not only "transgression of the law of God," but "any lack of conformity to" that law. Because the law is ignored in the evangelical world (according to Gallup, few Christians can name the Ten Commandments), we have invented our own standards of righteousness. Thus, sin and righteousness are not measured by the degree to which we conform to the law in thought, word, and deed, but in being able to live above "known sins." But the Bible doesn't call us to be "fully surrendered"; it demands that we conform perfectly to the righteousness commanded in the law. And it condemns not only for "known," but also for "unknown sins." One unknown sin is enough of an affront to God's majesty to condemn a person for all eternity.

Whenever the law is diminished in its strict terror, we lose the stern taskmaster that leads us to Christ for salvation (Gal. 3:23–24). For the "victorious Christian life" teaching, sin is not a failure to conform to God's legal righteousness, but merely a failure to yield or surrender to the Spirit. If only we could "let go and let God," we could conquer sin in our lives. Again, the focus of grace in this scheme is subjective (the Holy Spirit's infusion of power within us) rather than objective (the imputation of Christ's legal righteousness to our charge). Salvation by "letting him do it all" is even more subjective and, therefore, less certain, than salvation by obedience to the law. How do I know when I have "let him do it all"? What if I get in there with "the flesh" and ruin it all? Salvation by letting go and letting God, then, becomes the source of great anxiety.

Here, then, is the explanation of the confusion which plagues the person in the pew these days when trying to understand the gospel in the light of "higher life" teaching: First, they tell us, we must not exert any effort in the matter of victory. It is given to us in its totality, as a gift. So far, the teaching seems to exalt grace, but beware of making too hasty a conclusion. The next few steps in their argument muddy the waters a bit.

Second, before we can be given this victory which is the gift of God, we must "surrender." "Surrender," wrote the movement's early leader, Charles Trumbull, "is *our* part in victory" (italics in original). The Holy Spirit doesn't subdue us; he is dependent on us for that. "Let us get subdued," Trumbull tells us, as though we are to plug in the connection to the divine electrical current. This sort of mysticism Luther would have understood perfectly as a monk. Thus, "Christ plus my receiving" is the formula for "the hope of victory."

Third, *surrender* is defined as "the uttermost giving up of all that we have and all that we are to the mastery of Jesus." And it means that "I am without sinning immediately and completely" upon receiving this "victory."[9]

Now let's put all of this together. If "surrender" is the human contribution to this whole thing and surrender is "the uttermost giving up of all that we have and all that we are to the mastery of

Jesus," assuring us that we are "without sinning immediately and completely," and all of this is required *before* God will give us victory, how on earth can this be called a free gift? We are told we must not exert any effort (after all, that keeps the Spirit from living his life through us), and yet, without effort of the most strenuous sort (cessation from sinning) we cannot achieve a victory which is ostensibly given to us as a gift. Princeton theologian Benjamin B. Warfield saw this emerging movement and sarcastically caricatured the leaders as saying, "We must remember, of course, 'that everything must depend upon Christ and His work, in the matter of victory.' But this only 'after we have surrendered our lives to Him.' That He does the work on which everything depends itself depends absolutely on us. Thus everything ultimately is in our hands."[10] So much for "letting go and letting God."

The results of this "higher life" teaching are, according to Warfield, quite plain:

> The law of God having been pushed out of sight His grace becomes obscured with it. . . . He is no longer greatly feared, neither is He any longer greatly loved. Nor is He trusted. Our dependence is put in our own trust, not in God, and as errant a work-salvation results as was ever taught. . . . Pelagius, when he hung salvation on works, at least demanded perfect righteousness as its ground. In this teaching perfect righteousness is dispensed with. . . . The type of piety engendered by the preaching of a conditional salvation is naturally in polar opposition to that engendered by the preaching of a free salvation.[11]

In opposition to all of this, once again, we have that great doctrine of union with Christ set before us. He himself *is* "our righteousness, holiness, and redemption" (1 Cor. 1:30). We don't "let" him become our righteousness or holiness. We are baptized into *his* death, burial, and resurrection; so we talk about *his* victory, *his* full surrender to the will of the Father, *his* yielding. We have our victory not by our surrendering, but by his. That is the focus of the gospel message. Notice the words of Calvin in this regard, which seem to knock down in one bold stroke all of the ladders we climb in order to try to convince ourselves that sinning can be conquered all at once, through our use of various spiritual techniques:

> We see that our whole salvation and all its parts are comprehended in Christ. We should therefore take care not to derive the least portion

of it anywhere else. If we seek salvation, we are taught by the very name of Jesus that it is "of Him." If we seek any other gifts of the Spirit, they will be found in *His* anointing.

If we seek strength, it lies in *His* dominion; if purity, in *His* conception; if gentleness, it appears in *His* birth. For by His birth He was made like us in all respects that He might learn to feel our pain. If we seek redemption, it lies in His passion; if acquittal, in His condemnation; if remission of the curse, in *His* cross; if satisfaction, in *His* sacrifice; if purification, in *His* blood; if reconciliation, in *His* descent into hell; if mortification of the flesh, in *His* tomb; if newness of life, in *His* resurrection; if immortality, in the same; if inheritance of the Heavenly Kingdom, in *His* entrance into heaven; if protection, if security, if abundant supply of all blessings, in *His* Kingdom; if untroubled expectation of judgment, in the power given to Him to judge. In short, since rich store of every kind of good abounds in Him, let us drink our fill from this fountain, and from no other.[12]

Christian Liberty

Christian liberty was so important to the Reformers that Martin Luther devoted an entire treatise to it *(The Freedom of the Christian Man)* and Calvin referred to it as "an appendix to justification." In other words, said Calvin:

> He who proposes to summarize gospel teaching ought by no means to omit an explanation of this topic. For it is a thing of prime necessity, and apart from a knowledge of it consciences dare undertake almost nothing without doubting; they hesitate and recoil from many things; they constantly waver and are afraid. But freedom is especially an appendage of justification and is of no little avail in understanding its power.[13]

Many Christians will heartily agree that we are saved by grace alone, but their piety is marked by scrupulous attachment to extrabiblical rules. Prohibitions against dancing, moderate drinking, movie-going, card-playing, and the like become a test of Christian maturity in such circles, when in fact Paul refers to those who have scruples about things indifferent as "weaker brothers." These folks will insist that we must oppose any theology of works-righteousness, but their actual practice undermines the gospel of grace! Grace does not free us to live to ourselves; it frees us to serve God sincerely for the first time. Nevertheless, it is a grand service, an expression of inestimable gratitude. To include in any definition of genuine Christian piety or holiness extrabiblical guidelines—even if they are put forward as having been "deduced" from Scripture—is to fall under God's judgment first issued through Isaiah and then repeated by our Lord: "You hypocrites! Isaiah was right when he prophesied about you: 'These people honor me with their lips, but their hearts are far from me. They worship me in vain; their teachings are but rules taught by men'" (Matt. 15:8–9). In fact, Jesus seemed utterly baffled by the religious leaders: "To what can I compare this generation? . . . For John came neither eating nor drinking, and they say, 'He has a demon.' The Son of Man came eating and drinking, and they say, 'Here is a glutton and a drunkard, a friend of tax collectors and "sinners"'" (Matt. 11:16–19).

Calvin acknowledged in his day that there were many who argued that in things "indifferent" (i.e., things not expressly forbidden or commanded in Scripture), freedom should be cast aside: "Shall we say good-by to Christian freedom, thus cutting off occasion for such dangers?" After all, if it is going to cause problems, let's just refrain from presenting the option. In our day, this takes the form of "taboos," where even among Christian groups or institutions where it might be acknowledged that the Bible does not expressly forbid something, the institution nevertheless prohibits or limits individual liberty to engage in these activities. "But, as we have said," writes Calvin, "unless this freedom be comprehended, neither Christ nor gospel truth, nor inner peace of soul, can be rightly known." Isn't that overstating it a bit? What's the big problem in requiring everybody in a particular Christian group or institution to abide by a common set of moral guidelines—even if they are not expressly taught in Scripture—for the good of Christian peace and unity? It's a big problem because it is too high a price to pay for the ease of not having to think for oneself and exercise self-control. For being liberated from the tyranny of the world, the flesh, and the devil was too great a victory not to be experienced and enjoyed by every believer. If one cannot *experience* and *enjoy* justification before God, the practical value of this amazing truth is lost even if it is given assent by those who deny Christian liberty.

One more extended observation from Calvin will suffice on this matter of Christian freedom:

But these matters are more important than is commonly believed. For when consciences once ensnare themselves, they enter a long and inextricable maze, not easy to get out of. . . . If he boggles at sweet wine, he will not with clear conscience drink even flat wine, and finally he will not dare touch water if sweeter and cleaner than other water. To sum up, he will come to the point of considering it wrong to step upon a straw across his path, as the saying goes. . . . To sum up, we see whither this freedom tends: namely, that we should use God's gifts for the purpose for which he gave them to us, with no scruple of conscience, no trouble of mind. With such confidence our minds will be at peace with him, *and will recognize his liberality toward us.* . . . Its whole force consists in *quieting frightened and disturbed consciences before God—* that are perhaps disturbed and troubled over forgiveness of sins, or anxious whether unfinished works, corrupted by the faults of our flesh, are pleasing to God, or tormented about the use of things indifferent. . . . And we have not been forbidden to laugh, or to be filled, or to join new possessions to old or ancestral ones, or to delight in musical harmony, or to drink wine. (italics added)[14]

As we saw earlier, legalism leads to license. Those who have been raised in very strict homes are often the ones who will probably go off the deep end in college. We must all learn self-control, a habit that must grow with our character, but self-control cannot be learned at all where it is replaced with a rigid set of prohibitions. Furthermore, if one is brought up in an environment of primarily negative ethics, that person will undoubtedly have a confused understanding of God and the gospel, even if the diet in church and in the home is solidly evangelical and orthodox. God will be seen as a stern judge instead of a loving Father. Calvin said we need to know our Christian liberty in order to "recognize his [God's] liberality toward us." In other words, when I enjoy a really fine meal and a bottle of superb wine with some friends, I can say, "Well, I hope God isn't looking. This is the last time I'll do this," or, more likely, "Who cares who's looking. I'm sick of those stupid rules. If God exists to tell me where to part my hair, I've had it with religion." Or, on the other hand, I can silently thank God and think of him as the loving provider of this meal. As we laugh, tell stories, and catch up on old news, it is almost as if God is there at the table, just sitting there, laughing right along, like a father who takes pleasure in the delight of his children. In fact, this is not an image one has to conjure up; one may find it quite clearly in the life of our Lord, God incarnate, "friend of sinners." To think of abusing a gift of God one must completely deny or ignore this image, so, ironically, when we see in such everyday experiences an opportunity to "recognize his liberality toward us," we are less likely to take advantage of the moment as an occasion for sin. This attitude breeds moderation and gratitude to the liberal giver.

The apostle Paul spoke of "the weak and the strong" in Romans 14:

> Accept him whose faith is weak, without passing judgment on disputable matters. One man's faith allows him to eat everything, but another man, whose faith is weak, eats only vegetables. The man who eats everything must not look down on him who does not, and the man who does not eat everything must not condemn the man who does, for God has accepted him. Who are you to judge someone else's servant? To his own master he stands or falls. And he will stand, for the Lord is able to make him stand.
>
> One man considers one day more sacred than another; another man considers every day alike. Each one should be fully convinced in his own mind. He who regards one day as special, does so to the Lord. . . . Therefore let us stop passing judgment on one another. Instead, make up your mind not to put any stumbling block or obstacle in your brother's way. [vv. 1–6, 13]

The counsel of that last sentence is often used by legalists to restrict other believers' freedom. But Paul makes clear that this advice cuts both ways.

From these and similar passages the Reformers challenged the medieval church's authority to govern the conscience. Only God may command the conscience. The church may—indeed, must—issue God's commands in Scripture, but it may not issue its own commands beyond it. The Reformers called this "grey area" *adiaphora,* the Greek word Paul uses here for "disputable matters." They insisted that there was such a category in Christian ethics and that those with a weaker conscience should not be tyrannized by those who have no problem exercising their liberty in matters some might consider doubtful, and vice versa. The bottom line for Paul is this: "Therefore let us stop passing judgment on one another" (v. 13). Stronger Christians must stop judging weaker Christians for having doubts or reservations about certain things. They must not "lord it over" the weaker

Christians simply to flaunt their freedom. In fact, in a situation where it is possible for a weaker believer to become deeply disturbed or confused, love must rule the moment. Otherwise, the "liberated" brother or sister is just as rule-oriented as the legalist—he or she just falls out on a different side of the argument. Nevertheless, what often happens is that the legalist will quote passages here, such as, "It is better not to eat meat or drink wine or to do anything else that will cause your brother to fall" (v. 21), in support of abstinence from drinking alcohol. And yet, this believer will probably have no trouble enjoying a choice slice of prime rib, even though some Christians are strict vegetarians.

Paul's point here is not that the stronger believers must always give up their liberty, but that in certain instances they ought to exercise their judgment, wisdom, and charity, being governed by what is best for their brothers and sisters, not for themselves. And whatever point the apostle is making here, it leaves no room for the legalist to abuse his or her authority in trying to impose absolute rules in matters of "indifference"—grey areas. That is why Calvin argued, "None but the weak is made to stumble by the first kind of offense, but the second gives offense to persons of bitter disposition and pharisaical pride. Accordingly, we shall call the one the offense of the weak, the other that of the Pharisees. Thus we shall so temper the use of our freedom as to allow for the ignorance of our weak brothers, but for the rigor of the Pharisees, not at all!"

At the same time, we must remember that, just as Paul moved, in Galatians 5, from telling the church to "stand firm" in its liberty and to "not let yourselves be burdened again by a yoke of slavery" (vv. 1–15), to informing them of how they have been freed in order to live for God and each other (vv. 16–26), so too we must use our liberty as an opportunity to glorify God and enjoy him forever. If we can enjoy an activity, a product, or a relationship that is within the guidelines of Scripture and do so as an expression of gratitude to the God who gave it, we are at liberty to accept these gifts from God's liberal hands. "But," Calvin warns us, "where there is plenty, to wallow in delights, to gorge oneself, to intoxicate mind and heart with present pleasures and be always panting after new ones—such are very far removed from a lawful use of God's gifts."[15] We must never use our liberty as a pretext to "outstrip [our] neighbors in all sorts of elegance." To be sure, one Christian might buy an economy car and another might purchase a luxury automobile, and these are "things indifferent." But greed is not, and each believer must judge for himself or herself whether a decision has crossed from this "grey area" into that clearly forbidden realm.

In short, let no one be lord of your conscience but God, and do not give up your Christian liberty to those who might wish to dictate the more difficult decisions we all have to make. At the same time, use your liberty as an opportunity to acknowledge God's liberality toward you and calm your fears, doubts, and questions about his goodness or favor. Use it also as an opportunity to serve your brother or sister for whom Christ died.

This chapter opened with a story about Duke George and his words of comfort and hope to his dying son. After hearing the Duke's impassioned words about justification, the son's wife asked, "Father, why may not such truths be preached publicly?" to which the Duke answered, "It may be told to the dying only, not to those who are well." Duke George was afraid that such "strong meat" was too much for someone to bear who was not on his or her way out. But we must side with his daughter-in-law. The only real comfort we can ever have in this life of ups and downs is that God is a kind Father toward us and not a stern judge. And the only way we can be confident of that is not to flatter ourselves with thoughts of God's general goodness or benevolence, for we know that "the wicked will not go unpunished" (Prov. 11:21) and that we are wicked. Thus, "simultaneously justified and sinful" is the biblical remedy. Until we are glorified, we must endure the war within, the conflict between the old and new life. But this war within can be waged when the war without (between God and us) finds a peace settlement. With the heavenly verdict on our side—"there is therefore now no condemnation"—we are able to engage in battle, knowing that the outcome is already decided.

Study Questions

1. Can a person still be considered a Christian and be confident that he is acceptable before God even if he continues to sin? (See Rom. 7.)

2. Are we justified by God by Christ's work for us and outside of us or by his work within us? Distinguish between imputation and infusion.

3. Explain the relationship between the first Adam (original sin) and the Second Adam (justification) in the light of Romans 5:16, 19.

4. What is meant by "union with Christ," and how does this help explain the relationship between justification and sanctification? (See especially Rom. 6.)

5. Can Jesus be one's Savior if one does not accept him as Lord? (See John 14:15; 15:16; Rom. 10:8–13.)

6. Discuss the nature and history of the Pietist movement. To what extent does it influence you and the churches with which you are most familiar?

7. Critique the following phrases about the Christian life:
   (a) "Let go and let God"
   (b) "The victorious Christian life"
   (c) "Complete surrender"

ten

No Lost Causes

My grandmother was the queen of canning. She was known throughout the community for her incredible preserves. I remember well sitting on a stool in the kitchen and, like an obnoxious cat, watching her every move as she made her famous goods.

I would ask, "Bigmama [we never called her Grandma], why are you always melting that wax over the fruit?" I didn't understand how wax could make any positive contribution to the flavor.

She answered, "The wax seals the jar tightly so the fruit can't be contaminated. If I didn't seal it, the fruit would eventually rot."

As an amateur in the canning business, I could see the importance of the picking, purchasing, and canning stages. But I saw little importance in the sealing of the preserves.

You and I are God's preserves. What good would it do for God to choose us, redeem us, and call us into union with his Son if he did not have a plan for preserving us as heirs of the eternal kingdom? "And you also were included in Christ when you heard the word of truth, the gospel of your salvation. Having believed, you were marked in him with a seal, the promised Holy Spirit, who is a deposit guaranteeing our inheritance until the redemption of those who are God's possession—to the praise of his glory" (Eph. 1:13–14).

Christendom is not entirely at one on this matter of the security of the Christian. I must also concede that many of those who have espoused this doctrine have also been guilty of taking God's grace for granted. Even though one might not come right out and state it, often a person will live in such a way as to say, "I made my decision. Jesus is my Savior, and all my sins—past, present, and future—are forgiven and forgotten. So I don't have to deal any more with those moments of weakness." Professor Robert Godfrey once rather sarcastically caricatured this tendency as saying, "God loves to forgive; I love to sin, so that makes for a good relationship." That is not what God's sealing is all about.

A Slogan That's Best to Avoid

Some who believe that Christians are eternally secure give their doctrine the slogan "once saved, always saved," but that slogan is very misleading. The slogan suggests that once persons make a decision for Christ, they can then go off and do their own thing, fully confident that no matter what they do or how they live, they are "safe and secure from all alarm." That simply is not biblical.

The new birth, to be sure, is an event. In other words, at some point in your life, the Holy Spirit moves and creates new life in your soul. But salvation is more than that. Justification, too, is a one-time declaration, but salvation also involves a *process* of, over time, becoming righteous, which is called *sanctification*.

Sanctification is the Christian life, the daily pursuit of God and the transformation of the heart, mind, and will. Our priorities and our view of life are drastically altered, revolutionized, and reversed. We did not cooperate in our justification. But we must cooperate with God in our sanctification.

Some Christians have the idea that they must sit back and let the Spirit do everything. But, as we have seen, the process toward maturity in Christ is not based on a passive view of life. Another way of saying *sanctification* is "taking the bull by the horns." We do not wait for the Holy Spirit to perform some supernatural number on our lives: He already has done this for us! We actively pursue holiness and Christ-centeredness in our lives, recognizing that the same One who commands us to work, persevere, and obey gives us the supernatural ability to do so. Just do it! *You* do the work; but recognize that, if the work is done, *God* has done it in and through you.

So then, when we speak of "once saved, always saved," we are not taking into account the full scope of salvation. We have been saved (justified), we are being saved (sanctified), and we will one day be saved (glorified). You cannot claim to have been "saved" (justified) unless you are being sanctified. Jesus Christ is Savior *and* Lord.

Jesus made it plain throughout his ministry that one could not become his disciple (and, therefore, could not receive eternal life) unless that person was willing to "take up his cross daily" and follow Jesus. The New Testament emphasizes denying yourself, dying to sin, and deferring to others.

These terms identify a concept that is not in vogue today. When even many church leaders are telling people "believe in yourself" and are preaching a gospel that is more concerned with fulfilling our desires than God's, we have difficulty falling unreservedly into the arms of the Savior in whom we find our only confidence. But of course, we cannot ever tailor-make the gospel to fit our self-serving expectations.

The Chain of Salvation

Romans 8:30 makes clear the chain of salvation, a chain whose links cannot be broken: "And those he predestined, those he also called; those he called, he also justified; he justified, he also glorified." Can one be predestined, called, justified, and lost? This verse teaches us that when God starts something, God finishes it. Did you grant yourself salvation? Did you gain it yourself in the first instance? No, salvation was a gift. Remember, God justifies and condemns: "Who will bring any charge against those whom God has chosen? It is God who justifies. Who is he that condemns?" (Rom. 8:33–34).

Those whose hearts and minds have been (and are being) renewed by God's grace should not be obsessed with worry about falling away because, although we will always have periods of wandering around in the wilderness and falling into various temptations and sins, we really are becoming new persons. The ugly duckling is turning into a beautiful swan, to our surprise!

God never plants trees that do not bear fruit: "You did not choose me, but I chose you and appointed you to go and bear fruit—fruit that will last" (John 15:16). And the conclusion we can draw from James is, if you don't have the fruit, check the root!

Since God initially gives us the grace to believe in him and to turn from self, why would he not give us the grace to *keep on* trusting him? One simply cannot believe in the possibility of losing salvation through moral failure and in salvation by grace at the same time.

If we expect ourselves to maintain our faith and keep everything going, we fall under the reprimand of the apostle Paul, as he confronted the Galatian church: "You foolish Galatians! Who has bewitched you? . . . I would like to learn just one thing from you: Did you receive the Spirit by observing the law, or by believing what you heard? Are you so foolish? After beginning with the Spirit, are you now trying to attain your goal by human effort?" (Gal. 3:1–3).

We always approach God on his terms. Admittedly this fact does serious injury to our pride because it tells us that we are saved in spite of rather than because of ourselves.

Free Will

Still another issue is involved as we see security in the light of the new birth or regeneration—the matter of free will.

"Nobody can take a believer out of Christ but the believer himself," someone has said. However, God's Word states that "[no] created thing shall be able to separate us from the love of God which is in Christ Jesus our Lord" (Rom. 8:39 NKJV). That love of God which is "in Christ" for those who are "in Christ" is much too powerful.

If we fit the description of a "created thing," then even we cannot undo what God has done. If God loved us enough to choose us, purchase us with his Son's blood, and bring us into union with himself, then it would be silly to wonder if God would keep on demonstrating his affection by preserving us in that love.

Once God truly changes someone, that person never really wants to undo what God has done!

"Sure I was saved, but that was Tuesday!" Many people see their salvation in terms of a decision they made, and since their assurance of salvation is based upon the shifting sands of human decision, they are faced with having to return frantically to the mirror every hour on the hour rather than resting in the character, plan, and purpose of a sovereign God.

Think of the decisions you make every day. How about that decision to change employment or to move? Or what about your decision to go on that blind date the other night? Boy, was that a disappointment! Wouldn't you fear having your eternal destiny hinging on your decision-making ability, an ability that might lead you to commit yourself to a new course one minute and to reject it the next? What a terrible way to live!

I am not downplaying the necessity of making decisions, especially the decision for your eternal destiny. But it is nice to know that you can gauge your life by God's decision for you and not the other way around. You can keep on going when you know that this is God's program, God's project, and that God's interest in you creates within you an interest in him.

I remember how I used to ask Jesus into my heart as a child over and over again. Each time I intended to make absolutely certain that I was saved. Why do we do that? Why is it in some churches that we see the same people walking down the aisle week after week? Perhaps it is because we are looking to something *we* can do, or have done, to secure the kind of assurance we need. But we can't trust our feelings or our abilities of either will or effort, so we're left with having to trust in the ability of God, "who is able to keep you from falling" (Jude 24).

We have the responsibility to "go on to maturity" (Heb. 6:1). So we are responsible *to* persevere, but not *for* our perseverance. We are responsible *to be* saved, but not *for* our salvation.

To lose our salvation, we would have to return to a condition of spiritual death. Of what sort of regeneration would the Holy Spirit be the author if those whom he has resurrected and given eternal life are capable of dying spiritually again? "Well, can't we commit spiritual suicide?" one might ask. Not if we take seriously the claim of 1 Peter 1:23: "For you have been born again, not of perishable seed, but of imperishable."

All in the Family

If God really is our father and we have been legally adopted by his design and will, then we are members of his eternal covenant family. Certainly I may fall from the fellowship of my earthly parents, but it would be nonsense to say, "I'm no longer your son; I hereby declare that you, Mother, did not give birth to me, and that you, Dad, are not my natural father." That would be ridiculous.

Because we have been born into this royal family with an imperishable seed, we have been given the gift of perseverance to stand in the middle of frustration and despair and say, "[I am] confident of this, that he who began a good work in [me] will carry it on to completion" (Phil. 1:6).

Earlier, I said that one of the chain links of salvation is the fact that we are justified or declared righteous. That is an act. The matter of being sanctified or made righteous has been presented as a process. We cannot see justification. Nor can we monitor justification, as we can, at least to a certain extent, sanctification. But we do believe God's Word that we are declared righteous even though we are still sinful.

In the matter of justification, we see a Judge; we picture a courtroom. In the matter of sanctification, we see a Father and the image of a home. I referred to the ugly duckling's becoming the beautiful swan. Sanctification involves that kind of transformation. Don't lose heart! If God starts this thing, he will finish it!

A Nation of Sheep

Sheep do indeed stray from the shepherd. After all, if sheep did not tend to stray, why would they need a shepherd? But notice that the shepherd is always there to bring the sheep back.

Of course, we pay a penalty for straying. When we are living in a period of rebellion as children of God, life is "hell on earth." Sure, we enjoy our brief moments of self-gratification. But the gains do not compare with the unrest and disappointment. "We died to sin; how can we live in it any longer?" was the apostle Paul's question (Rom. 6:2). Living in rebellion against God goes against our grain now. We remember how exciting and pleasurable those former experiences were, but now they have lost their glamor. We are unhappy in sin—like a fish out of water—if our nature has truly been changed. It is still enjoyable, but eventually unbearable.

Backsliding can never be a crutch for having a fling. Doing so is a serious matter. "For certain men whose condemnation was written about long ago have secretly slipped in among you. They are godless men, who change the grace of our God into a license for immorality" (Jude 4).

In the book of Hosea God called his people to repentance:

> Take words with you
> and return to the LORD.
> Say to him:
> "Forgive all our sins
> and receive us graciously,
> that we may offer the fruit of our lips. . . ."
> [And God said] "I will heal their waywardness
> and love them freely,
> for my anger has turned away from them." [Hos. 14:2, 4]

Backsliding is one thing; apostasy is yet another: "They went out from us [they abandoned the Christian fellowship—that's apostasy], but they did not really belong to us. For if they had belonged to us, they would have remained with us; but their going showed that none of them belonged to us" (1 John 2:19). John also says, "Anyone who runs ahead and does not continue in the teaching of Christ does not have God; whoever continues in the teaching has both the Father and the Son" (2 John 9). In Revelation 17:14, we see Christ in victory, and "those who are with Him are called, chosen, and faithful (NKJV)." Notice that it does not say, "only those of God's called and chosen who are faithful." Rather, it actually describes his followers as those who *are* "called, chosen, and faithful." That they remain faithful is as much a gift of God's grace as their election and calling.

And remember, even the motions of perseverance do not save us. When the Scriptures warn, "he who stands firm to the end will be saved" (Matt. 24:13), it is still God's perseverance with us that enables us to respond in faithfulness to him.

The Christian faith flies in the face of social Darwinism and its principles of perfection. Ours is not the "survival of the fittest" but the "survival of the weakest." That is, those alone who come to terms with their spiritual impotence are granted the grace of God to persevere in his strength. You will fall. Stop trying to live the "victorious Christian life" and simply live, as you feed on God's Word and grow by his Spirit.

The Christian life cannot be described as "Three Easy Steps to Happiness." As many who have been believers for some time can testify, the Christian life is not easy, and it is not always happy. The Christian life is a road that can be traveled only by God's sovereign grace—a rough road, filled with temptations and fears, rewards and failures, joys and frustrations. But we can take our eyes off the storm of our own lives and look up to Christ, as Stephen did, where he stands at our defense. Then we are reminded of God's promise that things are fitting into a pattern for our good and his glory, that God is still in charge.

"If God is for us, who can be against us?" the apostle Paul asked enthusiastically (Rom. 8:31). God is pulling for you in this race of life, if you are in his family. He will see to it that you win over the obstacles. God is shaping you into something of which he can be proud. Your stubbornness, faithlessness, doubt, and self-will cannot stand in God's way. Indeed, "[nothing] will be able to separate us from the love of God that is in Christ Jesus our Lord" (Rom. 8:39).

To him who is able to keep you from falling and to present you before his glorious presence without fault and with great joy—to the only God our Savior be glory, majesty, power and authority, through Jesus Christ our Lord, before all ages, now and forevermore! Amen. [Jude 24–25]

Study Questions

1. Is there a difference between the Reformed doctrine of the perseverance of the saints and the teaching of eternal security? Explain, especially in the light of Matthew 24:13.
2. Discuss the "chain of salvation" in Romans 8:29–39. What happens if one link in the chain is lost?

3. Is regeneration (i.e., the new birth) something that can be lost or undone? (See Phil. 1:6; 1 Peter 1:23.)

4. How can we explain the situations we all know about where someone "falls away" and walks away from the faith even after making a decision, joining the church, and openly confessing Christ? (See 1 John 2:19.)

5. What comfort does the doctrine of the perseverance of the saints bring?

eleven

Two Keys to Spiritual Growth

If I hear one more sermon or see another book offering, "Five Steps to" or "Five Keys to" this or that, I'm going to go nuts. So why "Two Keys to Spiritual Growth"? It is intended to be "two keys to end all keys!"

Suppose we were to make a list of aids to spiritual growth. What might top the list? Prayer, Bible study, fasting, devotions, evangelism, and perhaps even singing in the choir. But how many of us would put the sacraments at the top? Would they even make the list? One wonders.

Some time ago I addressed a group of pastors in a city in the South. The meeting was organized by someone who was familiar with my work and wanted me to share the "doctrines of grace" with his fellow pastors. I don't usually look for a provocative opening, but having been raised in the particular denomination I now addressed, I felt something come over me. I was possessed (by what or whom, I'll leave up to the reader) to ask, "How many of you here are Roman Catholic priests?" Now, these brothers were Baptists, and the looks I got ran anywhere from confused to irritated. One pastor spoke up: "Boy, if you think there are any Catholic priests here, you're about as lost as a ball in tall grass."

I continued.

"What's that thing," I asked, "that you have at the end of the service?" After a few blank stares, another pastor answered tentatively, "The altar call."

"The altar call?" I responded. "We were supposed to have gotten rid of altars in the Reformation, substituting the Lord's Table, since Christ was crucified once and for all at Calvary!" (It's indeed ironic that the Holiness leader Phoebe Palmer even used the Roman Catholic terms: "If the gift is on the altar, the altar sanctifies the gift."[1])

Then I went on to give a blow-by-blow description of what I remember taking place. "With every head bowed and every eye closed," the pastor would himself do some accounting. "Yes, I see that hand," he would say, acknowledging the sinner. What purpose would there be in a pastor acknowledging the sinner's hand, while everybody else is supposed to avoid so much as peeking? "No looking around," the pastor would say, as though some hocus-pocus were taking place between the penitents and him.

Finally, those who slipped up their hands and were acknowledged by the pastor were to make their way down to the altar (not that new folks actually knew this when they put their hand up). Once at the front, with the pastor flanked by his choir, those seeking salvation would repeat word-for-word the pastor's prayer, like a saving formula. After the "sinner's prayer," the pastor would pronounce "absolution." "If you prayed that prayer after me and really meant it," he would say, "you are now a child of God."

The problem is, many of those down front were going through all of this for the umpteenth time! If Saturday night had been particularly rowdy, Sunday morning could be an opportunity to fill up the leaky bathtub with sacramental grace again. Rededication became for many, including myself, the equivalent of the Mass, sacrificing Christ again and again, hoping each time that I now had the amount of grace I needed to make it. "This time I'm really going to surrender all." Salvation by surrender eclipsed anything I may have heard in passing about salvation by grace.

Of course, if this sounds like the medieval system, it should. There are, after all, surprising similarities. What I expected when I went forward to the altar for rededication and what my Catholic friends meant when they went forward to the altar for penance were pretty similar. The terms were different, but the point was not.

Then, too, one can almost wonder whether the Roman Catholic "altar call" is at least more biblical. After all, it grew out of the scriptural sacrament of Holy Communion, whereas, *our* altar call is little more than a century old.

You might remember that one of the Reformation's central concerns was that the addition of sacraments to the two commanded in Scripture obscured Christ and confused the gospel. Couldn't the same be said today? Of course, evangelicals hardly ever use terms like *sacrament,* but the rituals we've invented play the same role in our Christian life that the seven sacraments played in medieval times.

Earlier I mentioned that the sacrament of rededication fulfills a similar function to the medieval sacrament of penance. According to the great medieval theologian Thomas Aquinas, "Penance is a second plank after shipwreck." It is for "a man on his return to God." Divine forgiveness is once again given, after the backslider "grieves for his sin, with the purpose of submitting himself by confession and satisfaction to the keys of the Church, in the hope of receiving forgiveness again through the power of Christ's cross." Hence, a penance is fulfilled when "a man shows external signs of sorrow, confesses his sins verbally to the priest who absolves him, and makes satisfaction for his sins according to the judgment of the priest." This should, according to Aquinas, include "weeping and tears of sorrow." This sacrament is required, he added, because "on account of free will, grace once possessed, can be lost. . . . It is therefore evident that penance can be repeated many times."[2]

Indeed, by the number of times I went forward and watched my friends go forward, this sacrament is alive and well in contemporary evangelicalism. During part of my youth, my parents managed a Christian camp at Lake Tahoe. My childhood memories of camp are many. Of course, the last night was decision and rededication night—the last chance to pilot the wary teens into the faith. It was during the *Thief in the Night* film craze, and I can recall how tense we would become—some of us watching it for the tenth time—as the rapture caught half the film's characters off-guard. After the terrifying movie the camp leader would talk about how important it was to be ready for the rapture. We didn't want God to come back while we were saying a four-letter word. Fear of missing the rapture overshadowed any sense of fear of God's holiness and justice or trust in God's eternally satisfying grace. After being threatened with the terrors of living through the tribulation because we weren't ready, we were invited by the leader to write a list of our sins and throw them into the bonfire. Temporarily at least, it was a cathartic relief. At least for the time being I knew I wouldn't miss the rapture.

Evidently, my experiences are not isolated. Randall Balmer, a professor at Columbia University, recalls his experience at camp: "I sat next to a fire and shifted uneasily on the stony ground. My repeated attempts to appropriate the faith of my parents were desultory and imperfect, as I realized even then. Summer camp was where I tried annually to get it right, to conjure the same piety that my elders showed, to claim the elusive 'victory in Christ' that they professed."[3]

The point to all of this is that evangelicals have founded as many extrabiblical means of grace, satisfactions, and penances as medieval believers could ever have been plagued with. And yet, the Scriptures teach us that God's righteousness is *imputed* to our charge, so that we are forgiven already, not only for past sins, but for all future sins as well. Rededication, like a New Year's resolution, is often little more than an attempt to get back in God's good graces. The weeping is there; a prayer is prayed after the minister; and the tears are expected to wash away recent blemishes. I remember trying to force myself to cry, hoping that a sacrifice of tears might move God to compassion.

It should also be noted that even we evangelicals have satisfactions we make as part of penance. If we have blown it, we promise God (often when we're up at the altar) that we will have a regular quiet time every day. When we miss, we feel guilty, as though grace were leaking from the bathtub once again. This is a slavery not altogether different from the Office of Hours prescribed by the medieval church, especially for monks. Martin Luther, as a monk, never missed his daily quiet time ("office"), but not because he loved the Scriptures. Rather, it was because he was afraid of what might happen if he didn't. Better to jump through the hoops than to tempt the unknown. But when Luther left the monastery and the theology undergirding it, prayer became as natural as breathing. "The Christian's heart," he said, "is constantly sending up sighs and petitions to God, regardless of whether he happens to be eating or drinking or working." There are other ways we make satisfaction for our sins. We decide we will give something up, as a medieval believer might give something up for Lent or as satisfaction in penance. For instance, something we really enjoy, like watching football, will be replaced with spiritual duties, in order to show God we mean business.

You might be able to add to this list of "evangelical sacraments." Once again, like the Reformers before us, we must strip our faith of accumulated traditions which find no biblical warrant. We, too, must revive the centrality and importance of God's chosen sacraments. But that is a negative way of looking at a tremendously positive and exciting truth. One of the Reformation's goals was to rid the church of sacraments our Lord never commanded in order to spotlight the two he had: baptism and the Lord's Supper. Let's take a look, then, at these neglected "means of grace."

The Sacraments

Many evangelicals are put off by the term *sacrament,* viewing it as a sort of throwback to Roman Catholicism. And yet, the Latin term *sacramentum* means "anything that's sacred or consecrated." The Latin word is translated from the Greek *musterion* (mystery), which is found in Ephesians 1:9; 3:9; 5:32; Colossians 1:27; 1 Timothy 3:16; and Revelation 1:20 and 17:7. In New Testament times, a *musterion* was the signification for a secret—for instance, a rite which only they knew and accepted who embraced the mystery. As Latin replaced Greek, so the term *sacramentum* replaced *musterion,* but they are still the same thing. Outside the religious context, the oath sworn by a new Roman soldier was called a *sacramentum;* it sealed the new recruit's position. The biblical writers had in mind, then, that idea of the holy mystery we find when we approach baptism and the Lord's Supper. A sacrament is a visible sign of invisible grace. But surely a sacrament is still more than that.

According to Richard Muller, in his *Dictionary of Latin and Greek Theological Terms*, a *sacramentum* is "a holy rite that is both a sign and a means of grace."[4] Not only do baptism and the Lord's Supper remind us of Christ and his death; these sacraments are actually channels of God's grace, linked to faith. (Baptism looks forward to faith; the Lord's Supper strengthens faith.)

The Roman Catholic church accepted seven sacraments, but the Reformers were convinced that the Bible only commanded two. Furthermore, a sacrament had to have an evangelical (i.e., "gospel") reference point, which, of course, marriage and other so-called sacraments do not have. Because Christ commanded baptism and the Lord's Supper, the Reformers argued, and because these two sacraments were evangelical (gospel-oriented), they are alone "means of grace" alongside the written Word of God, the Bible.

According to the Lutheran Augsburg Confession (1530), sacraments "are signs and testimonies of God's will toward us for the purpose of awakening and strengthening our faith." Similarly, the Heidelberg Catechism (1563) teaches, "They are visible, holy signs and seals instituted by God in order that by their use He may the more fully disclose and seal to us the promise of the gospel, namely, that because of the one sacrifice of Christ accomplished on the cross, He graciously grants us the forgiveness of sins and eternal life. . . . The Holy Spirit creates faith in our hearts by the preaching of the holy gospel and confirms it by the use of the holy Sacraments." The Presbyterian Westminster Confession concurs. The Anglican Thirty-nine Articles (1571) add, "Sacraments ordained of Christ are not only badges or tokens of Christian men's profession, but rather they be certain sure witnesses, and effectual signs of grace, and God's good will towards us, by which means He works invisibly in us, and not only quickens but greatly strengthens and confirms our faith in Him."

Now, let's take a look at the biblical definition of a sacrament. Since the Bible does not read like a catechism, with everything neat and tidy, we have to do a little bit of deduction from the texts treating the sacraments. These visible signs and seals of inward and invisible grace abound in the Old Testament. Circumcision separates the children of believers from those of unbelievers and places them within the protective wings of the covenant (Gen. 17:10–12). This was an outward sign of invisible grace. In other words, the physical circumcision of the flesh pointed to a circumcision of the heart that all Israelites were to recognize (Deut. 10:16). It was not enough for God's people to be inwardly circumcised; they had to bear *on their bodies* a visible sign of invisible grace.

Likewise, the Passover was more than a memorial of the liberation of Israel from Egyptian captivity. The sprinkling of the blood on the doorpost marked those who trusted God, and the firstborn children of those who did not apply the blood to the doorpost were killed by the avenging angel. In this case, too, the visible sign became intimately and inseparably connected with the salvation it signified and sealed.

In the New Testament, this sacramental way God has of communicating his grace is not abandoned. He still uses common, everyday elements to draw us into himself, to confirm us in the gospel, and to conform us to Christ's likeness. Let's look, then, at the two New Testament sacraments against the backdrop of their Old Testament counterparts.

Baptism: Beginning Grace

When God established his covenant with Abraham, he commanded, "This is my covenant with you and your descendants after you, the covenant you are to keep: Every male among you shall be circumcised. You are to undergo circumcision, and it will be the sign of the covenant between me and you" (Gen. 17:10–11).

It's difficult for us as individualistic Americans to appreciate the covenantal solidarity that forms the shape and texture of biblical history. God does not work with individuals primarily, but with families. This is his way of creating his church. "You and your descendants after you, unto a thousand generations" is a common phrase throughout both testaments. God, therefore, established a covenantal sign which separated the children of the believers unto the Lord. Their circumcision not only signified that separation; it *was* that separation. "The LORD's curse is on the house of the wicked. . . . but those who are righteous will go free" (Prov. 3:33; 11:21). Children of believers are not considered unregenerate pagans, "for they are the seed of the blessed of the LORD, and their offspring with them" (Isa. 65:23 KJV). Nevertheless, there were many who, though outwardly circumcised, were uncircumcised inwardly: "You stiff-necked people, with uncircumcised hearts and ears!" Stephen called his contemporaries (Acts 7:51).

Why did God command the circumcision of Israel's infants? Abraham believed and was justified when he could make a responsible decision, and yet God commanded the patriarch to institute the rite, beginning with his own children. Why didn't God simply wait until Abraham's son, Isaac, was old enough to make his own decision? It is because salvation is God-centered, not human-centered. The focus is not on our choosing, but on God's. God comes to us and to our children in love and grace, placing his mark of ownership on his covenant people. Circumcision was not something a convert did to show he meant business, but was something *God* did to show *he* meant business!

In the New Testament, God still wants to save families. When Peter preached his evangelistic sermon on the temple steps in Jerusalem, he did not announce a radical departure from this covenantal, family model. In fact, after telling his hearers to repent and be baptized, he proclaimed, "The promise is for you and your children and for all who are far off—for all whom the Lord our God will call" (Acts 2:39). Notice that the orientation here is not on God sitting around waiting for our children to make an individual choice, but on *his* calling. He calls us and then calls our children through baptism and the Word. He is actively pursuing us and our household. The apostle Paul assured us that one believing parent sanctified the children even if the other parent was an unbeliever, "Otherwise your children would be unclean, but as it is, they are holy" (1 Cor. 7:14). Why would the apostles accept the Old Testament's covenantal distinction between the "clean" and the "unclean" children if, in fact, there is no difference between the children of believers and those of unbelievers?

Recognizing the distinction is not enough, however. The *mark* that distinguishes the covenant children is baptism.

Our Lord himself "took a little child and had him stand among them [the disciples]. Taking him in his arms, he said to them, 'Whoever welcomes one of these little children in my name welcomes me; and whoever welcomes me does not welcome me but the one who sent me'" (Mark 9:36–37). Those who seek to enter the kingdom of God must imitate the little children (Mark 10:15). Further, when the Philippian jailer was converted, Paul and Silas told him, "Believe in the Lord Jesus, and you will be saved—you and your household" (Acts 16:31). Consequently, "he and all his family were baptized" (v. 33). Some critics of infant baptism have argued that "household" here could refer to either grown children or to servants. And yet, the assurance of household salvation seems to depend not on the individual decisions of those in the jailer's household, but upon the jailer's faith in Christ, which brings his family into the covenant of grace. Furthermore, it is difficult to conceive of a jailer being wealthy enough to support a staff of servants. The natural reading, at least in my opinion, is that the jailer's own immediate family is in view. In addition, the apostle Paul confessed to a household baptism: "Yes, I also baptized the household of Stephanas" (1 Cor. 1:16). In all of these cases are we to believe that each and every member of the household converted from deeply rooted paganism? It would seem that the common-sense reading of these instances would suggest infant as well as adult baptism.

Secondarily, this was the practice of the early church. The earliest postapostolic documents demonstrated an unchallenged practice of infant baptism. If that is true, the burden of proof in the debate falls on the shoulders of those who *deny* the practice. In other words, the relative silence of the New Testament with regard to announcing more specifically *who* should be baptized should be taken as an assumption that Christian baptism, in replacing Hebrew circumcision, was to still include covenant children. If Old Testament covenant children received the sign of the covenant, known then as circumcision, then New Testament covenant children are equally entitled to the sign of the covenant. If, in other words, New Testament Christians were to give up including their children in the covenant by sacrament, would that not have been a major subject taken up somewhere in the New Testament? And could the disciples of the apostles have held to infant baptism in opposition to their mentors? One would think that if a practice of baptizing infants was something new in the second- and third-generation church, there would have been a debate, but there was none. There was perfect continuity on this issue from New Testament to postapostolic times. Therefore, the burden falls on the shoulders of the opponents of infant baptism to demonstrate where the New Testament and the early church departed from the Old Testament practice of infant inclusion. It would seem that with the references mentioned above, a shift is difficult, if indeed possible, to detect.

What Baptism Does

The Bible doesn't beat around the bush here. Whatever baptism accomplishes, the sign and seal (water and the Word) are inseparably linked to the reality (washing of regeneration) itself (Tit. 3:5). John the Baptist's baptism was still an Old Testament Jewish ritual washing. The Jews had many such washings, usually rituals of rededication after lapses. The Baptist informed his converts, "I baptize you with water for repentance. But after me will come one who is more powerful than I, whose sandals I am not fit to carry. He will baptize you with the Holy Spirit and with fire" (Matt. 3:11). In other words, the Coming One will do more than offer rededication ceremonies. He will actually unite believers to himself through the work of the Holy Spirit. Therefore, this new baptism will need no repetition; the Holy Spirit himself will be given in this baptism. But he will also baptize with fire. This refers, of course, to judgment, as the next verse makes clear: "His winnowing fork is in his hand, and he will clear his threshing floor, gathering his wheat into the barn and burning up the chaff with unquenchable fire." Thus, there are, as it were, two fonts—the font of salvation and the font of damnation. Christian baptism, when joined by the Word and faith, assures us that our baptism will be of the former type.

Baptism is, in effect, a "sprinkling by his [Christ's] blood" (1 Peter 1:2). "God . . . made us alive with Christ even when we were dead in transgressions—it is by grace you have been saved. And God raised us up with Christ and seated us with him in the heavenly realms in Christ Jesus" (Eph. 2:5–6). The apostle Paul further described this New Testament rite:

"Or don't you know that all of us who were baptized into Christ Jesus were baptized into his death? . . . in order that, just as Christ was raised from the dead through the glory of the Father, we too may live a new life. If we have been united with him like this in his death, we will certainly also be united with him in his resurrection" (Rom. 6:3–5).

In other words, Christ was baptized with God's wrath so that we could be baptized with God's grace. In baptism we are identified with Christ and united to him. He as truly saves us from God's wrath as Moses saved the Israelites while condemning the Egyptians in the Red Sea.

The apostle Peter compared baptism to Noah's ark:

> In it only a few people, eight in all, were saved through water, and this water symbolizes baptism that now saves you also—not the removal of dirt from the body but the pledge of a good conscience toward God. It saves you by the resurrection of Jesus Christ, who has gone into heaven and is at God's right hand—with angels, authorities and powers in submission to him. [1 Peter 3:20–22]

And the apostle Paul compared baptism in Christ to the Israelites' wilderness experience when "They were all baptized into Moses in the cloud and in the sea" (1 Cor. 10:2). That cloud was the presence of God following and guiding the children of Israel (Exod. 33:8–11) and the sea, of course, was the Red Sea. Baptism for the apostles, then, was the descent of the indwelling presence of God and the "proof of purchase," guaranteeing that we have already escaped the raging waters of divine wrath. While there are, of course, exceptions (for instance, the thief on the cross), the general rule is "Whoever believes and is baptized will be saved, but whoever does not believe will be condemned" (Mark 16:16). If we refuse baptism, we are refusing the promise God makes and seals to us and to our children. While we are saved by grace alone through faith alone, it is impossible to separate baptism and salvation, as though we can have the gift, but refuse the box in which it comes. We are justified by grace through faith alone; baptism nevertheless promises the new life of the convert or child of the believer and attests to the fact that God has come to nurture us even in our earliest days.

Holy Communion: Sustaining Grace

"Grace for the journey" is one way of thinking about this second sacrament. You will remember in our discussion of justification that objective grace is imputed—when we believe we are declared righteous. But then the process of sanctification begins; this is subjective grace and it is imparted. That is, it is a grace that actually transforms us from within. For a somewhat crude illustration, imagine a teen who, upon earning his driver's license, is given a car by his parents. Furthermore, the parents paid for gasoline, too, by credit card. All the elated youth would have to do is present the card to the attendant and fill the tank. In a similar way, God has already paid for our salvation, and there is nothing we can do to have our name erased from the "pink slip." But God has given us something in addition to that gift. He has also ensured that we will never have to pay for our own "fuel," either. Justifying grace comes all at once, when God declares us righteous while we are still sinners. Our sins are paid in full, and complete and total salvation is already ours for good. Yet, God wants to keep us constantly "fueled" in our faith, too.

The danger comes when we invent "sacraments." In the Middle Ages, the church came up with as many as seven to thirty sacraments or "means of grace." The problem is that we begin to become preoccupied with the means rather than the end. With so many "means of grace," we lose sight of the Giver himself. This is why the Reformers insisted on only these two sacraments: baptism and Holy Communion. They point to Christ alone and reinforce the gospel of grace. Like medieval Rome, however, contemporary evangelicalism seems to have invented a host of new sacraments. I remember an evangelical missions conference in which the leader even *said*, "There are so many means of grace, and you've got to get into the flow." A short-term mission, a daily quiet time and prayer journal, or even rededication at the end of a conference could serve as examples of such "means of grace." Of course, one doesn't even have to mention Christ. One could commit to a short-term mission or do his devotions or rededicate himself without thinking of the gospel. This, once again, is "do this" religion, not "believe this" religion. That is why we need to refuel—but at the station God has appointed.

First, let's understand what Holy Communion is *not*. According to Rome, baptism washed away original sin in the infant and, to use an illustration, filled the bathtub of grace. But every time the believer committed a venial ("little") sin, grace would leak; a mortal ("big") sin could empty the tub altogether! That's where sacraments like communion came in; they could fill the tub up again. This, of course, is not the view the Protestant Reformers held, and it is, I believe, far from the biblical view. The impartation of grace we find in Holy Communion is not a grace that saves but a grace that restores the believer's confidence in the Word's pronouncement, "Not guilty." Communion is a refueling station not because we continually need to recover lost merits, but because we need to recover lost steam. We are weak; our hearts are easily cooled, and our souls need to feed on Christ just as truly as our bodies need to feed on bread. Holy Communion strengthens us not only because it *symbolizes* or *represents* something great, but because it really *is* something great. It is the actual nourishment of Christ himself who offers his body and blood for spiritual food. To those wearied by a tough week at the home or office or to those whose consciences never let them forget a sin they commit during the week, the sacrament of Holy Communion is there to communicate Christ and his forgiveness. There is no conscience that cannot be instructed and overcome by this powerful sacrament. Rather than using it as a means of filling up a leaky bathtub, we must view it as God's chosen reminder that we are always and everywhere forgiven people.

What the Bible Says about the Lord's Supper

The Passover is to the Lord's Supper what circumcision is to baptism. "The Season of Our Freedom," the Passover feast is known to Jews as the most cherished holy day. Acting as the celebrant-priest, the head of the household raises the cup and the bread, saying, "Behold! This is as the bread of affliction that our fathers ate in the land of Egypt." "Now we are here," they say, "may we be next year in the land of Israel! Now we are slaves— may we be free men in the year to come!" God commanded the Hebrew exiles in Egypt to "take a bunch of hyssop, and dip it in the blood" from a sacrificial lamb, and to place the blood on "the two side posts." "And none of you shall go out at the door of his house until the morning." This is because "the LORD will pass through to smite the Egyptians; and when he seeth the blood . . . the LORD will pass over the door, and will not suffer the destroyer to come in unto your houses to smite you" (Exod. 12:22–23 KJV).

As baptism marks our having passed through the waters from death unto life (drawing heavily upon the exodus), so Holy Communion is a sign and seal that God's anger has passed over us. Christ himself endured the cup of God's wrath so we could drink the cup of salvation. This language is common to both Old and New Testaments. The psalmist boasts, "I will lift up the cup of salvation and call on the name of the LORD" (Ps. 116:13). But that same cup can be a dangerous drink for the enemies of God. Before, God tells Isaiah, Israel had been forced to drink God's cup of wrath. But the tables have turned: "See, I have taken out of your hand the cup that made you stagger; from that cup, the goblet of my wrath, you will never drink again. I will put it into the hands of your tormentors" (Isa. 51:22–23). Conversely, Habakkuk warns the people of his day, "The cup from the LORD's right hand is coming around to you, and disgrace will cover your glory" (Hab. 2:16). In the Revelation, we read that those who follow the Beast are made to "drink of the wine of God's fury, which has been poured full strength into the cup of his wrath" (Rev. 14:10).

This language and imagery is carried on into the New Testament. When Jesus celebrated the Passover with his disciples, he "took bread, gave thanks and broke it, and gave it to his disciples saying, 'Take and eat; this is my body.' Then he took the cup, gave thanks and offered it to them, saying, 'Drink from it, all of you. This is my blood of the covenant, which is poured out for many for the forgiveness of sins'" (Matt. 26:26–28). Later that night when Jesus slipped out to Gethsemane, he prayed, "My Father, if it is possible, may this cup be taken from me. Yet not as I will, but as you will" (v. 39). The cup he raised earlier that night was the cup of salvation: "This is my blood of the covenant, which is poured out for many for the forgiveness of sins." The cup he had on his mind in Gethsemane was of a different hue. He drank the cup of divine wrath so we could quench our thirst with the cup of salvation. Thus, he told his followers,

"I am the bread of life. He who comes to me will never go hungry, and he who believes in me will never be thirsty" (John 6:35). "If anyone eats of this bread," he promised, "he will live forever. This bread is my flesh, which I will give for the life of the world." The Jews were as confused by its language as many Christians are today. "How can this man give us his flesh to eat?" they asked. Instead of explaining the theological intricacies of this feast, our Lord simply said, "unless you eat the flesh of the Son of Man and drink his blood, you have no life in you." He added, "Whoever eats my flesh and drinks my blood has eternal life, and I will raise him up at the last day. For my flesh is real food and my blood is real drink. Whoever eats my flesh and drinks my blood remains in me, and I in him" (John 6:51–56).

The apostle Paul employs this language, too. "You cannot drink the cup of the Lord and the cup of demons," he warns the Corinthians. "You cannot have a part in both the Lord's table and the table of demons" (1 Cor. 10:21). Then, after reminding them of the words of institution—"This is my body. . . . This cup is the new covenant in my blood"—the apostle to the Gentiles adds that "whoever eats the bread or drinks the cup of the Lord in an unworthy manner," as the Corinthians were doing by turning communion into a drunken orgy, "will be guilty of sinning against the body and blood of the Lord" (1 Cor. 11:27). Notice the connection Paul makes here between the elements of bread and wine and the actual body and blood of Christ himself. He does not say, ". . . will be guilty of sinning against the wine, which evokes the image of his blood, or of sinning against the bread, which reminds us of his body."

"Therefore, whoever eats the bread or drinks the cup of the Lord in an unworthy manner will be guilty of sinning against the body and blood of the Lord" (1 Cor. 11:27). In other words, by turning communion into a sacrilege, the Corinthians were maintaining a dangerously low view of the sacrament—such a low view, in fact, that by eating the bread and drinking the "cup of salvation" without discerning the seriousness of what was taking place, they were inviting divine wrath. The "cup of salvation" for them became, as the waters of the Red Sea were to the Egyptians, a "cup of wrath." This issue, then, of properly discerning the nature of communion and considering its weight is no small matter. Some "laid back" churches in southern California have replaced the solemnity of Holy Communion with a "punch and cookies" approach; some have even replaced bread and wine with pizza and Coke! To these the apostle Paul would repeat his warning to the Corinthians: "Is not the cup of thanksgiving for which we give thanks a participation in the blood of Christ? And is not the bread that we break a participation in the body of Christ?" (1 Cor. 10:16). "Participation" (*koinonia*) in that verse is also translated "sharing" or "communion." The bread and the cup, we are told by the apostle Paul, is actually a sharing with and participation in the body and blood of Christ.

To be sure, there is much about this sacrament which invites our curiosity to anxiously probe. Nevertheless, we are treading on holy ground—a mystery beyond human comprehension. That we truly feed on Christ must be maintained. And yet, Christian unity must not be determined by particular explanations which seek to determine more than God has revealed.

We are weak. God knows that. Instead of attacking Thomas's doubt, our Lord invited him to see and feel his wounds. Similarly, he indulges our weakness and doubt, offering us physical, tangible tokens of inward grace. Instead of condemning us for doubt, fear, anxiety, and faithlessness, Christ offered himself as food for the journey in the desert—the Bread of heaven. Just as surely as we take the bread do we take Christ's body, and just as surely as we drink the cup do we take his blood for our salvation. Just as surely as we cannot sustain our bodies without food and drink, so we cannot hope to flourish in the Christian life without this heavenly meal.

> Welcome, sweet, and sacred feast; welcome life!
>   Dead I was, and deep in trouble;
> But grace, and blessings came with thee so rife,
>   That they have quicken'd even drie stubble;
> Thus souls their bodies animate . . .
>
> And now by these sure, sacred ties,
>   After thy blood
>   (Our sov'rain good)
>   Had cleared our eyes,
>   And given us sight;
> Thou dost unto thyself betroth

Our souls and bodies both
In everlasting light.

'Twas not enough that thou hadst payd the price
    And given us eyes
When we had none, but thou must also take
    Us by the hand
And keep us still awake,
    When we would sleep,
    Or from thee creep,
Who without thee cannot stand . . .

'Twas not enough to lose thy breath
And blood by an accursed death,
    But thou must also leave
    To us that did bereave
Thee of them both, these seals the means
    That should both cleanse
    And keep us so,
    Who wrought thy wo?
O rose of Sharon! O the Lily
    of the valley!
How art thou now, thy flock to keep,
Become both *food,* and *Shepherd* to thy sheep!

Henry Vaughan (1622–1695)[5]

Study Questions

1. Discuss the "altar call" and the theology underlying it.
2. What is a sacrament, historically and biblically defined?
3. Define infant baptism, and explain the arguments in favor of it. Are these arguments valid? Using Scripture, argue for or against the position.
4. Explain the significance of "household salvation" in both testaments. (See Acts 2:39; Acts 16:31, 33; 1 Cor. 1:16; 1 Cor. 7:14.)
5. What does baptism mean? (See Matt. 3:11–12; Mark 16:16; Rom. 6:3–5; 1 Cor. 10:2; Eph. 2:5–7; 1 Peter 1:2; 1 Peter 3:20–22.)
6. Explain the meaning of communion. Is it a) just a symbolic memorial of Christ's death; b) a change of the substance of

bread and wine into the physical body and blood of Christ; c) a spiritual feeding on Christ in which he is truly, but not physically, present in the bread and wine.

7. What does the Bible say about the importance of communion? (See Exod. 12:22–23; Ps. 116:13; Matt. 26:26–28; 1 Cor. 10:10–21; 11:24–29.) What does 1 Corinthians 10:16 mean when it calls communion "a participation" or "sharing" in Christ's body and blood? Is this how we usually think of it?

twelve

A Kingdom of Priests

Our Lord announced it when the Pharisees asked him when the kingdom of God would come: "The kingdom of God does not come with your careful observation, nor will people say, 'Here it is,' or 'There it is,' because the kingdom of God is within you" (Luke 17:20–22). "And I confer on you a kingdom," Jesus told his disciples, "just as my Father conferred one on me, so that you may eat and drink at my table in my kingdom and sit on thrones, judging the twelve tribes of Israel" (22:29–30). Standing before Pilate, Jesus announced, "My kingdom is not of this world. If it were, my servants would fight to prevent my arrest by the Jews. But now my kingdom is from another place" (John 18:36). "You are a king, then!" Pilate responded. Our Lord's answer was sharp and to the point: "You are right in saying I am a king. In fact, for this reason I was born, and for this I came into the world, to testify to the truth. Everyone on the side of truth listens to me" (John 18:37).

In these brief explanations, our Lord announced the present reality of the kingdom of God, conferred it upon his disciples, and indicated that it was a heavenly kingdom, not an earthly one; headquartered in the heavenly Jerusalem, not the earthly one. In fact, observers will not be able to point to it as though it were a literal, earthly kingdom and say, "There it is." Further, the signpost of this kingdom is truth. Its mission, character, and activity is not geopolitical, sociological, or racial, but theological. The kingdom shall be extended by the proclamation of the truth about God and us, known as the gospel.

Eschatology, or the study of last things, has, it seems, been the chief preoccupation of evangelicals over the last several decades. Lewis Sperry Chafer, founder of Dallas Theological Seminary, argued: "It is obvious that, apart from the knowledge of dispensational truth, the believer will not be intelligently adjusted to the present purpose and will of God in the world."[1] That, of course, was a curious and bold remark considering that "dispensational truth" was never held anywhere in the Christian church until the late nineteenth century. The churches of my youth required adherence to dispensational premillennialism as though it were the test of one's faith. There were even instances in which the statement of faith did not include definitions of God, Christ, or justification, but explained the dispensational, pretribulation-rapture point of view with missionary zeal. Dominating Bible and prophecy conferences, and even a good number of weekly sermons, dispensationalism has overshadowed, and in some cases replaced, the gospel itself in the minds of many of us who come from this tradition.

Christians are not to divide over such peripheral matters as the grace of God and human activity, we are told, and yet, to deny the rapture (which is mentioned nowhere in Scripture) marks a heretical departure.

The fact is, Christians have always held conflicting theories about the end times. Premillennialism holds that Christ will set up a future kingdom on earth in the literal precincts of Jerusalem. Christ will return *before* the literal millennium. Postmillennialism insists that Christ will return *after* a literal era of peace, prosperity, and worldwide conversion. The amillennial interpretation argues that we are currently experiencing the reign prophesied in Scripture. Since the reference to a millennium only occurs in Revelation 20, and only in an apocalyptic, symbolic literary genre, amillennialists argue, the sole mission and meaning of the kingdom is the proclamation of the gospel and the ingathering of believers into the church. Where the Word is rightly preached and the sacraments rightly administered, there is the kingdom of God. Amillennialists believe the question is answered by Christ's remarks concerning the heavenly, spiritual character of the kingdom which spreads by the peace and blessing of being reconciled to God (i.e., the gospel).

History has often influenced the dominance of one position over the others. For instance, when the early church was suffering tremendous persecution and difficulty, premillennialism dominated (though not the dispensational form). When Constantine declared Christianity the state religion in the fourth century, amillennialism and postmillennialism shared the spotlight, as premillennialism was reduced to a "superstition" by a church council. In our own time, the optimism of a nineteenth-century society that saw itself progressing toward world peace and prosperity maintained the dominance, since colonial times, of postmillennialism. As the "gay 90s" gave way to the First World War, Americans, stunned by the savage brutality of the war, became pessimistic. It was in this climate that premillennialism gained dominance, in evangelical circles, at least, for the first time since at least the fourth century A.D.

For the children of the Reformation, end-times speculation is, at best, a waste of time; at the very worst it is an inordinate preoccupation that further obscures Christ and replaces the gospel's emphasis on union with Christ and justification with an obsessive concern over the time and details of a rapture the Bible does not even mention.

But notice, I said end-times *speculation,* not end-times *truth.* After all, with believing Christians of twenty centuries, I "look for the resurrection of the dead and the life of the world to come" (Apostles' Creed). But that is all the creed says on the subject. To deny the second coming of Christ *is* indeed heretical (2 Tim. 1:17–19; 1 Cor. 15, etc.). Nevertheless, charity must allow variance over the hows and whens of his coming.

The heirs of the Reformation have held all three positions on the millennium. Nevertheless, dispensationalism cannot be reconciled with a tradition which emphasizes the sovereignty of God and the *progress* of redemption. Let me explain what I mean.

Leading dispensationalist Lewis Sperry Chafer wrote that even the "dispensation of grace" is a failure: "Under grace, however, failure also was evident as grace produced neither worldwide acceptance of Christ nor a triumphant church."[2] Furthermore, even when the millennium does arrive, says Chafer, "The kingdom will also be a period of failure."[3] According to dispensationalism, Christ offered the Jews the kingdom and they rejected it. It is as though our Lord had to scramble for an alternative and decided to create a church in the meantime, while he was preparing himself for a second try with Israel. This is not a caricature; it's the language dispensationalists themselves use. God's plan is not the progressive unfolding of redemptive history, but the cycles of attempt and failure.

Even the Old Testament sacrifices will be revived in this kingdom, according to many dispensationalists. "There is no solid reason," wrote Chafer, "for not accepting both the temple and the sacrificial system as literal prophecy."[4] Chafer defended this statement against charges of blasphemy by arguing that the character of such sacrifices would be memorial, looking back to the cross. Nevertheless, the entire book of Hebrews labors the point that the sacrifices were ended when the perfect sacrifice came. That whole epistle was designed to teach the suffering believers that Jeremiah's prophecy of a new covenant and a new kingdom (Jer. 31, quoted in Heb. 8:8–13) is fulfilled in the church, not in a future restoration of the nation of Israel. "The point of what we are saying is this: We do have such a high priest, who sat down at the right hand of the throne of the Majesty *in heaven,* and who serves in the sanctuary, the *true* tabernacle set up by the Lord, not by man" (Heb. 8:1–2, italics added). The kingdom is eternal; the tabernacle is heavenly; the sacrifice is complete. This is the recurring theme of Hebrews.

The Church and Israel

God himself takes the promises he made to Old Testament Israel and applies them to the New Testament church. In Isaiah 43:20–21, God refers to the Hebrews as "my chosen, the people I formed for myself that they may proclaim my praise." In Exodus 19:5–6, God informed them, "Although the whole earth is mine, you will be for me a kingdom of priests and a holy nation." And then in 1 Peter 2:9, the Christians were told, "But you are a chosen people, a royal priesthood, a holy nation, a people belonging to God, that you may declare the praises of him who called you out of darkness into his wonderful light." Thus, the Old Testament reference was applied to New Testament believers, as the transfer from an earthly theocratic kingdom (the shadow of things to come) was replaced by the heavenly reign of Christ in his body, the church. Lest we think that Peter, in this text, was referring to Jewish believers who shared the designation of Exodus 19:6 by virtue of their nationality, the apostle added, "Once you were not a people, but now you are the people of God; once you had not received mercy, but now you have received mercy." Who could be his reference but Gentiles as well as Jews?

In his discussion of the identity of the "true Israel," St. Paul quoted Hosea 1:10 and 2:23 in reference to those whom God called "not only from the Jews but also from the Gentiles": "I will call them 'my people' who are not my people; and I will call her 'my loved one,' who is not my loved one." . . . "It will happen that in the very place where it was said to them, 'You are not my people,' they will be called 'sons of the living God'" (Rom. 9:24–26).

There was no discussion of the church as a "Plan B" group, or as an intermission between the Jewish rejection and acceptance of the kingdom. The church *is* the kingdom! Believers *are* the new people of God, taken "from every tribe and language and people and nation" to be made "a kingdom and priests to serve our God" (Rev. 5:9–10). After reminding the Galatians that "There is neither Jew nor Greek" and that "if you belong to Christ, then you are Abraham's seed, and heirs according to the promise" (Gal. 3:28–29), the apostle Paul referred to the church as "the Israel of God" (Gal. 6:16). It seems clear from these passages, and many more like them, that Christians are the true descendants of Abraham; that they form the true Israel, a new nation, as the rightful heirs of the promises God made to Abraham concerning Israel. God does not take notice of one's nationality; his kingdom is universal wherever his gospel has spread. "A man is not a Jew if he is only one outwardly, nor is circumcision merely outward and physical," wrote the apostle to the Gentiles. Do Jews have a special place in God's economy, apart from that of the church? "No, a man is a Jew if he is one inwardly; and circumcision is circumcision of the heart, by the Spirit, not by the written code" (Rom. 2:28–29).

The Nature of the Kingdom

Like Camelot, the kingdom of God is at once sought in the form of castles, knights in shining armor, and the implementation of universal peace, order, justice, and tranquillity. After all, Isaiah did prophesy of the Messiah that "the government will be on his shoulders. And he will be called Wonderful Counselor, Mighty God, Everlasting Father, Prince of Peace. Of the increase of his government and peace there will be no end." Further, "He will reign on David's throne and over his kingdom, establishing and upholding it with justice and righteousness from that time on and forever. The zeal of the LORD Almighty will accomplish this" (Isa. 9:6–7). But does this speak of a geopolitical, earthly millennial reign? And does this kingdom come all at once, or successively? Notice that there is an "*increase* of his government." It is not as though his government comes all at once, but that it progressively stretches its boundaries to the ends of the earth.

In order to understand the nature of the kingdom of God in the present context, we have to understand its nature in the past. The Bible, from Genesis to Revelation, is a story of successive theocracies (literally, "God-reigns").

In Eden, God reigned, symbolized by the tree of life in the middle of the garden. Placed over creation as viceroy, Adam was to ensure that every earthly activity served to bring praise and glory to God. The Old Testament scholar Meredith Kline has distinguished throughout these theocracies the union of cult (worship) and culture (worldly activity). God ruled Eden through Adam's kingship in such a way that all human activities served under the general heading of "worship." In other words, Eden was *literally* a "heaven on earth." Everything was ruled by miracle. It was heaven in miniature. When Adam sinned, however, the unity of worship and culture was dissolved. The kingdom was taken back up into the heavenlies, and humans could only worship God and hope for salvation through types and shadows, promises for a future time. By trusting God's Word that such a time would come when the kingdom would return and its King would grant pardons and set everything right between believers and God, Adam and Eve were saved.

Much later in world history, God decided to destroy a world that had become filled with rebellion and evil. He selected a man named Noah to build an ark from which a "new creation" would emerge. A remnant from each living creature was carried on the waters of divine wrath inside this miniature theocracy, Noah's ark. Here again, God led his people through a king and by miracle. He judged righteously as the wicked were destroyed and the righteous delivered.

When God called Abraham and promised him that he would be "the father of many nations," a new kingdom was born. Israel became the theocracy. A tabernacle was set up and, later, a temple was built. The temple wasn't Eden, but it wasn't an obnoxious-smelling ark either. It was a glorious accomplishment. Once again, cult (worship) and culture (human activity) merged, and God ruled directly by miracle. The people of God had been delivered by water again, as the Red Sea had parted for them and collapsed to engulf the enemies of God's people. They had been fed miraculously in the wilderness and had been led by the cloud during the day, and by the pillar of fire at night. The kingdom was among them. They had access to God through the high priest.

Eventually, God established a king. David became the center of Jewish royal history, and the type or shadow of the coming King, uniting cult and culture in his offices as priest and king. God not only commanded Israel through David concerning issues of salvation, prayer, liturgy, and "spiritual" matters, but dictated every facet of cultural, civic, social, political, and business life.

In each of those theocracies there was a temple, a prophet, a priest, and a king, and there were sacrifices. Eden was God's first theocratic temple; Noah's ark became the second; Solomon's temple dominated the Old Testament. As for the offices of prophet, priest, and king, one viceroy normally shared all three offices in the theocracy. As for sacrifices, God himself sacrificed an animal to provide fallen Adam and Eve with skins to cover their nakedness (Gen. 3:21) and promised a final sacrifice for sins, of which this animal sacrifice was merely a type (3:15). After the flood, Noah "built an altar to the LORD and, taking some of all the clean animals and clean birds, he sacrificed burnt offerings on it" (Gen. 8:20). Sacrifices were at the center of the Abrahamic and Davidic theocracies. And all theocracies were directed by miracle. God was speaking, revealing, saving, and showing.

But something changed on that solemn night in Nazareth, when a Jewish virgin conceived God incarnate by the Holy Spirit. The One prefigured by the past prophets, priests, and kings arrived when the fullness of time had come. His theocracy once again ushered in a new stage of miracles, revelations, and redemptive acts. Once again, God brought heaven to earth in the person of Christ and the presence of his kingdom. "The Word became flesh and made his dwelling [literally, pitched his tent] among us," St. John announced (John 1:14), drawing from the imagery of the tabernacle in the wilderness. As we learned from earlier chapters, Jesus Christ himself was the new temple, which exceeded the splendor of Solomon's at its zenith.

Since the presence of the miraculous was tied to the theocracy, our Lord announced, "But if I drive out demons by the Spirit of God, then the kingdom of God has come upon you" (Matt. 12:28). Since he was, in fact, driving out demons by the Spirit of God, it is apparent that the kingdom of God came when Christ appeared the first time. Nevertheless, upon his ascension, the kingdom was to advance as a heavenly, not earthly, theocracy, in an age marked by providence rather than miracle. Heaven is not on earth because Christ is in heaven, but Christ's kingdom is spiritually present as the gospel is believed around the world. Rather than being literally led through the Red Sea or through the flood in an ark, we are led through the waters of judgment.

Christ himself is the temple, but he is also the prophet. He *is* the announcement, the Word of God incarnate. "No one has ever seen God, but God the One and Only, who is at the Father's side, has made him known" (John 1:18). He is our priest, mediating between a holy God and sinful humans. He is our king, reigning in glory from the heavenlies. According to Hebrews, Christ was ascended, and "*Since that time* he waits for his enemies to be made his footstool, because by one sacrifice he has made perfect forever those who are being made holy" (Heb.

10:13–14, italics added). Notice that he has been reigning and his kingdom progressively conquering and that this making footstools out of his enemies is achieved by his sacrifice on the cross, turning enemies into friends. It is not a political or social agenda, although the implications for public faith are numerous. Finally, Christ is the sacrifice. He is the temple, the prophet, the priest, and the king, and he himself is our Passover Lamb, sacrificed for our sins. He supplies the chief form of mediation, sacrificing the only offering that is entirely spotless and without blemish, prefigured by the offering of "clean" animals.

This interpretation of biblical history is Christ-centered rather than end-times-centered. It is more concerned with comprehending the breadth and depth of redemptive history than predicting, calculating, and speculating on the evening news. It takes into account the realization that our generation is not the center of history, but part of a long and progressive unfolding of God's purpose for this world.

Practical Benefits

Whether of the historic premillennial, amillennial, or postmillennial variety, Reformation Christians have always been optimistic about the future because of God's sovereignty. Yet they are realistic because of their serious view of sin as a condition which, like a giant octopus, grips the world in its tentacles, eluding human attempts to chop the tentacles off one by one. Octopi just grow new arms, and sin simply finds another avenue of expression. This is why moral, political, or social solutions will always fall short. That does not mean we should not attempt them, but that we should not confuse the establishment of the kingdom with the legislation of our agenda.

The Reformation tradition stands in contrast both to dispensational "otherworldliness" on one end and triumphalistic views of "Christian politics" on the other. Chafer asserts that dispensationalism will save the believer "from undertaking the impossible world transforming program belonging to the dispensation which is to come."[5] This has had a crippling effect on the evangelical social witness in our century.

During the nineteenth century, when postmillennialism reigned, and to a lesser extent, amillennialism, conservative, Bible-believing evangelicals had a tremendous sense of responsibility for the social evils of their time. It was these evangelicals who protested slavery and actually launched the women's suffrage movement. The evangelical revival in England was largely responsible for new child labor legislation. Benjamin B. Warfield, the Princeton theologian who coined the term *inerrancy* and articulated a defense for Scripture which has yet to be answered, was a champion of the integration of the emancipated slaves and an early member of the Audubon Society.

While dispensationalism encourages some of its adherents to throw up their hands and give up trying to "polish the brass on the Titanic," some zealous postmillennialists in our day are in danger of turning the law into gospel and confusing salvation and earthly utopia. "Man is summoned to create the society God requires," according to R. J. Rushdoony.[6] Gary North adds that God is "waiting for His people to challenge the rulers of the earth, and take the steering wheel from them. . . . the battle for the earth is currently going on."[7] But this seems to fly in the face of what has already been demonstrated against a dispensational interpretation of the kingdom as geopolitical. "My kingdom is not of this world" (John 18:36). The kingdom's struggle is a battle for believers, for people who will worship in Spirit and in truth (John 4:23). It is not a battle for control, but for conversion. It is not a battle for dominion, but for reaching a lost, guilt-ridden, self-destructive generation with the gospel and for reconciling sinners to God.

Obviously the gospel has wide implications. Once we are justified before God, justice takes on a different light. Once we are forgiven by a God who had every right to condemn us, mercy comes into sharper focus. We begin to see our Christian calling as the command "To act justly and to love mercy and to walk humbly with your God" (Mic. 6:8). Once we begin to realize that this is our Father's world and that we are part of the problem, we should wake up to the fact that we have responsibilities to our neighbors. The Ten Commandments (generally rejected by strict dispensationalists as having no New Testament application) show us our duty to God and to our neighbors, and those in the Reformation tradition have had a profound sense of this duty. Christian social responsibility, for Calvin especially, was neither escape nor dominion, but godly influence: reformation, not reconstruction.

Furthermore, theology for the Reformers was never allowed to be reduced to ideology. This is amply demonstrated in their responses to both left-wing and right-wing political fanaticism during the Reformation. Against those who insisted that Christians ought to be separated from the world and give up on social improvement, The Geneva Confession of 1536 declared, "Since in performing their office they serve God and follow a Christian vocation, whether in defending the afflicted and innocent, or in correcting and punishing the malice of the perverse . . . we ought to regard [civil officials] as vicars and lieutenants of God."[8] This was both in opposition to the church-controlled state known to medieval Christendom and to a rejection of involvement in worldly affairs, characteristic of most Anabaptists of the period.

The Anabaptists, ancestors of the Mennonite and Amish communities, declared in the Schleitheim Confession of 1527, "Since all who do not walk in the obedience of faith . . . are a great abomination before God, it is not possible for anything to grow or issue from them except abominable things. . . . He [God] further admonishes us to withdraw from Babylon and the earthly Egypt that we may not be partakers of the pain and suffering which the Lord will bring upon them."[9] And yet, one radical Anabaptist sect led by Thomas Münzer toppled a city in Germany, turning it into a communist, polygamous, and violent state. Unwilling to stop at anything short of a full-scale city of God on earth, the Münzerite Anabaptists turned to civil disobedience and revolution instead of withdrawing like other Anabaptist groups had. The Reformation steered a calmer course through both elements within the radical Reformation and rewarded our own modern age with advances toward democracy, toleration, and human rights, notwithstanding setbacks and self-contradictions.

Because we are a kingdom of priests, we have a duty to demonstrate visibly and tangibly the *fruit* of faith in the form of good works. And good works, for the Reformation's heirs are not private, navel-gazing exercises. They actually serve some useful purpose for others. In a number of ways, we are sent out as ambassadors of Christ's kingdom, and this must shape our reflection on every activity. The connection between the kingdom of God, therefore, and the kingdoms of this world is the connection between faith and the gospel, on one hand, and good works, on the other. Although we are "simultaneously justified and sinful," as Luther put it, we are new creatures in Christ and are "created in Christ Jesus to do good works" (Eph. 2:10). Similarly, although we will never create a *perfect* society, we should not shrink from helping create a *better* one. This does not mean we all have to be more active in politics, but that we begin to see our daily callings as parents, children, employers, employees, neighbors, and friends as the sphere of "good works."

The Priesthood of All Believers

In the medieval church, the Sacrament of Holy Orders entered those who were really "sold out" for the Lord into "full-time Christian ministry." Christians were separated into "secular" and "religious" callings, as though those who decided to work for the church or Christian ministries were somehow more spiritual than those who engaged in "worldly" vocations. Luther recorded, "Whoever looked at a monk fairly drooled in devotion and had to be ashamed of his secular station in life."[10] To be sure, not all believers are *ministers;* God has called some to hold offices in his church. However, those who are not are no less committed to God in their secular vocations.

Against this "sacrament," the Reformers launched their biblical notion known to us as "the priesthood of all believers." This doctrine insists that the milkmaid has as God-honoring a calling and contributes as much as any priest, though in a different way. One need not be a monk (i.e., an employee of a Christian organization). Christians ought to be involved with the world, as salt and light. "For the right faith," urged Luther, "does not make people give up their calling and begin a 'spiritual' one, like the monks do. They imagined that they were not truly Christian unless they appeared different outwardly from other people."[11] Each Christian, whatever his or her calling, serves God, and that person's calling—whether making shoes, practicing law, dressing wounds, caring for children, or plowing the fields—is a ministry to the community on God's behalf. What a revolutionary idea! It can be again. If even a pagan ruler can be described as ministering on God's behalf (Rom. 13:4), surely believers can see their secular work as fulfilling an important task in God's world.

The Reformation produced great artists who were liberated from the almost exclusively religious themes commissioned by the church. The only way a medieval artist could feed himself was to secure an ecclesiastical commission to paint an altarpiece or to sculpt a religious statue. Of course, there were exceptions—for instance, the tombs of wealthy clergymen or nobles. But the Reformation shifted the emphasis from the church to the world. Zurich's Reformer, Ulrich Zwingli, took music out of the church entirely and, himself a musician, founded that city's symphony. Others, like Luther, retained music in the church, but insisted on congregational participation. Bach's chief ambition was to represent the Reformation in music both in secular as well as in church scores. In fact, he signed *all* of his compositions (secular and religious) with the Reformation slogan, *Soli Deo Gloria,* "To God Alone Be Glory." Rembrandt, the Dutch master, brought the reality of this world to the canvas. Medieval artists consistently depicted the light in a scene emanating from heavenly rays or from the halos of the biblical heroes and saints. But for Rembrandt, and for many of the Protestant painters, there was natural light. For instance, in medieval paintings of the Nativity, the source of the light was Christ and the holy family; in Protestant baroque art, the source of light was more often a beam of light coming in through the window from the sun or moon. These subtle differences marked a shift in the way people looked at the world and their place in it.

There was a tremendous sense among the Reformation's adherents that *this* world is terribly important too. To be sure, heaven is the believer's ultimate hope, but it is in *this* world where God has chosen to reveal, act, redeem, and restore. As one hymn puts it, "This is my Father's world."

Where are today's Bachs, Handels, Miltons, Rembrandts, Dürers, Cranachs, Herberts, and Donnes? Some of them might be found working two or three jobs to put food on the table. Others have been intimidated by well-meaning but ill-informed brothers and sisters who are convinced that unless artists are producing something useful for the church (i.e., an evangelistic tract, shirt, or bumper sticker or a church bulletin), art is a waste of God's time. Once again, the "full-time Christian ministry" thing, which the Reformers knew as "monkery," is the criterion for determining the legitimacy of a Christian's work. Painting, singing, playing an instrument, composing, writing, directing, acting, sculpting—these activities are callings which require no evangelistic justification. All God requires of a Christian is the very best, most creative, and profound work he or she can produce. The response of one young man in a study of the evangelical subculture by Randall Balmer captured the new monasticism. This man gave up his calling to make films for what he was convinced were godly reasons:

> I said, "Lord, all I want to do is what You want me to do. If you want me to make church movies for the rest of my life, then praise God, hallelujah, I'll make church films. I just want to do what You want me to do. I don't want to make theatricals if You don't want me to." The time came when I had to make a decision, so I got down on my knees. In the end, it wasn't difficult. All I had to do was choose God first, and the rest would fall into line. I told them, No, I wouldn't do it.[12]

In the church I used to pastor, we had a member who had trained some of Hollywood's leading actors and directed the graduate drama studies at Yale and Stanford. When he came to southern California to an evangelical college, he had a dream to help Christians fulfill their callings. But he soon learned that, unlike the serious students he was used to, many of his students now were bent on using drama in church or in evangelistic ministries. For many, the thought of actually going into Hollywood and acting on a "secular" stage wasn't even a passing fancy. My friend was hounded for doing "worldly" plays, until, eventually, he realized the dream was not to be, at least not yet, not here.

Of course, liberating the laity with this "priesthood of all believers" includes all callings. The band Loverboy, mentioned earlier, sings about "working for the weekend." Too many Christians work for the weekend; in fact, I know many who feel guilty if they don't do some volunteer "Christian work" on the side. But Christians are called by God to work for the *week!* The Reformation is credited with the Protestant work ethic, sometimes called the Puritan work ethic. You see, if you are a *priest*—not only on Sunday, but throughout the week, and not only in the church, but at work or at home—what you do during the week is not a job, but a *calling*. This term, *calling*, appears again and again in the Reformers' writings. Calvin wrote, "The Lord bids each one of us in all life's actions to look to his calling." This is necessary, he says, because we are fickle and require a steady vocation. We ought not to transgress our calling, he says, and meddle where we have neither the calling nor the expertise:

> Each will bear and swallow the discomforts, vexations, weariness, and anxieties in his way of life when he has been persuaded that the burden was laid upon him by God. From this will arise also an impressive consolation: that no task will be so sordid and base, provided you obey your calling in it, that it will not shine and be reckoned very precious in God's sight.[13]

Luther argued that God is more impressed with the milkmaid, milking her cow to the glory of God, than with all the lavish and pious exercises of the monks.

Unfortunately, Christians don't have the best reputation in some circles of employment. My dad, himself a devout Christian, used to say he would prefer to hire a non-Christian or to take his car to a non-Christian mechanic because of past experiences with believers who did not take their work in *this* world very seriously. In my area, we have the *Christian Yellow Pages,* a phone book with ads for Christians in business; I remember overhearing a businessman at church one day cynically remarking to his wife, "Honey, grab one of those; I've got to see who I *won't* do business with." What a tragedy! There are horror stories of employers who want to strangle Christian employees who read the Bible, pray, or evangelize on company time. And sometimes these brothers and sisters don't even put their effort and energy into the job when they *are* working. The Protestant work ethic has deteriorated even in Christian circles, it seems. But God expects Christians to think hard, to work hard, and to play hard during the breaks he has provided for our refreshment.

When Christians begin to see that it is as godly to be a businessperson, lawyer, homemaker, artist, garbage collector, doctor, or construction worker, as it is to be a missionary, evangelist, pastor, youth leader, or employee of a Christian organization, they will once again become salt and light. Once a young Christian woman realizes it is just as spiritual to sing for the Metropolitan Opera as it is to sing in the church choir, we will begin to see a new generation of liberated Christians calling attention to their Maker and Redeemer.

The doctrines of the Reformation produced leadership in the arts, in education (Harvard, Dartmouth, Yale, Brown, Rutgers, and Princeton were founded by Reformed believers), in industry, and in the crafting of democratic states. When all believers become priests once again, we will see the end of full-time Christian ministry as a separate and superior calling.

Our Blessed Hope

Our being "a kingdom of priests" has profound implications for our lives here and now. But it also shapes our future hope.

The Apostles' Creed ends with the line, "And I believe in the resurrection of the dead, and the life of the world to come." Here all Christians agree: Christ is coming back! Nevertheless, there is a question raised by some believers today that has never been raised until this century: Are we looking forward to a rapture or to the Second Coming? And if we are awaiting *two* comings, why don't we speak of Christ's coming in judgment as the *third* coming? Dispensationalism argues that there are essentially two future returns of Christ: the first, his coming "*for* the saints"; the second, "*with* the saints." The first coming, then, is the rapture of the church before the tribulation.

But does the Bible teach us to look for a rapture? The text dispensationalists turn to for support is 1 Thessalonians 4:16–17: "For the Lord himself will come down from heaven, with a loud command, with the voice of the archangel and with the trumpet call of God, and the dead in Christ will rise first. After that, we who are still alive and are left will be caught up together with them in the clouds to meet the Lord in the air." But is there a rapture in this text? It appears, at least on the surface, to be a simple reference to the Second Coming. For instance, dispensationalism maintains that the rapture is Christ's return *for* his saints, but verse 14 of this text reads, "We believe that Jesus died and rose again and so we believe that God *will bring with Jesus those who have fallen asleep in him*" (italics added). This, however, is the description usually given for what dispensationalists consider Christ's "third coming" *with* his saints. Further, in the verses immediately following the text, the apostle indicates to the Thessalonians that he has just been talking about "the day of the Lord," which, in both testaments, always refers to Christ's coming in judgment, not to a rapture.

If Reformation Christians are not looking for a rapture, what do they anxiously anticipate? The answer is, with the Apostles' Creed, "the resurrection of the body and the life of the world to come." Instead of being preoccupied with guesses about the Antichrist and end-time curiosities, Christians ought to find in the hope of the resurrection a feast of delight.

The doctrine of the resurrection was especially important to the early church. The apostle Paul made it clear that our resurrection depends entirely on Christ's (1 Cor. 15), since we are members of his body. One of the most destructive heresies of the period was known as *gnosticism,* which drew a sharp contrast between matter and spirit, the realm of darkness and the realm of light. All that was natural, human, and material was considered evil; the spirit was the only thing that mattered. Therefore, the incarnation was denied. How could God become flesh if flesh is inherently evil? Jesus, they insisted, only *appeared* to have a physical body. Thus, the resurrection was also denied. After all, the goal of salvation, for the gnostics, was the spirit's release from the "prison-house" of the body, not being saddled with a body for eternity!

Much in the New Testament epistles forms a defense against this type of thinking. In the Bible, the body was created by God and was an inseparable aspect of what made us human. We don't just *have* a body; we *are* bodily. Therefore, when the body and soul are separated at death, due to the fall, a profoundly sad and disruptive thing takes place. It is not good to be separated from one's body—that's part of what makes us who we are. But the good news is that the body will be reunited in all of its perfection and splendor one day. And it will be a real body—the same body we had, but perfect in splendor and function. Job contented himself with the vision, that, "Though . . . worms destroy this body, yet *in my flesh* shall I see God" (Job 19:26 KJV, italics added).

Gnostic tendencies can be seen in contemporary attitudes toward the body within the church. Sexual organs, which God created and included in his pronouncement, "good," we call "naughty parts." Pleasure or sensual enjoyment is suspect in some Christian circles. "We ought not to take part in the world" is a sentiment with which the gnostics would have fully agreed. But it is an attitude foreign to the earthly orientation of Scripture. Many of us can probably remember funerals where the mourners were told something like, "Eunice is finally free of her body, and her spirit is able to worship God without hindrance." But, however tremendous it is to be with the Lord, the separation of the soul from the body, even for a time, is not a cause for celebration.

Mysticism often bends toward the gnostic error, as though there were a good realm of the spirit and an evil realm of the body. But God created the body. And not only that, "In Christ all the fullness of the Deity lives in bodily form" (Col. 2:9); he rose again *physically* from the dead and ascended *in his resurrected flesh* to the right hand of the Father, and he is going to restore our bodies at the resurrection.

The resurrection was a favorite subject among the Puritans, who not only took *this* world seriously, but did so because they looked forward to the next. Thomas Watson is a case in point:

> Not in another flesh, but in my flesh shall I be resurrected. Some hold that the soul shall be clothed with a new body; but then it would be improper to call it a resurrection. Rather, it would be a creation. If the body did not rise again, a believer would not be completely happy; for, though the soul can subsist without the body, yet it has a desire of reunion with the body. If the soul should go to heaven, and not the body, then a believer would be only half saved.[14]

The Puritans insisted that the body and soul together were redeemed and that it would be unjust for God to bar from heaven the body that worshiped him, while allowing the soul entrance:

"They have served God with their bodies; their bodies have been members of holiness; their eyes have dropped tears for sin; their hands have relieved the poor; their tongues have set forth God's praise; therefore justice and equity require that their bodies should be crowned as well as their souls."[15]

The effects of this are, of course, far from limited to the next world. This future hope spurs us on in this life, as we realize that we are living right now in the presence of God as members of Christ's body. It makes sense of the commands in Scripture to "offer yourselves to God, as those who have been brought from death to life; and offer the parts of your body to him as instruments of righteousness" (Rom. 6:13). Since our bodies will share in that glorious resurrection, we ought to conduct them now in a godly manner. There is another effect. If we really believe that God cares about the whole person—not just his or her soul—evangelism will require its corollaries: justice and mercy. We cannot disregard the physical plight of our neighbors, caring only to save their souls. Of course, there is a priority of evangelism, since the death of the body is a foregone conclusion for believers and unbelievers alike. Ultimately, those who believe the gospel will inherit the resurrection, but they, too, will die when they grow old. Nevertheless, since the body will be raised, it is God's goal to encompass the care of body and soul together. That should lead us to include both concerns in our vision for outreach.

Jesus is coming again! That is no sentimental, wishful announcement for the religiously inclined. It will be as much a fact of history one day as his first coming is now. For centuries, the first coming of Christ was prophesied until that moment in Bethlehem. In nearly two thousand years, the most hostile critics have never been able to discredit the historicity of Christ and the fact of his resurrection. Absurd alternatives have been offered, but the evidence still rests on the side of Scripture. If the case is strong that two thousand years of biblical history *preceding* Christ were fulfilled in real time and space, the odds are fairly certain of the promise of a Second Coming being fulfilled. And to that, children of the Reformation join their voices with the chorus of all ages, chanting, "Even so, Lord Jesus, come quickly!"

Study Questions

1. What is the *nature* of Christ's kingdom? (See Luke 17:20–21; 22:29–30; John 18:36–37.)
2. Explain the different eschatological (end-times) positions: premillennialism, postmillennialism, amillennialism.
3. Consider the biblical arguments for each position.
4. What role does world history play in the dominance of a particular eschatology?
5. Explain the relationship between Israel and the church. (See Exod. 19:6; Isa. 43:21; Hosea 1:10; 2:23; Rom. 2:28–29; Rom. 9:24–26; Gal. 3:26–29; 1 Peter 2:9; Rev. 5:9; 6:16.)
6. Discuss the history of God's kingdom in this world. What do each of the theocracies (Eden, Noah's ark, Israel, the church) have in common? What do they *not* have in common?
7. Explain the "priesthood of all believers." What did the Reformers mean by this? Discuss the implications for work, creativity, enjoyment of the world, and duty to our neighbors.

Appendix

Theologian Donald Bloesch has said, "It's time for less dialogue, and more monologue—with God doing the talking!" When discussing doctrinal themes, many people say, "It's just too confusing; it isn't really clear in Scripture." But the confusion seems to be more appropriately charged to the account of the theological rhetoricians on both sides of the debate than to the Scriptures.

God has offered comment—at length—on the subjects we have raised in this book. To substantiate this, I now invite you to study closely a selection of passages related to the human condition, election, particular redemption, the new birth, and security. Though the listing is incomplete, no doubt you will be surprised to discover some new scriptural insights!

Not only does Scripture speak definitively in proclaiming God's electing grace; the historic, catholic, apostolic church affirms these truths as the truly orthodox position of the church of Jesus Christ. To substantiate this claim, I have also prepared an abbreviated historical sketch from church fathers to the present, including church creeds, that clearly affirms the doctrines of grace.

Let us join hands with the saints of the past and move into the future with God's Word and God's message for the present time.

The Witness of Scripture

Adam, the prototype of ourselves, representing our race before God was warned of the fatal consequences of eating from the tree of the knowledge of good and evil:

Genesis 2:17: "for when you eat of it you will surely die."

Because Adam chose disobedience and independence from God's restraints, he and our entire race experienced spiritual suicide. Hence, every person at birth is separated from God, without hope and with no potential within grasp of believing the gospel or of loving God truly.

Job 15:14: "What is man, that he could be pure, or one born of woman, that he could be righteous?"

Psalm 51:5: "Surely I was sinful at birth, sinful from the time my mother conceived me."

Psalm 58:3: "Even from birth the wicked go astray; from the womb they are wayward and speak lies."

Psalm 130:3: "If you, O LORD, kept a record of sins, O LORD, who could stand?"

Proverbs 20:9: "Who can say, 'I have kept my heart pure; I am clean and without sin'?"

Ecclesiastes 7:20: "There is not a righteous man on earth who does what is right and never sins."

Ecclesiastes 7:29: "This only have I found: God made mankind upright, but men have gone in search of many schemes."

Ecclesiastes 9:3: "The hearts of men, moreover, are full of evil and there is madness in their hearts while they live."

Isaiah 53:6: "We all, like sheep, have gone astray, each of us has turned to his own way."

Isaiah 64:6: "All of us have become like one who is unclean, and all our righteous acts are like filthy rags."

Jeremiah 17:9: "The heart is deceitful above all things and beyond cure. Who can understand it?"

Mark 7:21–23: "For from within, out of men's hearts, come evil thoughts, sexual immorality, theft, murder, adultery, greed, malice, deceit, lewdness, envy, slander, arrogance and folly. All these evils come from inside and make a man unclean."

John 3:19: "Men loved darkness instead of light."

John 8:34: "Jesus replied, 'I tell you the truth, everyone who sins is a slave to sin.'"

John 8:44: "You belong to your father, the devil, and you want to carry out your father's desire."

Romans 3:9–12: "What shall we conclude then? Are we any better? Not at all! We have already made the charge that Jews and Gentiles alike are all under sin. As it is written:

'There is no one righteous, not even one;

there is no one who understands,

no one who seeks God.

All have turned away,

they have together become worthless;

there is no one who does good, not even one.'"

Romans 5:12: "Therefore, just as sin entered the world through one man, and death through sin, and in this way death came to all men, because all sinned."

Romans 6:20: "You were slaves to sin."

Romans 8:7–8: "The sinful mind is hostile to God. It does not submit to God's law, nor can it do so. Those controlled by the sinful nature cannot please God."

1 Corinthians 2:14: "The man without the Spirit does not accept the things that come from the Spirit of God, for they are foolishness to him, and he cannot understand them, because they are spiritually discerned."

Ephesians 2:1–3: "You were dead in your trangressions and sins, in which you used to live when you followed the ways of this world and of the ruler of the kingdom of the air, the spirit who is now at work in those who are disobedient. All of us also lived among them at one time, gratifying the cravings of our sinful nature and following its desires and thoughts. Like the rest, we were by nature objects of wrath."

Clearly, our condition is so desperate that we can do nothing about it under our own power.

Job 14:4: "Who can bring what is pure from the impure? No one!"

Jeremiah 13:23: "Can the Ethiopian change his skin or the leopard its spots? Neither can you do good who are accustomed to doing evil."

Matthew 7:18: "And a bad tree cannot bear good fruit."

John 6:44: "No one can come to me unless the Father who sent me draws him, and I will raise him up at the last day."

2 Corinthians 3:5: "Not that we are competent in ourselves to claim anything for ourselves, but our competence comes from God."

Because of the shocking reality of human impotence, the initiative rests with God. We wait in the dark silence to hear God speak and deliver his decision. We expect nothing from God's hand but wrath and eternal hatred. But we are surprised that instead God decides (in fact, decided from all eternity) to act in mercy and compassion by selecting a large number of people from every walk, every nation and tribe, every ethnic and racial background to form a new race, establishing the Son as the new head, the second Adam, of this kingdom.

Psalm 33:12: "Blessed is . . . the people he chose for his inheritance."

Psalm 65:4: "Blessed are those you choose and bring near to live in your courts!"

Psalm 106:5: "that I may enjoy the prosperity of your chosen ones."

Matthew 22:14: "For many are invited, but few are chosen."

Matthew 24:22, 24, 31: "If those days had not been cut short, no one would survive, but for the sake of the elect those days will be shortened. . . . For false Christs and false prophets will appear and perform great signs and miracles to deceive even the elect—if that were possible. . . . And he will send his angels with a loud trumpet call, and they will gather his elect from the four winds."

Luke 18:7: "And will not God bring about justice for his chosen ones, who cry out to him day and night?"

Romans 8:28–30: "And we know that in all things God works for the good of those who love him, who have been called according to his purpose. For those God foreknew [those with whom he had a prior relationship], he also predestined to be conformed to the likeness of his Son, that he might be the firstborn among many brothers. And those he predestined, he also called; those he called, he also justified; those he justified, he also glorified."

Romans 8:33: "Who will bring any charge against those whom God has chosen?"

Romans 11:28: "As far as the gospel is concerned, they are enemies on your account; but as far as election is concerned, they are loved on account of the patriarchs."

Colossians 3:12: "Therefore, as God's chosen people, holy and dearly loved, clothe yourselves with compassion, kindness, humility, gentleness and patience."

1 Thessalonians 5:9: "For God did not appoint us to suffer wrath, but to receive salvation through our Lord Jesus Christ."

Titus 1:1: "Paul, a servant of God and an apostle of Jesus Christ for the faith of God's elect."

1 Peter 1:1–2: "To God's elect, strangers in the world, . . . who have been chosen according to the foreknowledge of God the Father, through the sanctifying work of the Spirit, for obedience to Jesus Christ and sprinkling by his blood."

1 Peter 2:8–9: "They stumble because they disobey the message—which is also what they were destined for. But you are a chosen people."

Revelation 17:14: "and with him will be his called, chosen, and faithful followers."

God's choice is not based on anything in us—not even our decision to accept the gospel. After all, we accept the gospel only because God has accepted us in Christ through election. So our salvation is based on a decision God made in eternity past, without respect to our personal choices or actions. Hence, salvation is by grace alone.

Exodus 33:19 (and Rom. 9:15): "I will have mercy on whom I will have mercy, and I will have compassion on whom I will have compassion."

Matthew 20:15: "Don't I have the right to do what I want with my own money?"

John 15:16: "You did not choose me, but I chose you and appointed you to go and bear fruit—fruit that will last."

Acts 13:48: "and all who were appointed for eternal life believed."

Romans 9:11–13, 16: "Yet before the twins [Jacob and Esau] were born or had done anything good or bad—in order that God's purpose in election might stand: not by works but by him who calls—she [Rebekah] was told, 'The older will serve the younger.' Just as it is written: 'Jacob I loved, but Esau I hated.' . . . It does not, therefore, depend on man's desire or effort, but on God's mercy."

Romans 9:20–21, 23: "But who are you, O man, to talk back to God? 'Shall what is formed say to him who formed it, "Why did you make me like this?"' Does not the potter have the right to make out of the same lump of clay some pottery for noble purposes and some for common use? . . . What if he did this to make the riches of his glory known to the objects of his mercy, whom he prepared in advance for glory."

Romans 11:5–6: "So too, at the present time there is a remnant chosen by grace. And if by grace, then it is no longer by works; if it were, grace would no longer be grace."

Romans 11:7: "What then? What Israel sought so earnestly it did not obtain, but the elect did. The others were hardened."

Romans 11:33–36: "Oh, the depth of the riches of the wisdom and knowledge of God! How unsearchable his judgments, and his paths beyond tracing out!

'Who has known the mind of the Lord?
Or who has been his counselor?'

'Who has ever given to God,
that God should repay him?'
For from him and through him and to him are all things.
To him be the glory forever! Amen."

1 Corinthians 1:27–29: "But God chose the foolish things
. . . God chose the weak things . . . the lowly things of this
world and the despised things . . . so that no one may boast
before him."

Ephesians 1:4–5, 11–12: "For he chose us in him before the
creation of the world to be holy and blameless in his sight.
In love, he predestined us to be adopted as his sons through
Jesus Christ, in accordance with his pleasure and will. . . .
In him we were also chosen, having been predestined
according to the plan of him who works out everything in
conformity with the purpose of his will, in order that we,
who were the first to hope in Christ, might be for the praise
of his glory."

1 Thessalonians 1:4–5: "For we know, brothers loved by God,
that he has chosen you, because our gospel came to you not
simply with words, but also with power, with the Holy Spirit
and with deep conviction."

2 Thessalonians 2:13: "from the beginning God chose you
to be saved through the sanctifying work of the Spirit and
through belief in the truth."

2 Timothy 2:10: "Therefore I endure everything for the sake
of the elect."

James 2:5: "Has not God chosen those who are poor in the
eyes of the world to be rich in faith and to inherit the kingdom he promised those who love him?"

2 Peter 1:10: "Therefore, my brothers, be all the more eager
to make your calling and election sure. For if you do these
things, you will never fall, and you will receive a rich welcome into the eternal kingdom of our Lord and Savior Jesus
Christ."

Revelation 13:8: "All inhabitants of the earth will worship the
beast—all whose names have not been written in the book
of life belonging to the Lamb that was slain from the creation of the world."

Having marked us out for an eternal relationship before the world was ever created, the Father placed us "in Christ." Christ, just before his crucifixion, prayed, "not . . . for the world, but for those you have given me, for they are yours" (John 17:9). The elect, fallen in sin, needed a Savior to satisfy the righteous demands of God's justice. Jesus died as a sacrifice for the eternal family of God, securing everything necessary for eternal life and redemption. Christ's saving work, freely offered to all, guaranteed the salvation of the elect, clearing them from every charge against them.

The following verses establish the atonement as a saving thing. Not only did Christ's work make salvation possible, nor is it merely the basis for redemption—it *is* redemption. And all for whom Christ died are or will eventually be saved.

Matthew 1:21: "and you are to give him the name Jesus, because he will save his people from their sins."

Romans 3:24: "and are justified freely by his grace through the redemption that came by Christ Jesus."

Romans 5:8–9: "But God demonstrates his own love for us in this: While we were still sinners, Christ died for us. Since we have now been justified by his blood, how much more shall we be saved from God's wrath through him!"

Romans 5:10: "For if, when we were God's enemies, we were reconciled to him through the death of his Son, how much more, having been reconciled, shall we be saved through his life!" [To be reconciled by Christ's death is to be, in fact, saved.]

Galatians 1:3–4: "Grace and peace to you from God our Father and the Lord Jesus Christ, who gave himself for our sins to rescue us from the present evil age, according to the will of our God and Father."

Galatians 3:13: "Christ redeemed us from the curse of the law."

Colossians 1:21–22: "once you were alienated from God and were enemies in your minds because of your evil behavior. But now he has reconciled you by Christ's physical body through death to present you holy in his sight, without blemish and free from accusation."

1 Timothy 1:15: "Christ Jesus came into the world to save sinners."

Titus 2:13–14: "while we wait for the blessed hope—the glorious appearing of our great God and Savior, Jesus Christ, who gave himself for us to redeem us from all wickedness and to purify for himself a people that are his very own, eager to do what is good."

Hebrews 9:12: "He did not enter by means of the blood of goats and calves; but he entered the Most Holy Place once for all by his own blood, having obtained eternal redemption."

1 Peter 3:18: "For Christ died for sins once and for all . . . to bring you to God."

The Bible states clearly that Christ came to earth with a mission that involved a particular number of people. He came to fulfill the contractual agreement made within the Trinity from all eternity. Given to the Son by the Father, the elect alone are purchased at the cross.

Matthew 20:28: "the Son of Man did not come to be served, but to serve, and to give his life as a ransom for many."

Matthew 26:28: "This is my blood of the covenant, which is poured out for many for the forgiveness of sins."

John 6:36–40: "But as I told you, you have seen me and still you do not believe. All that the Father gives me will come to me. . . . For I have come down from heaven not to do my will but to do the will of him who sent me. And this is the will of him who sent me, that I shall lose none of all that he has given me, but raise them up at the last day."

John 10:11, 14–15, 24–26: "'I am the good shepherd. The good shepherd lays down his life for the sheep. . . . I am the good shepherd; I know my sheep and my sheep know me—just as the Father knows me and I know the Father—and I lay down my life for the sheep.' . . . [The accusers said] 'If you are the Christ, tell us plainly.' Jesus answered, 'I did tell you, but you do not believe. . . . because you are not my sheep.'" [Christ gives his life for the sheep, of which these particular unbelievers are not.]

John 11:50–52: "'You do not realize that it is better for you that one man die for the people than that the whole nation perish.' He did not say this on his own, but as high priest that year he prophesied that Jesus would die for the Jewish nation, and not only for that nation but also for the scattered children of God, to bring them together and make them one."

John 17:1–2, 4, 9–11: "After Jesus said this, he looked toward heaven and prayed: 'Father, the time has come. Glorify your Son, that your Son may glorify you. For you granted him authority over all people that he might give eternal life to all those you have given him. . . . I have brought you glory on earth by completing the work you gave me to do. . . . I pray for them. I am not praying for the world, but for those you have given me, for they are yours. All I have is yours, and all you have is mine. And glory has come to me through them. I will remain in the world no longer but they are still in the world, and I am coming to you. Holy Father, protect them by the power of your name—the name you gave me—so that they may be one as we are one.'"

Acts 20:28: "Be shepherds of the church of God, which he bought with his own blood."

Romans 5:19: "For just as through the disobedience of the one man the many were made sinners, so also through the obedience of the one man the many will be made righteous."

Romans 8:32–34: "He who did not spare his own Son, but gave him up for us all—how will he not also, along with him, graciously give us all things? Who will bring any charge against those whom God has chosen? It is God who justifies. Who is he that condemns?"

Ephesians 1:4–5, 7: "For he chose us in him before the creation of the world to be holy and blameless in his sight. In love he predestined us. . . . In him we have redemption through his blood, the forgiveness of sins, in accordance with the riches of God's grace."

Ephesians 5:25–27: "Husbands, love your wives, just as Christ loved the church and gave himself up for her to make her holy, cleansing her by the washing with water through the word, and to present her to himself as a radiant church, without stain or wrinkle or any other blemish, but holy and blameless."

Hebrews 9:15: "For this reason Christ is the mediator of a new covenant, that those who are called may receive the promised eternal inheritance—now that he has died as a ransom to set them free from the sins committed under the first covenant."

Hebrews 9:28: "Christ was sacrificed once to take away the sins of many people."

Revelation 5:9: "You are worthy to take the scroll and to open its seals,

because you were slain,

and with your blood you purchased men for God

from every tribe and language and people and nation."

Chosen *in* Christ, redeemed *by* Christ, and now brought into union *with* Christ, the people of God are born again—spiritually resurrected, given the gift of faith, justified, and baptized into the church.

The following verses underscore the reality that our new birth is the result of God's will and action, not ours. We are saved, not because we found Christ, but because he found us.

Isaiah 65:1: "I revealed myself to those who did not ask for me; I was found by those who did not seek me."

Ezekiel 11:19: "I will give them an undivided heart and put a new spirit in them; I will remove from them their heart of stone and give them a heart of flesh."

Ezekiel 37:3–9: "He asked me, 'Son of man, can these bones live?' I said, 'O Sovereign LORD, you alone know.' Then he said to me, 'Prophesy to these bones and say to them, "Dry bones, hear the word of the LORD! This is what the Sovereign LORD says to these bones: I will make breath enter you, and you will come to life. I will attach tendons to you and make flesh come upon you and cover you with skin; I will put breath in you, and you will come to life. Then you will know that I am the LORD."' So I prophesied as I was commanded. And as I was prophesying, there was a noise, a rattling sound, and the bones came together, bone to bone. . . . Then he said to me, 'Prophesy to the breath; prophesy, son of man, and say to it, "This is what the Sovereign LORD says: Come from the four winds, O breath, and breathe into these slain, that they may live."' So I prophesied as he commanded me, and breath entered them; they came to life and stood up on their feet— a vast army." [This is, by the way, an excellent illustration of what happens when we share the gospel with people. We "prophesy," that is, preach the message, and God causes the individual to respond.]

Daniel 4:35: "All the peoples of the earth are regarded as nothing. He does as he pleases with the powers of heaven and the peoples of the earth. No one can hold back his hand or say to him: 'What have you done?'"

[Take some time to read the entire fourth chapter for deeper insight on this point.]

Luke 17:5: "The apostles said to the Lord, 'Increase our faith!'"

John 1:12–13: "Yet to all who received him, to those who believed in his name, he gave the right to become children of God—children born not of natural descent, nor of human decision or a husband's will, but born of God."

John 6:29, 37, 44, 63–66: "Jesus answered, 'The work of God is this: to believe in the one he has sent.' . . . 'All that the Father gives me will come to me, and whoever comes to me I will never drive away.' . . . 'No one can come to me unless the Father who sent me draws him, and I will raise him up at the last day.' . . . 'The Spirit gives life; the flesh counts for nothing. The words I have spoken to you are spirit and they are life. Yet there are some of you who do not believe.' . . . He went on to say, 'This is why I told you that no one can come to me unless the Father has enabled him.' From this time many of his disciples turned back and no longer followed him."

John 15:5, 16, 19: "apart from me you can do nothing. . . . You did not choose me, but I chose you. . . . I have chosen you out of the world."

Acts 11:18: "When they heard this, they had no further objections and praised God, saying, 'So then, God has granted even the Gentiles repentance unto life.'"

Acts 13:48: "When the Gentiles heard this, they were glad and honored the word of the Lord; and all who were appointed for eternal life believed."

Acts 16:14: "One of those listening was a woman named Lydia, a dealer in purple cloth from the city of Thyatira, who was a worshiper of God. The Lord opened her heart to respond to Paul's message."

Romans 2:4: "Or do you show contempt for the riches of his kindness, tolerance and patience, not realizing that God's kindness leads you toward repentance?"

Romans 9:15–16: "For he says to Moses, 'I will have mercy on whom I have mercy, and I will have compassion on whom I have compassion.' It does not, therefore, depend on man's desire or effort, but on God's mercy."

Romans 11:5–7, 29: "So too, at the present time there is a remnant chosen by grace. And if by grace, then it is no longer by works. . . . What then? What Israel sought so earnestly it did not obtain, but the elect did. The others were hardened. . . . for God's gifts and his call are irrevocable."

1 Corinthians 2:14: "The man without the Spirit does not accept the things that come from the Spirit of God, for they are foolishness to him, and he cannot understand them, because they are spiritually discerned."

1 Corinthians 4:7: "For who makes you different from anyone else? What do you have that you did not receive [from God]? And if you did receive it, why do you boast as though you did not?" [Here Paul rebukes the pride of the Corinthians in thinking that their spiritual inheritance is inherently theirs, forgetting that they don't have anything that was not given to them as a gift from God.]

2 Corinthians 3:4–5: "Such confidence as this is ours through Christ before God. Not that we are competent in ourselves to claim anything for ourselves, but our competence comes from God."

Ephesians 1:18–19: "I pray also that the eyes of your heart may be enlightened in order that you may know the hope to which he has called you . . . and his incomparably great power for us who believe. That power is like the working of his mighty strength." [We believe by the working of God's power.]

Ephesians 2:1–9: "As for you, you were dead in your transgressions and sins, in which you used to live when you followed the ways of this world, and of the ruler of the kingdom of the air, the spirit who is now at work in those who are disobedient. All of us also lived among them at one time, gratifying the cravings of our sinful nature. . . . Like the rest, we were by nature objects of wrath. But because of his great love for us, God, who is rich in mercy, made us alive with Christ even when we were dead in transgressions—it is by grace you have been saved. And God raised us up with Christ and seated us with him in the heavenly realms in Christ Jesus, in order that in the coming ages he might show the incomparable riches of his grace, expressed in his kindness to us in Christ Jesus. For it is by grace you have been saved, through faith—and this not from yourselves, it is the gift of God—not by works, so that no one can boast."

Philippians 2:13: "for it is God who works in you to will and to act according to his good purpose."

2 Timothy 2:25: "gently instruct, in the hope that God will grant them repentance leading them to a knowledge of the truth."

James 1:18: "He chose to give us birth through the word of truth."

We all understand our bent toward independence and infidelity. If the security of our salvation depends on our ability to choose and hang on to Christ, we will be caught on the treadmill of a self-centered works-righteousness. Once God starts something, he finishes it. A truly born-again person can do nothing to lose salvation; it is eternal. But we are responsible to persevere. If we do not, it is not because we have lost salvation, but because we never had it in the first place.

The following verses assure us of the security of our relationship with God in Christ.

Isaiah 54:10: "'Though the mountains be shaken and the hills be removed, yet my unfailing love for you will not be shaken nor my covenant of peace be removed,' says the LORD."

Jeremiah 32:40: "I will make an everlasting covenant with them: I will never stop doing good to them, and I will inspire them to fear me, so that they will never turn away from me."

Matthew 18:12–14: "What do you think? If a man owns a hundred sheep, and one of them wanders away, will he not leave the ninety-nine on the hills and go to look for the one that wandered off? And if he finds it, I tell you the truth, he is happier about that one sheep than about the ninety-nine that did not wander off. In the same way your Father in heaven is not willing that any of these little ones should be lost."

John 3:16: "For God so loved the world that he gave his one and only Son, that whoever believes in him shall not perish but have eternal life."

John 3:36: "Whoever believes in the Son has eternal life."

John 5:24: "I tell you the truth, whoever hears my word and believes him who sent me has eternal life and will not be condemned; he has crossed over from death to life." [Once we are given eternal life, we are no longer in the position where we can come into judgment ever again.]

John 6:37, 39: "All that the Father gives me will come to me, and whoever comes to me I will never drive away. . . . And this is the will of him who sent me, that I shall lose none of all that he has given me, but raise them up at the last day."

John 10:27–29: "My sheep listen to my voice; I know them, and they follow me. I give them eternal life, and they shall never perish; no one can snatch them out of my hand. My Father, who has given them to me, is greater than all; no one can snatch them out of my Father's hand."

John 17:11: "Holy Father, protect them by the power of your name—the name you gave me."

Romans 8:1: "Therefore, there is now no condemnation for those who are in Christ Jesus."

Romans 8:29–39: "For those God foreknew he also predestined to be conformed to the likeness of his Son, that he might be the firstborn among many brothers. And those he predestined, he also called; those he called, he also justified; those [not just some of those] he justified, he also glorified. What, then, shall we say in response to this? If God is for us, who can be against us? . . . Who will bring any charge against those whom God has chosen? It is God who justifies. Who is he that condemns? . . . Who shall separate us from the love of Christ? Shall trouble or hardship or persecution or famine or nakedness or danger or sword? . . . No, in all these things we are more than conquerors through him who loved us. For I am convinced that neither death nor life, neither angels nor demons, neither the present nor the future, nor any powers, neither height nor depth, nor anything else in all creation, will be able to separate us from the love of God that is in Christ Jesus our Lord."

1 Corinthians 1:7–9: "Jesus Christ . . . will keep you strong to the end, so that you will be blameless on the day of our Lord Jesus Christ. God, who has called you into fellowship with his Son Jesus Christ our Lord, is faithful."

1 Corinthians 10:13: "God is faithful; he will not let you be tempted beyond what you can bear. But when you are tempted, he will also provide a way out so that you can stand up under it."

Ephesians 1:5, 13–14: "he predestined us to be adopted as his sons through Jesus Christ, in accordance with his pleasure and will. . . . And you also were included in Christ when you heard the word of truth, the gospel of your salvation. Having believed, you were marked in him with a seal, the promised Holy Spirit, who is a deposit guaranteeing our inheritance until the redemption of those who are God's possession—to the praise of his glory."

2 Timothy 4:18: "The Lord will rescue me from every evil attack and will bring me safely to his heavenly kingdom. To him be glory for ever and ever. Amen."

Hebrews 10:14: "By one sacrifice he has made perfect forever those who are being made holy."

Hebrews 12:28: "Therefore, since we are receiving a kingdom that cannot be shaken, let us be thankful, and so worship God acceptably with reverence and awe."

1 Peter 1:3–5: "Praise be to the God and Father of our Lord Jesus Christ! In his great mercy he has given us new birth into a living hope through the resurrection of Jesus Christ from the dead, and into an inheritance that can never perish, spoil or fade—kept in heaven for you, who through faith are shielded by God's power until the coming of the salvation that is ready to be revealed in the last time."

1 John 2:19, 25: "They went out from us, but they did not really belong to us. For if they had belonged to us, they would have remained with us; but their going showed that none of them belonged to us. . . . And this is what he promised us—even eternal life." [When people apostasize, that is, repudiate the Christian faith and leave the church altogether, it is evidence that they were never Christians to begin with.]

1 John 5:4, 11–13, 20: "for everyone born of God overcomes the world. This is the victory that has overcome the world, even our faith. . . . And this is the testimony: God has given us eternal life, and this life is in his Son. He who has the Son has life. . . . I write these things to you who believe in the name of the Son of God, so that you may know that you have eternal life. . . . We know also that the Son of God has come and has given us understanding, so that we may know him who is true. And we are in him who is true—even in his Son Jesus Christ. He is the true God and eternal life."

Jude 1: "To those who have been called, who are loved by God the Father and kept by Jesus Christ."

Jude 24–25: "To him who is able to keep you from falling, and to present you before his glorious presence without fault and with great joy—to the only God our Savior be glory, majesty, power and authority, through Jesus Christ our Lord, before all ages, now and forevermore! Amen."

Witness of the Saints

The witness of the saints through the ages yields a forthright, dogmatic, and dynamic testimony to the centrality of these truths in the life of the holy, apostolic, catholic church of Christ. Periods of intense impact curiously coincide with the periods in which these teachings are vigorously defended and faithfully proclaimed.

The following excerpts, though incomplete, should present a clear and definitive statement concerning the position of the church from its early years to more recent history. Here, then, one finds not only an appeal from Scripture, but a decisive call from the historic church as well.

Human Inability

Barnabas, the associate of Paul, said in A.D. 70:

> Learn: before we believed in God, the habitation of our heart was corrupt and weak.

The celebrated church father Ignatius in A.D. 110, said:

> They that are carnal [unbelievers] cannot do the things that are spiritual. . . . Nor can the unbelievers do the things of belief.

By this Ignatius meant that an unbeliever cannot do something that is entirely foreign to the person's nature. The reason people do not choose Christ is that, in their own natural state, they do not have the disposition or desire to be ruled by God.

Justin Martyr concurred strongly with this conviction when, in A.D. 150, he wrote:

> Mankind by Adam fell under death, and the deception of the serpent; we are born sinners. . . . No good thing dwells in us. . . . For neither by nature, nor by human understanding is it possible for men to acquire the knowledge of things so great and so divine, but by the energy of the Divine Spirit. . . . Of ourselves it is impossible to enter the kingdom of God. . . . He has convicted us of the impossibility of our nature to obtain life. . . . Free will has destroyed us; we who were free are become slaves and for our sin are sold. . . . Being pressed down

by our sins, we cannot move upward toward God; we are like birds who have wings, but are unable to fly.

"Like birds who have wings, but are unable to fly"—what a lucid metaphor Justin Martyr uses to paint the realistic if unfortunate picture of people's spiritual abilities! We all have a will. If you reject Christ, you do it *willingly*. Nevertheless, your will is in bondage to sin and the selfish nature owned by each of us.

It is interesting that wings and flying have been used most frequently to give us the sensation of our spirit. Clement of Alexandria (A.D. 190) repeated the metaphor:

The soul cannot rise nor fly, nor be lifted up above the things that are on high, without special grace.

The earlier period of church history proved to be a challenging one. Spin-off heresies were abundant, and one early father in particular, named Origen, was charged with such departure. Nevertheless, he was compelled to say with the broad consensus of early Christianity:

Our free will . . . or human nature is not sufficient to seek God in any manner.

And Eusebius, the famous church historian, said in A.D. 330,

The liberty of our will in choosing things that are good is destroyed.

We have read a great deal lately about "secular humanism," that is, the teaching that we have within ourselves whatever it takes to better ourselves and our world on our own—without God. This, far from being a recent development, is but a contemporary reappearance of the ancient heresy known to the church as Pelagianism.

The monk Pelagius taught that by nature humans are neither depraved nor good, but neutral. The will is free to choose either to accept Christ and his gospel or reject it. Furthermore, a Christian could lose favor and hence be lost if he or she failed to cooperate (do *his or her* part) with God in salvation. A modified and more moderate view, called appropriately "semi-Pelagianism," arose. Both movements were eventually uprooted by the Roman Catholic Church and officially declared heretical in the ancient Council of Orange (to which you will find a detailed reference later on).

The person most responsible for calling the church to the defense of the gospel of God's free and omnipotent grace was St. Augustine, hailed by Protestants and Roman Catholics alike as being the virtual founder of the Western church.

Here is just one of Augustine's many defenses against the error, from A.D. 370:

> If, therefore, they are servants of sin (2 Cor. 3:17), why do they boast of free will? . . . O, man! Learn from the precept what you ought to do; learn from correction, that it is your own fault you have not the power. . . . Let human effort, which perished by Adam, here be silent, and let the grace of God reign by Jesus Christ. . . . What God promises, we ourselves do not through free will of human nature, but He Himself does by grace within us. . . . Men labor to find in our own will something that is our own, and not God's; how they can find it, I know not.

Though the church had taken a stand, men and women rather quickly began to forget this message, led more by the feelings and impressions of their human nature than by the Spirit of God. Hence began what were to be called the Dark Ages. Flickering light shone here and there—for instance, Anselm of Canterbury in the eleventh century and the Gottschalk renewal in the ninth. Thomas Aquinas brought these teachings back into scholarly debate, and he was an able defender of this message, recalling the memory of Augustine.

But soon the church had become so corrupt both in doctrine and practice that it was virtually indistinguishable from the pagan world except in outward form, ritual, and legalistic regulations. The errors condemned by the church in the fifth century were now the popular religion of the day, from peasant to pope.

Now we come to the sixteenth-century Reformation, one of the most profound movements in the tradition of the ancient gospel. The most luminous figure of the era, Martin Luther, was clear in his defense of this gospel (A.D. 1530):

> A man without the Spirit of God does not do evil against his will, under pressure, as though he were taken by the scruff of the neck and

dragged into it; no, he does it spontaneously and voluntarily. . . . On the other hand, when God works in us, the will is changed under the sweet influence of the Spirit of God. . . . With regard to God and in all that bears on salvation or damnation, man has not "free-will," but is a captive, prisoner, and bondslave. . . .

Unconditional Election

Fortunately, the Scriptures do not leave us in the garden of Eden, fallen, torn, twisted, and ruined; neither does the gospel of the fathers of our faith. Faced with such a helpless and impotent condition, one must conclude that God will have to decide to do something about this mess if, in fact, he does anything at all (to which he is not even remotely obligated). The Christian gospel refers to this decision of God as "unconditional election." We do not place ourselves in Christ when we choose him; rather, the Father placed us in Christ when he chose us before creation.

In A.D. 69, Clement of Rome, possibly the same Clement mentioned in Paul's epistle to the Philippians (4:3), had this to say:

Let us therefore approach Him in holiness of soul, lifting up pure and undefiled hands unto Him, with love towards our gentle and compassionate Father because He made us an elect portion unto Himself. . . . Seeing then that we are the special elect portion of a holy God, let us do all things that pertain unto holiness. . . . There was given a declaration of blessedness upon them that have been elected by God through Jesus Christ our Lord. . . . Jesus Christ is the hope of the elect. . . .

And Clement prayed:

Creator, guard intact unto the end of the number that hath been numbered of Thine elect throughout the whole world, through Your beloved Son Jesus Christ. . . . For You chose the Lord Jesus Christ, and You chose us through Him for a peculiar people.

In a conversation with Trypho the Jew, Clement compared the election of the nation Israel to the election of people from every nation to form a new spiritual nation:

God, out of all nations, took your nation to Himself, a nation unprofitable, disobedient, and unfaithful; thereby pointing toward those that are chosen out of every nation to obey His will, by Christ, whom also He calls Jacob, and names Israel.

To the Ephesians (the same local church to whom Paul sent his inspired epistle), Ignatius wrote:

To the predestined ones before all ages, that is, before the world began, united and elect in a true passion, by the eternal will of the Father. . . .

This was a common salutation the fathers of the church gave in addressing their letters. Can you imagine how vigorously these teachings were taught and how excited the early Christians were about them that the fathers' common letters were addressed to the churches in this manner!

The church of Smyrna (mentioned in the Book of Revelation) circulated a letter to the other churches reminding them of their commitment to the gospel (A.D. 157):

It behooveth us to be very scrupulous and to assign to God the power over all things. . . .

Later in the letter, the church of Smyrna refers to examples in which it would appear that evangelists of the church had been preaching to crowds, and the people watching noticed that some responded passionately and others violently rejected the message. Why do some choose Christ and others reject him? The church of Smyrna writes further:

The multitude marveled that there should be so great a difference between the unbelievers and the elect. . . . The Lord maketh election from His own servants. . . . Glory be unto God for the salvation of His holy elect.

Earlier I referred to Justin Martyr's discussions with Trypho the Jew. His evangelistic appeal to Trypho using this doctrine of election as a common point of discussion might give us a clue as to how we can effectively use this teaching in our evangelism, particularly in speaking with Jews:

In all these discourses I have brought all my proofs out of your own holy and prophetic writings, hoping that some of you may be found of the elect number which through the grace that comes from the Lord of Sabaoth, is left or reserved [set apart] for everlasting salvation.

Let's turn now to a different sort of conversion—this time, a discussion between Octavius (a Christian) and Coecilius (a heathen). Coecilius charges that the Christian teaching of election is essentially no different from the pagan notion of fate:

Whatsoever we [pagans] ascribe to fate, so you to God; and so men desire your sect not of their own free will, but as elect of God; wherefore you suppose an unjust judge, who punishes in men lot or fortune, and not on the basis of their will.

Of course, Coecilius misunderstood the church's teaching on election. That is to be expected from a non-Christian. After all, look at how many *Christians* today would have the same misconception! Unfortunately, we do not have any record of Octavius's response to the charge. However, Irenaeus, the disciple of the martyr Polycarp (who was a disciple of the apostle John), wrote in A.D. 198:

God hath completed the number which He before determined with Himself, all those who are written, or ordained unto eternal life. . . . Being predestined indeed according to the love of the Father that we would belong to Him forever.

And contrast the following description of the early church by Irenaeus with the contemporary scenario:

The tower of election being everywhere exalted and glorious.

Clement of Alexandria, in A.D. 190, explains election somewhat and encourages those to whom he is writing in their own standing:

Through faith the elect of God are saved. The generation of those who seek God is the elect nation, not the place [i.e., not an earthly, political nation] but the congregation of the elect, which I call the Church. . . . If every person had known the truth, they would all have leaped into the way, and there would have been no election. . . . You are those who are chosen from among men and as those who are predestined from among men, and in His own time called, faithful, and elect, those who before the foundation of the world are known intimately by God unto faith; that is, are appointed by Him to faith, grow beyond babyhood.

This concise statement resembles the declaration of Paul's side-kick, Barnabas, in A.D. 70:

We are elected to hope, committed by God unto faith, appointed to salvation.

Cyprian said (A.D. 250):

This is therefore the predestination which we faithfully and humbly preach.

Can we say today that our churches are "faithfully and humbly" preaching the glory of God in election?

Ambrose of Milan (A.D. 380) buttressed the beauty, grandeur, and mystery of the church with this doctrine:

In predestination the Church of God has always existed.

Today, many people will consent to God's having chosen them. But, to circumvent the humbling and intimidating impact of the real doctrine of election, they will invent their own. One of these responses is cased in the form of this argument: "Yes, God chose me, but it's because he knew I would choose him." You see, here you and I still get to maintain that salvation is based on us—or something we did. Conditional election (God's choosing me because he knew I would choose him) is no election at all; it's nothing more than advanced knowledge of something that we would do of our own will and resources.

This argument is by no means new. Read Augustine's response, and I think you will see what I mean (A.D. 380):

Here certainly, there is no place for the vain argument of those who defend the foreknowledge of God against the grace of God, and accordingly maintain that we were elected before the foundation of the world because God foreknew that we would be good, not that He Himself would make us good. This is not the language of Him who said, "You did not choose Me, but I chose you" (John 15:16).

William Tyndale, the English Reformer, wrote clearly and directly on the subject.

> Now may not we ask why God chooseth one and not another; for God hath power over all of His creatures to do as He pleaseth.

The Reformation was not a crusade against indulgences, papal infallibility, or rituals. Indulgences only became an issue as they cheapened (and in fact replaced) the doctrine of grace. The pope's infallibility was challenged only when he began to challenge the doctrine of sovereign grace. No, the real issue was that the church would simply not give in to Paul's affirmation: "It does not, therefore, depend on man's desire or effort, but on God's mercy" (Rom. 9:16). Martin Luther said:

> Although this matter is very hard for the "prudence [thinking] of the flesh," which is made even more indignant by it and brought even to the point of blasphemy, because here it is strangled to death and reduced to absolutely nothing, man understands that salvation comes in no way from something working in himself, but only from outside himself, namely, from God, who elects. But those who have the "prudence of the Spirit" delight in this subject with ineffable pleasure.

Martin Luther's dialogue with Erasmus of Rotterdam (the church's defender against Luther) is well known. In it Luther commends Erasmus for at least being willing to discuss the issue of election. He found that nobody really wanted to talk about the subject. People just did not think the doctrine of election was all that important. Of course they didn't! After all, who wouldn't think a humbling doctrine of this nature to be unimportant! Luther said:

> I give you hearty praise on this, Erasmus—that you alone, in contrast with all others, have attacked the real thing, that is, the essential issue. You have not wearied me with those extraneous issues about the papacy, purgatory, indulgences and such like—trifles, rather than issues. . . . You, and you alone, have seen the hinge on which everything turns, and aimed for the vital spot.

Furthermore, according to Luther:

There are two causes which require such things to be preached. The first is the humbling of our pride and knowledge of the grace of God. The second is, the future of the Christian faith itself.

Luther said that because "God is thus robbed of His power to elect" he might as well take a vacation and go "to an Ethiopian feast," since he is not much of a God at all.

We will not indulge in excerpting quotes from the other Reformers: Zwingli, Calvin, Bucer, and Knox, to name a few. Suffice it to say that the essence of the Reformation—its *raison d'etre,* if you will—was at the heart a defense of this great truth of the gospel.

The "prudence of the flesh" (as Luther would call it) again rolled onto the shores of history as fog dominates the early morning. The Pilgrims had brought the faith of the Reformers to America, but by the turn of the eighteenth century Deism and semi-Pelagianism had gained the ascendancy. This condition called for another great movement for the gospel of grace. This movement did come, and many historians credit the impact of this event with the American Revolution. It was, of course, the Great Awakening. Its leaders all held to doctrines of the Reformation. In fact, its most acclaimed leader, Jonathan Edwards, wrote:

> From my childhood up, my mind had been full of objections to the doctrine of God's sovereignty, in choosing whom He would to eternal life; and rejecting whom He pleased. . . . But I have often, since that first conviction, had quite another kind of sense of God's sovereignty than I had then. I have often since had not only a conviction, but a *delightful* conviction. The doctrine has very often appeared exceedingly bright and sweet. Absolute sovereignty is what I love to ascribe to God. . . . And wherever the doctrines of God's sovereignty with regard to the salvation of sinners were preached, there with it God sent revival.

Edwards was joined in his effort by the powerful English evangelist George Whitefield. Whitefield and John Wesley had begun the movement that would be called Methodism. Eventually their theological convictions drew them into controversy, and Wesley cut himself off entirely from fellowship with Whitefield (for which estrangement Whitefield lamented the rest of his life). Yet even Wesley had to confess about him:

Have we read or heard of any person who called so many thousands, so many myriads of sinners to repentance?

Whitefield preached the gospel to more people than any person of his day—thousands at one time, with no modern sound amplification system. He was asked by many of his deistic friends (like Benjamin Franklin) why he made so much of election. He responded:

> This is one reason, among many others, why I admire the doctrine of election, and am convinced that it should have a place in the gospel ministry, and should be insisted on with great faithfulness and care. . . . I shall only say, it is the doctrine of election that mostly presses me to abound in good works. This makes me preach with comfort, because I know that my salvation does not depend upon my free will, but the Lord makes me willing in the day of His power; and can make use of me to bring some of His elect home, when and where He pleases.

"When" God pleased was often, and "where" he pleased was nearly everywhere in England and America. It is no accident that the greatest missionary heroes (William Carey, Hudson Taylor, John Patton, David Livingstone) were well-versed and passionately concerned about this truth. Evangelism takes on real meaning because we are now preaching "the power of *God* unto salvation." No better modern example can one find of this principle than the famed Baptist evangelist of England Charles Haddon Spurgeon:

> Brethren, we must always believe this and preach it, for it is the sum of all true doctrine. If you do not make salvation to be wholly of the Lord, mark my word, you will have to clip salvation down, and make it a small matter. I have always desired to preach a great salvation, and I do not think that any other is worth preaching. . . . We cannot preach the gospel unless we preach the electing, unchangeable, eternal, immutable, conquering love of Jehovah.

Definite Atonement

The late professor of theology Lewis Sperry Chafer reflected a popular view in evangelical circles with regard to the death of Christ when he said: "The death of Christ upon the cross does not save anybody—either actually or potentially. It makes all men saveable." If one is not convinced by Scripture—the highest standard and only objective guide for truth—then it should be undeniable that the faith of our fathers sharply condemns this popular denial of the power of the cross.

When Jesus died for us, he paid the price for our sins; he actually redeemed us and cleared us of all charges, taking them upon himself. In short, he saved us. That is the message of the gospel. Our Lord came with a mission: to redeem the elect of God, not to make possible the redemption of every person.

Once again we turn to Paul's partner in ministry, Barnabas, who, in A.D. 70, said:

> [Christ speaking] I see that I shall thus offer My flesh for the sins of the new people.

Justin Martyr (A.D. 150) said:

> He endured the sufferings for those men whose souls are [actually] purified from all iniquity. . . . As Jacob served Laban for the cattle that were spotted, and of various forms, so Christ served even to the cross for men of every kind, of many and various shapes, procuring them by His blood and the mystery of the cross.

The Bible says that Christ died "a ransom for all" (1 Tim. 2:6). But *all* does not always means "each and every person," as can be evidenced from many other passages in which *all* appears. Here is how the church of Smyrna handled Christ's being "the Savior of the world" (A.D. 169):

> Christ suffered for the salvation of the whole world of them that are saved.

And here is how Irenaeus (A.D. 180) handled the *all* of 1 Timothy:

> He came to save all, all, I say, who through Him are born again unto God, infants, and little ones, and children, and young men, and old men.

In other words, Christ died not just for one particular kind of people, one special ethnic group or age, sex, or geographical area. He died for everybody—all nationalities, and so on. Irenaeus continued:

> Jesus is the Savior of them that believe; but the Lord of them that believe not. Wherefore, Christ is introduced in the gospel weary. . . . promising to give His life a ransom, in the room of, many.

Tertullian (A.D. 200) said plainly:

> Christ died for the salvation of His people . . . for the church.

Cyprian, in A.D. 250, said:

> All the sheep which Christ hath sought up by His blood and sufferings are saved. . . . Whosoever shall be found in the blood, and with the mark of Christ shall only escape. . . . He redeemed the believers with the price of His own blood. . . . Let him be afraid to die who is not reckoned to have any part in the cross and sufferings of Christ.

In the year 320, Lactantius elaborated on this teaching:

> He was to suffer and be slain for the salvation of many people . . . who having suffered death for us, hath made us heirs of the everlasting kingdom, having abdicated and disinherited the people of the Jews. . . . He stretched out His hands in His passion and measured the world, that He might at that very time show that a large people, gathered out of all languages and tribes, should come under His wings, and receive the most great and sublime sign.

In response to "who gave Himself up for us *all*," Eusebius replied (A.D. 330):

> To what "us" does he refer, unless to them that believe in Him? For to them that do not believe in Him, He is the author of their fire and burning. The cause of Christ's coming is the redemption of those that were to be saved by Him.

Julius said in A.D. 350:

> The Son of God, by the pouring out of His precious blood, redeemed His set apart ones; they are delivered by the blood of Christ.

In A.D. 363 Hilarion said:

He shall remain in the sight of God forever, having already taken all whom He hath redeemed to be kings of heaven, and co-heirs of eternity, delivering them as the kingdom of God to the Father.

St. Ambrose (A.D. 380) tied the Father's election before creation to the Son's mission on earth:

Before the foundation of the world, it was God's will that Christ should suffer for our salvation.

God is just. He will not punish both the Redeemer and the redeemed. God can only collect a debt once. If one must pay his or her own debt for sin, clearly Jesus did not take that debt upon himself. No one for whom Christ died will be in hell, as Pacian supports (A.D. 380):

Much more, He will not allow him that is redeemed to be destroyed, nor will He cast away those whom He has redeemed with a great price.

In the same vein, Ambrose said in A.D. 380:

Can He damn thee, whom He hath redeemed from death, for whom He offered Himself, whose life He knows is the reward of His own death?

Epiphanius raised the dander of some pagans when he told them that if they rejected the gospel, Christ never died for them in the first place (A.D. 390):

If you are redeemed. . . . *If* therefore ye are bought with blood, thou art not of the number of them who were bought with blood, O Manes, because thou deniest the blood. . . . He gave His life for His own sheep.

And Hieronymus (Jerome) said, in A.D. 390:

Christ is sacrificed for the salvation of believers. . . . Not all are redeemed, for not all shall be saved, but the remnant. . . . All those who are redeemed and delivered by Thy blood return to Zion, which Thou hast prepared for Thyself by Thine own blood. . . . Christ came to redeem Zion [a metaphor for the church] with His blood. But lest we should think that all are Zion or every one in Zion is truly redeemed of the Lord, who are redeemed by the blood of Christ form the Church.

. . . He did not give His life for every man, but for many, that is, for those who would believe.

Anselm lost a lot of friends over this one:

If you die in unbelief, Christ did not die for you.

In A.D. 850 Remigius reasoned, based on Scripture:

Since only the elect are saved, it may be accepted that Christ did not come to save all and did not die on the cross for all.

William Tyndale who, you will remember, was one of the English Reformers, was clear in his convictions on the matter:

Christ's blood only putteth away the sins of them that are elect. . . . We are elect through Christ's blood. . . . Thou art elect to life everlasting by Christ's blood, whose gift and purchase is thy faith.

Martin Luther left little question as to where he stood on the matter:

For in an absolute sense, Christ did not die for everyone, because He says: "This is My blood which is poured out on you" and "for many"— He does not say: for every person—"for the forgiveness of sins." As the Apostle says, "Everything for the sake of the elect."

The celebrated Anglican evangelist George Whitefield had much to say about the definite atonement or particular redemption of God's people. Notice his practical appeal:

Universal redemption is a notion sadly adapted to keep the soul in its lethargic, sleepy condition; and therefore so many natural men admire and applaud it. . . . Infidels of all kinds stand on the universal side of redemption: Deists, Arians, Socinians—they all arraign God's sovereignty, and stand up for universal redemption. . . . The doctrine of universal redemption is really the highest reproach upon the dignity of the Son of God, and the merit of His blood.

How could that be? Whitefield explains himself:

Consider, therefore, whether it be not blasphemy to say, "Christ not only died for those that are saved, but also for those that will perish." But blessed be God, our Lord knew for whom He died. . . .

Again, Charles Spurgeon, England's famed Baptist evangelist, asserts:

Some persons love the doctrine of universal atonement. . . . Yet if it was Christ's intention to save every man, how deplorably has He been disappointed, for there is a lake of fire, and into that pit of woe have been cast some of the very persons who, according to the theory of universal redemption, were bought with His blood. . . . We cannot preach the gospel unless we base it upon the special and particular redemption of His elect and chosen people which Christ wrought upon the cross.

Irresistible Grace

It happens every day—whether in Los Angeles or Liverpool—no matter what the social conditions are. People undergo an internal conversion. Their views change; their disposition and interests are altered. They are suddenly at peace, experiencing the deep love of God in Christ.

This event is called the new birth. It is an act of God, who tenderly and yet powerfully invades the darkness and death of the human soul, creating new life and enabling a person to respond positively in faith.

You are not "born again" because you accept Christ; rather, you believe because the Holy Spirit has resurrected your soul and given you the gift of faith. Once alienated, stubborn, independent, and rebellious—disinterested in the things of God—now you recognize your desperate need of Christ and cry out, "Lord, be merciful to me, a sinner."

This teaching is especially comforting when we are faced with loved ones who appear to us to be beyond the possibility of conversion. After all, repentance is not only difficult; it's downright impossible unless it is the work of God within the individual. This point is made well by the noble father, Ignatius.

Pray for them, if so be they may repent, which is very difficult; but Jesus Christ, our true life, has the power of this.

In that same line of thinking, Justin Martyr said (A.D. 150):

> Having sometime before convinced us of the impossibility of our nature to obtain life, hath now shown us the Savior, who is able to save them which otherwise were impossible to be saved. . . . Free will has destroyed us; we are sold into sin.

From these thoughts one gets the impression that repentance is not a natural ability we all possess, but rather a gift from God, given to whomever he chooses at whatever time he is pleased to grant it. Notice the earlier comment of Barnabas (A.D. 70) in this connection:

> God gives repentance to us, introducing us into the incorruptible temple.

Irenaeus, in A.D. 180, had this to say:

> Not of ourselves, but of God, is the blessing of our salvation. . . . Man, who was before led captive, is taken out of the power of the possessor, according to the mercy of God the Father, and restoring it, gives salvation to it by the Word; that is, by Christ; that many may experimentally learn that not of himself, but by the gift of God, he receives immortality.

In A.D. 200, Tertullian brought the debate to a simpler, more reasonable level. He asked,

> Do you think, O men, that we could ever have been able to have understood these things in the Scriptures unless by the will of Him that wills all things, we had received grace to understand them? . . . But by this it is plain, that it (faith) is not given to thee by God, because thou dost not ascribe it to Him alone.

The following are the words of Cyprian in the year A.D. 250:

> Whatsoever is grateful is to be ascribed not to man's power, but to God's gift. It is God's, I say, all is God's that we can do. Yea, that in nothing must we glory, since nothing is ours.

Addressing himself to the heathen, Arnobius says (A.D. 303):

You place the salvation of your souls *in yourselves,* and trust that you may be made gods by your inward endeavor, yet it is not in our own power to reach things above.

I find it interesting that in this, the fourth century when Christianity was just in its elementary stages, believers nevertheless had a handle on these teachings. After all, this same conversation Arnobius had with heathens one might well have today with a fellow Christian. That surely is a critical sign.

In A.D. 320 Lactantius said rather succinctly:

The victory lies in the will of God, not in thine own. To overcome is not in our own power.

Athanasius, who bears the name of the foundational Athanasian Creed, said in A.D. 350:

To believe is not ours, or in our power, but the Spirit's who is in us, and abides in us.

Similarly, George of Nazianzum (A.D. 370) said:

To will is from God.

Hieronymus (Jerome) said in A.D. 390:

This is the chief righteousness of man, to reckon that whatsoever power he can have, is not his own, but the Lord's who gives it. . . . See how great is the help of God, and how frail the condition of man that we cannot by any means fulfill this, that we repent, unless the Lord first convert us. . . . When He [Jesus] says, "No man can come to Me," He breaks the proud liberty of free will; for man can desire nothing, and in vain he endeavors. . . . Where is the proud boasting of free will? . . . We pray in vain if it is in our own will. Why should men pray for that from the Lord which they have in the power of their own free will?

In that same period, Augustine had made his stand for grace. In A.D. 370 he described the nature of faith and its relationship to our salvation. Obviously we do believe, that is, we make a conscious decision for or against Christ. But is that decision natural to us or must we be *first* converted before we can respond? Augustine said:

Faith itself is to be attributed to God. . . . Faith is made a gift. These men, however, attribute faith to free will, so grace is rendered to faith not as a gratuitous gift, but as a debt. . . . They must cease from saying this.

If ever there was a man who studied the meaning of faith in the Word of God and then experienced faith radically in his own life, that would have to be William Tyndale.

Tyndale had much to say about faith. And since our misunderstanding of this doctrine is so often linked to our misconception of the nature and substance of faith, let's take a look at Tyndale's instruction on unwinding ourselves from this confused view of faith (A.D. 1520):

Many have a certain imagination of faith. They think no farther than that faith is a thing which is in their own power to have, as do other natural works which men do. . . . But the right faith springeth not of man's fantasy, neither is it in any man's power to obtain it; but it is altogether the pure gift of God without deserving and merits, yea, without our seeking for it, even faith is God's gift and grace. . . . Faith rooteth herself in the hearts of the elect.

Is it not . . . perverse blindness to teach how a man can do nothing of his own self, and yet presumptuously take upon them the greatest and highest work of God, even to make faith in themselves of their own power, and of their own false imagination and thoughts?

Therefore, I say, we must despair of ourselves and pray to God to give us faith.

Martin Luther defended for God's free and omnipotent grace:

We become sons of God by a power divinely given us—not by any power of "free-will" inherent in us! . . . What is hereby attributed to man's own decision and free-will? What indeed is left but nothing! In truth, nothing! Since the source of grace is the predestinating purpose of God, then it comes by necessity, and not by any effort or endeavor on our part.

And in the nineteenth century, the "Prince of Preachers," Charles Spurgeon, said:

The Holy Ghost comes, not according to our own mind or will, but according to the gift and purpose of the Lord. From top to bottom this salvation is of the Lord.

The Final Perseverance of the Saints

As we noted in our chapter devoted to this discussion, it is apparently unscriptural to say, on the one hand, "I'm eternally secure, no matter what I do or how I live, or what I believe," or to say, on the other, "If we don't keep our end up, we may lose our salvation and perish in spite of our having been redeemed."

Rather, Scripture seems clearly to teach us that it is our responsibility to persevere in faith and conviction—with great determination even in the midst of formidable obstacles. Yet, that very perseverance is due ultimately to God's abiding grace and eternal love that will never allow us to undo what he has so graciously accomplished for us.

Clement of Rome, a contemporary of Paul's who was, as indicated earlier, mentioned in Paul's epistle to the Corinthian church, had this to say in A.D. 69:

> It is the will of God that all whom He loves should partake of repentance, and so not perish with the unbelieving and impenitent. He has established it by His almighty will. But if any of those whom God wills should partake of the grace of repentance, should afterwards perish, where is His almighty will? And how is this matter settled and established by such a will of His?

Said Clement of Alexandria in A.D. 190:

> Such a soul [of a Christian] shall never at any time be separated from God. . . . Faith, I say, is something divine, which cannot be pulled asunder by any other worldly friendship, nor be dissolved by present fear.

That "present fear" holds many millions of Christians in bondage today. Whereas the true gospel calls us to a present hope, this errant "gospel" leads people to look to themselves and their own performance as a standard of hope and security in Christ.

Tertullian didn't beat around the bush on this account. He said straight out:

> God forbid that we should believe that the soul of any saint should be drawn out by the devil. . . . For what is of God is never extinguished.

You see, that is the central issue. If our salvation is even in some measure of ourselves, then our security depends somewhat on what we do to keep things going. If, however, salvation is of God entirely, then "He who began a good work will complete it." Augustine connects this grace to persevere with the grace of election:

> Of these believers no one perishes, because they all were elected. And they are elected because they were called according to the purpose— the purpose, however, not their own, but God's. . . . Obedience then is God's gift. . . . To this, indeed, we are not able to deny, that perseverance in good, progressing even to the end, is also a great gift of God.

Believers, God takes your salvation seriously! God loves you with an everlasting, unconditional love. That means two things: God loves you too much to see you lose the grace he has given you and also God loves you too much to see you live a life that is inconsistent with your profession and his character. Both goals are sought and achieved by God as he works in us his good pleasure. William Tyndale said:

> Christ is in thee, and thou in Him, knit together inseparably. Neither canst thou be damned, except Christ be damned with thee: neither can Christ be saved, except thou be saved with Him.

And the English evangelist of the eighteenth century, George Whitefield, added:

> A true child of God, though he might fall foully, yet could never finally fall.

Finally, Charles Spurgeon, who became the leading evangelist of the following generation, left no question as to where he stood on the matter when he said:

> I cannot comprehend a gospel which lets saints fall away after they are called, and suffers the children of God to be burned in the fires of damnation after having believed in Jesus. Such a gospel I abhor.

Creedal Statements

The Council of Nicaea met in A.D. 325 to define the doctrine of the Trinity. Next on the agenda was the establishment of the official position on the nature of Christ as both God and man. The Council of Chalcedon (A.D. 451) was convened for this purpose, but the issue was far from settled. Against the backdrop of this debate over the nature of Jesus Christ—utterly basic to all Christian claims—the Second Council of Orange was held (A.D. 529). This particular council met to establish the official Christian position on human depravity, election, the effectiveness of grace, and God's sovereign prerogative. After defining this position, the church went back to the debate on the nature of Christ. Certainly these truths have played a central role in Christendom from the beginning.

The following are excerpts from Christian creeds through history, underscoring the role of these doctrines in perspective. The first is a selection of excerpts from the Council of Orange:

Council of Orange (A.D. 529)

If anyone says that the grace of God can be conferred as a result of human prayer, but that it is not grace itself which makes us pray to God, he contradicts the prophet Isaiah, or the Apostle who says the same thing, "I was found by them that did not seek Me; I appeared openly to them that asked not after Me." If anyone maintains that God awaits our will to be cleansed from sin, but does not confess that even our will to be cleansed comes to us through the infusion and working of the Holy Spirit, he opposeth the Holy Spirit Himself who says through Solomon, "The will is prepared by the Lord." If anyone says that not only the increase of faith but also its beginning and the very desire for faith, by which we believe—if anyone says that this belongs to us naturally and not by a gift of grace, that is, by the inspiration of the Holy Spirit amending our will and turning it from unbelief to faith and from godlessness to godliness, it is proof that he is opposed to the teaching of the Apostles. . . . For those who state that faith by which we believe in God is our own make all who are separated from the Church of Christ in some measure believers.

If anyone says that God has mercy upon us when, apart from His gift, we believe, will, desire, strive, labor, pray, etc., but does not confess that it is by the infusion and inspiration of the Holy Spirit within us that we even have the faith, the will, or the strength to do all these things we ought, he contradicts the Apostles. . . . If anyone affirms that we can form any right opinion or make any right choice which relates to the salvation of eternal life, or that we can be saved, that is, assent to the preaching of the gospel through our own powers . . . he is led away by a heretical spirit. . . . If anyone maintains that he comes through free will, it is proof that he has no place in the true faith.

Council of Valence (A.D. 855)

Three centuries before the Council of Valence, St. Augustine and the monk Pelagius had battled it out over these doctrines. The teachings of Pelagius were condemned by more church councils than any other heresy in history. In the ninth century, the Catholic church was again in need of renewal, and the theologian Gottschalk rose up to defend the doctrines of grace, though perhaps he went too far at times. The Council of Valence reaffirmed the theology of grace and divine sovereignty:

> We confess a predestination of the elect to life, and a predestination of the wicked to death; that, in the election of those who are saved, the mercy of God precedes anything we do, and in the condemnation of those who will perish, evil merit precedes the righteous judgment of God.

The Ten Conclusions of Berne (A.D. 1528)

In the early years of the Swiss Reformation, these Ten Conclusions provided a statement of faith:

> God has elected us out of grace. God has from the beginning freely, and of his pure grace, without any respect of men, predestinated or elected the saints, whom He will save in Christ. . . . We are elected or predestined in Christ. Therefore, not for any merit of ours, yet not without a means, but in Christ, and for Christ, did God choose us. . . . We are elected to a sure end. . . . This is therefore above all to be taught and well weighted, what great love of the Father toward us in Christ is revealed.

The Small Catechism by Martin Luther (A.D. 1529)

> I believe that by my own reason and strength I cannot believe in Jesus Christ, my Lord, or come to Him. But the Holy Spirit has called me through the Gospel, enlightened me with His gifts, and sanctified and

preserved me in true faith, just as He calls, gathers, enlightens, and sanctifies the whole Christian church on earth and preserves it in union with Jesus Christ in the one true faith.

Further, Luther said, we are awakened to take hold of Christ,

When the heavenly Father gives us His Holy Spirit so that by His grace we may believe.

The Augsburg Confession of the Lutheran Church (A.D. 1530)

All men are full of evil lust and inclinations from their mothers' wombs and are unable by nature to have true fear of God and true faith in God. . . . Rejected in this connection are the Pelagians . . . . For they hold that natural man is made righteous by his own powers. . . . Without the grace and activity of the Holy Spirit, man is not capable of making himself acceptable to God, of fearing God and believing in God with his whole heart. . . . This is accomplished by the Holy Spirit.

The Thirty-Nine Articles of the Church of England (A.D. 1563)

The following excerpt is taken from the articles of doctrine upon which the Church of England is founded. The entire Anglican Communion, including the Episcopal churches in America, is bound by this confession:

The condition of Man after the fall of Adam is such that he cannot turn and prepare himself, by his own natural strength or good works, to faith, and calling upon God. . . . Predestination to Life is the everlasting Purpose of God, whereby (before the foundations of the world were laid) He hath decreed by His counsel secret to us, to deliver from curse and damnation those whom He hath chosen in Christ out of mankind, and to bring them by Christ to everlasting salvation, as vessels made to honor. . . . The godly consideration of Predestination, and our Election in Christ is full of sweet, pleasant, and unspeakable comfort to godly persons. . . . It doth greatly establish and confirm their faith of eternal Salvation to be enjoyed through Christ, as because it doth fervently kindle their love towards God.

The Westminster Confession (A.D. 1646)

Earlier in the seventeenth century, kings, princes, electors, and theologians had held a conference in Dordrecht, the Netherlands. The great "Synod of Dort" convened leaders from the English church and scattered European churches to reaffirm the doctrines of grace. It was at Dort where the historic Five Points of Calvinism originated as a condemnation of the followers of Jacob Arminius. Arminianism had been spreading into the churches of the Reformation, reintroducing old Roman errors that were simply recast in Protestant terms. Dort was a decisive No! from the heirs of the Reformation to Arminianism. The Synod of Dort reasserted and clarified total depravity, unconditional election, limited atonement, irresistible grace, and perseverance of the saints (T.U.L.I.P.); and once again Augustinianism triumphed.

I have not included an excerpt from the Confession of Dort, since the entire creedal statement is devoted to these doctrines.

Instead, we will jump to the latter part of that century, when the British Parliament commissioned the kingdom's religious leaders to come up with a confession that would bring unity to the war-torn land. Here is an excerpt:

> God from all eternity did, by the most wise and holy counsel of His own will, freely and unchangeably ordain whatsoever comes to pass. . . . By the decree of God, for the manifestation of His glory, some men and angels are predestined unto everlasting life, and others foreordained to everlasting death. . . . Those of mankind that are predestinated unto life, God, before the foundation of the world was laid, according to His eternal and immutable purpose, and the secret counsel and good pleasure of His will, hath chosen in Christ unto everlasting glory, out of His mere free grace and love, without any foresight of faith or good works, or perseverance in either of them, or any other thing in the creature, as conditions, or causes moving Him thereunto; and all to the praise of His glorious grace. . . . Neither are any others redeemed by Christ, effectually called, justified, adopted, sanctified and saved, but the elect only.

Confession of Dositheus (1672)

This is the most recent document of the Eastern Orthodox Church to have ever received official conciliar Sanction. According to Philip Schaff, "The occasion for the creed was the work of Cyril Lucaris, who had been elected Patriarch of Alexandria in 1602 and Patriarch of Constantinople (the highest position in Orthodoxy) in 1621." Lucaris, with deep sympathies for the

Reformed (Calvinist) churches in teaching "the ancient faith," aroused hatred from the Jesuits (a Roman Catholic order). Although this is the most recent Orthodox statement, it has been repudiated by many within that communion:

> We believe the most good God to have from eternity predestinated unto glory those whom He had chosen, and to have consigned unto condemnation those whom He hath rejected.

The Helvetic Consensus Formula (1675)

> As Christ was from eternity elected the Head, Prince, and Lord of all who, in time, are saved by His grace, so also, in time, He was made Surety of the New Covenant only for those who, by the eternal Election, were given to Him as His own people, His seed and inheritance. . . . He encountered dreadful death in the place of the elect alone, restored only these into the bosom of the Father's grace, and these only He reconciled to God, the offended Father, and delivered from the curse of the law. . . . The Father's election, the Son's redemption, and the Spirit's sanctification is one and the same people.

The London Confession (Philadelphia Conference) of the Baptists (1742)

The American Baptists accepted this confession in 1742, although the English Baptists already had accepted it in the form of the London Confession (1688). This confession of faith is identical to the Westminster Confession—except on matters related to the sacraments. The purpose was to show common agreement on these doctrines of grace.

The New Hampshire Confession of the Baptists in America (1833)

> We believe that Election is the gracious purpose of God, according to which He graciously regenerates, sanctifies and saves sinners . . . that it is a most glorious display of God's sovereign goodness . . . that it excludes boasting, and promotes humility, love, prayer, praise, trust in God, and active imitation of His free mercy . . . that it is the foundation of Christian assurance; and that to ascertain it with regard to ourselves, demands and deserves our utmost diligence.

Abstract of Principles (1859)

This statement was first drawn up for the Southern Baptist denomination and its schools. It is still endorsed and accepted officially by the denomination.

> Election is God's eternal choice of some persons unto everlasting life—not because of foreseen merit in them, but of His mere mercy in Christ—in consequence of which choice they are called, justified and glorified. . . . The Son lives to make intercession for His people. . . . Regeneration is a change of heart, wrought by the Holy Spirit, who quickeneth the dead in trespasses and sins, enlightening their minds spiritually and savingly to understand the Word of God. . . . It is a work of God's free and special grace alone.

Conclusion

I have found it difficult to edit and limit this scriptural, theological, and confessional material. Needless to say, a wealth of material from Scripture and tradition gives unity of support to the truths of God's free grace.

One cannot help noticing that when the church affirms and proclaims this message, it awakens to the world and reawakens the world to God's activity. As for the confessions—the Baptists, Presbyterians, Lutherans, Anglicans and Episcopalians, Congregationalists, and other bodies are founded upon these truths. And the great heroes of our faith—the people who were used by God to usher us into the brightest eras of history, felt these themes at their very heartbeat. The Scriptures are the divine depository of these rich teachings and emphasize them with crystal-clear definition.

It would appear more than a whim or piece of prejudice that we should expect to see a new glorious dawn of God-centered Christianity on the horizon if we once again confess our faith in the Alpha and Omega of creation and salvation. Should we choose to remain in ignorance and apathy, the world will continue to sing other men's songs.

Let us work, for the hour is late. Amen.

Suggested Resources
for Digging Deeper

In this brief study I hope I have sparked your interest in the Reformed faith. To help fan that interest, I have provided the following annotated bibliography as a guide for further study. Even if you have never read a single book on the subject, you will get as much use out of this list as the advanced researcher. Now to explain three key words you'll run into below:

Beginner means that the book suggested requires no prior knowledge of the subject. Here's the place to start.

Intermediate indicates that the book requires some, but not a great deal of, prior study. Perhaps you have read a little bit in passing on the subject; here's your chance to dive a few feet deeper.

Advanced means you probably won't want to jump feet first into this one. There may be some technical words you will never have heard before and that might put you off a bit. But if you are fairly familiar already with the subject, dig in!

The History of the Reformation Churches

Cunningham, William. *The Reformers and the Theology of the Reformation* (Edinburgh: Banner of Truth, 1979). Professor of Historical Theology at New College, Edinburgh, Scotland, Cunningham (1805–61) takes a sympathetic, yet balanced, look at the development of Reformation theology (emphasizing the Reformed side of the family tree). *Intermediate.*

Dickens, A. G. *The English Reformation* (New York: Schocken, 1964). The dean of English Reformation studies makes this an interesting introduction for those who have some background in the larger Reformation picture. *Intermediate.*

Dillenberger, John, ed. *John Calvin: Selections from His Writings* (Missoula, Mont.: Scholars Press for the American Academy of Religion, 1975). *Intermediate.*

Dillenberger, John, ed. *Martin Luther: Selections from His Writings* (New York: Anchor, 1961). For something a little lighter than the previous entry, there is this popular (and more readily available) collection. Everything of Luther's you absolutely *must* read is here, although it's difficult to read mere selections from the Reformer's commentary on Galatians. *Beginner.*

Ganoczy, Alexandre. *The Young Calvin* (Philadelphia: Westminster, 1987). This excellent study, written by a Roman Catholic priest and professor of theology, is now available in English after it has already generated much discussion in Europe. This may be the best modern study of Calvin's theological and spiritual development to date as Ganoczy demonstrates a command of the primary as well as secondary sources. *Advanced.*

Hillerbrand, Hans, ed. *The Reformation: A Narrative History Related by Contemporary Observers and Participants* (Grand Rapids, Mich.: Baker, 1978). A fascinating collection of firsthand accounts. It reads like a movie script in places and includes Roman Catholic reaction in the Counter-Reformation. Illustrations and woodcuts from the period make this an extraordinary companion to a simple historical overview. *Intermediate.*

Lull, Timothy, ed. *Martin Luther's Basic Theological Writings* (Minneapolis: Fortress, 1989). At 755 pages, this is a pretty comprehensive collection of Luther's best. From informal correspondence to seasonal sermons, to a constitution for setting up a school system, this collection does not stop with the familiar essays on Christian liberty and justification. Even if you've read Luther's collections before, this one is likely to sneak in a few surprises. *Intermediate.*

McNeill, John Thomas. *The History and Character of Calvinism* (Oxford: Oxford University Press, 1979). A standard work on the subject. McNeill highlights the major contributions of the Reformed churches not only to the religious life of the West, but also to its cultural and social progress as well. Overall, a good "big picture" of the Reformed tradition from the sixteenth century to World War II. *Intermediate.*

Neill, Stephen. *Anglicanism,* 4th edition (New York: Oxford University Press, 1978). A helpful book for understanding the influence of the Reformation on the English Church within the larger discussion of its whole history. *Advanced.*

Noll, Mark A., ed. *Confessions and Catechisms of the Reformation* (Grand Rapids, Mich.: Baker, 1991). At last, an easy-to-read collection of the central documents of the Reformation churches. Even the Anabaptist confession and the Counter-Reformation Canons and Decrees of the Council of Trent are included. A terrific resource. *Beginner.*

Oberman, Heiko A. *Forerunners of the Reformation: The Shape of Late Medieval Thought* (Philadelphia: Fortress, 1981). Though Oberman is criticized by some as regarding the Reformation as something like a footnote to medieval scholasticism, this is a terrific collection of original sources that remind us that there was at least a tradition of staunch Augustinianism even before the Reformation. *Intermediate.*

Olin, John C., ed. *A Reformation Debate: Sadoleto's Letter to the Genevans and Calvin's Reply* (Grand Rapids, Mich.: Baker, 1976). With an appendix on the debate over justification, this handy 135-page book provides a terrific glimpse of the substance of the Reformation's debate. The Genevan cardinal had written a stirring appeal for his flock to return to the Roman Catholic fold, but the city council asked John Calvin himself to issue the reply. Here Calvin explains to the cardinal, and to the whole church, why the Reformation was necessary. *Beginner.*

Parker, T. H. L. *John Calvin: A Biography* (Philadelphia: Westminster, 1975). One of the most respected Calvin scholars, Dr. Parker writes a readable biography that has yet to be surpassed as a basic introduction. The BBC calls it "a rating good yarn about one of the greatest Christians of all time." *Beginner.*

Pauck, Wilhelm, ed. *Melanchthon and Bucer* (Philadelphia: Westminster, 1969). This is from the Library of Christian Classics and includes important contributions from Luther's associate and Calvin's mentor. *Advanced.*

Reid, W. Stanford, and Paul Woolley, eds. *John Calvin: His Influence in the Western World* (Grand Rapids, Mich.: Zondervan, 1982). If you really want to see the cultural implications, take a look at this collection from a handful of respected Calvin scholars. This book examines the historical impact of Calvinism not only on the well-known paths of Western Europe, but in Eastern Europe as well, where Calvinism gained a large initial following. This really is a terrific introduction to Calvinism's vast influence. *Beginner.*

Rupp, E. Gordon, and Philip S. Watson, ed. and trans. *Luther and Erasmus: Free Will and Salvation* (Philadelphia: Westminster, 1969). This is from the Library of Christian Classics and includes Erasmus's *Freedom of the Will* as well as Luther's celebrated *Bondage of the Will,* which Luther considered his most important work. "Must" reading. *Intermediate.*

Ryken, Leland. *Worldly Saints: The Puritans As They Really Were* (Grand Rapids, Mich.: Zondervan, 1986). A Wheaton College literature professor and respected author takes a fresh look at the misunderstood Puritans and admires them for many of the very qualities they are popularly assumed to have lacked. An introduction is provided from J. I. Packer. *Beginner.*

Spitz, Lewis W. *The Renaissance and Reformation Movements,* The Rand McNally History Series (Chicago: Rand McNally, 1971). A standard textbook by one of the world's leading Reformation scholars. Dr. Spitz is professor of history at Stanford University. *Intermediate.*

Wallace, Ronald S. *Calvin, Geneva and the Reformation* (Grand Rapids, Mich.: Baker, 1988). To those interested in the social and political as well as religious implications of the movement, here's one for you. *Intermediate.*

Wells, David F., and Roger R. Nicole, eds. *Reformed Theology in America: A History of Its Modern Development* (Grand Rapids, Mich.: Eerdmans, 1985). *Beginner.*

General Doctrinal Studies

Bavinck, Herman. *The Doctrine of God* (Grand Rapids, Mich.: Eerdmans, 1951). *Intermediate.*

————. *Our Reasonable Faith* (Grand Rapids, Mich.: Eerdmans, 1956). *Intermediate.*

Berkhof, Louis. *Systematic Theology,* 2d rev. and enl. ed. (Grand Rapids, Mich.: Eerdmans, 1941). Most contemporary Reformed students turn first to this volume for systematic theology. *Intermediate.*

Calvin, John. *The Institutes of the Christian Religion,* edited by John T. McNeill, trans. by Lewis Ford Battles, Library of Christian Classics (Philadelphia: Westminster, 1960). *Intermediate.*

Calvin, John. *The Institutes of the Christian Religion,* Tony Lane and Hilary Osborne, eds. (Grand Rapids, Mich.: Baker, 1987). An abridged edition of any book is like walking into the middle of a movie, and more so when it is a classic. Nevertheless, Lane and Osborne have done a service for people who are taking their first steps in the wisdom and insight of Calvin. *Beginner.*

Hoekema, Anthony A. *Created in God's Image* (Grand Rapids, Mich.: Eerdmans, 1986). The best study on the subject of the image of God in humans. *Beginner/Intermediate.*

Godfrey, W. Robert, and Jess L. Boyd, III, eds. *Through Christ's Word* (Phillipsburg, N.J.: Presbyterian and Reformed, 1985). A festschrift for Westminster professor, Philip E. Hughes, this volume includes a number of interesting chapters spanning the horizon of Reformed thought from New Testament studies (Ridderbos, Morris, Bruce); Old Testament studies (Kline, Dillard, and Smick); historical and theological studies, including one of the best essays to date on Arminianism, by J. I. Packer. Stanford Reid, Roger Nicole, and Robert Godfrey are among those rounding out this handy volume. *Advanced.*

Meeter, H. Henry. *The Basic Ideas of Calvinism,* 6th ed., revised by Paul A. Marshall (Grand Rapids, Mich.: Baker, 1990). *Beginner.*

Packer, J. I. *God's Words: Studies of Key Bible Themes* (Downers Grove, Ill.: InterVarsity, 1981). *Beginner.*

————. *Knowing God* (Downers Grove, Ill.: InterVarsity, 1979). This has become a classic. Packer has proved wrong the shibboleth "doctrine doesn't sell." The best popular/devotional introduction to the doctrine of God. *Beginner.*

————. *Knowing Man* (Westchester, Ill.: Cornerstone, 1978). *Beginner.*

Christ's Person and Work

Athanasius. *On the Incarnation,* trans. and edited by Sister Penelope Lawson (New York: Macmillan, 1946), with a terrific introduction by C. S. Lewis. *Intermediate.*

Bray, Gerald. *Creeds, Councils and Christ* (Downers Grove, Ill.: InterVarsity, 1984). In only 215 pages, an outstanding introduction to the development of the church's understanding of Christ. *Beginner.*

Cheeseman, John, Philip Gardner, Michael Sadgrove, and Tom Wright. *The Grace of God in the Gospel* (Edinburgh: Banner of Truth, 1976). Four Oxford undergraduates, all office-holders in the Oxford Inter-Collegiate Christian Union, seek a recovery of the gospel of grace in our time. *Beginner.*

Custance, Arthur. *The Sovereignty of Grace* (Phillipsburg, N.J.: Presbyterian and Reformed, 1979). *Beginner.*

Hoekema, Anthony. *Saved by Grace* (Grand Rapids, Mich.: Eerdmans, 1989). A "must." *Beginner.*

Kuiper, R. B. *For Whom Did Christ Die?* (Grand Rapids, Mich.: Baker, 1982). In 100 pages the reader is able to scan the basic arguments for particular redemption. *Beginner.*

Morris, Leon. *The Atonement* (Downers Grove, Ill.: InterVarsity, 1983). A readable, popular treatment. *Beginner/Intermediate.*

Muller, Richard A. *Christ and the Decree: Christology and Predestination in Reformed Theology from Calvin to Perkins* (Grand Rapids, Mich.: Baker, 1986). *Advanced.*

Murray, John. *Redemption Accomplished and Applied* (Grand Rapids, Mich.: Eerdmans, 1955). This is your best bet for a popular survey of the Reformed doctrine of salvation. *Beginner.*

Owen, John. *The Death of Death in the Death of Christ* (Edinburgh: Banner of Truth, 1983). As vice-chancellor of Oxford, Owen was perhaps the most articulate defender of orthodox Calvinism in the seventeenth century. In this volume he treats the subject of Christ's death—both its nature *and* extent. Packer's famous introduction is worth the price of the book. *Advanced.*

Pinnock, Clark. *The Grace of God and the Will of Man: A Case for Arminianism* (Grand Rapids, Mich.: Zondervan, 1989). For the other side, see this collection. *Intermediate.*

Valdes, Juan de, and Don Benedetto. *The Benefit of Christ,* James Houston, ed. (Portland, Ore.: Multnomah, 1984). Even before Luther, Juan de Valdes, a Spanish priest, discovered the doctrine of justification. This work bears striking similarity to the work of the other Reformers. An immensely practical, devotional approach to Christ's work. *Beginner.*

Warfield, B. B. *The Person and Work of Christ* (Phillipsburg, N.J.: Presbyterian and Reformed, 1958). The great Princeton theologian on his favorite subject. *Advanced.*

———. *Studies in Perfectionism* (Phillipsburg, N.J.: Presbyterian and Reformed, 1958). *Advanced.*

———. *Biblical and Theological Studies* (Phillipsburg, N.J.: Presbyterian and Reformed, 1958). *Advanced.*

———. *The Plan of Salvation* (Grand Rapids, Mich.: Eerdmans, 1980). Though no more than 100 pages, this brief survey outlines the particularism evident in God's plan of salvation and explains the meaning of Christ's being the Savior of the world. *Intermediate.*

The Doctrine of Justification

Luther, Martin. *Commentary on Galatians* (Grand Rapids, Mich.: Baker, 1975). Here is Luther at his best. *He* may have thought the *Bondage of the Will* was his best work, but this commentary is what most of his admirers regard as his most impressive treatise. Among them was John Bunyan, who wrote, "I do prefer this book of Martin Luther upon the Galatians, excepting the Holy Bible itself, before all books that I have ever seen." *Beginner.*

McGrath, Alister. *Justitia Dei* (Cambridge: Cambridge University Press, 1986). A sweeping study of the history of the doctrine in Christian history. *Advanced.*

————. *Justification by Faith: What It Means for Us Today* (Grand Rapids, Mich.: Zondervan, 1988). Here's a much more popular treatment directed to the layperson. *Beginner.*

The Christian Life

Alexander, Donald L., ed. *Christian Spirituality: Five Views of Sanctification* (Downers Grove, Ill.: InterVarsity, 1988). This volume explores the Lutheran, Reformed, Holiness/Pentecostal, and Contemplative traditions. Very helpful in pointing out the similarities between the Lutheran and Reformed views on one hand, and the other positions. *Intermediate.*

Bromiley, Geoffrey W. *Children of Promise* (Grand Rapids, Mich.: Eerdmans, 1979). I dare you to find a better defense of infant baptism in 100 pages. Bromiley exegetes the major texts. *Beginner.*

Hooker, Thomas. *The Poor Doubting Christian Drawn to Christ* (Grand Rapids, Mich.: Baker, 1981). We've all doubted a time or two, and this thin paperback has dried many an eye. An outstanding figure in English Puritanism, Hooker left to become one of the founders of Connecticut. Written in a conversational style, every Christian will find in it the comfort of knowing Christ is really enough. *Beginner.*

Knox, D. Broughton. *The Lord's Supper from Wycliffe to Cranmer* (London: The Paternoster Press, 1983). From the "Morningstar" to the full dawn of the Reformation, Knox traces the development of the English Reformed doctrine of communion. *Intermediate.*

Marcel, Pierre Ch. *The Biblical Doctrine of Infant Baptism,* Philip Hughes, trans. (Greenwood, S.C.: The Attic Press, 1981). This pastor of the French Reformed Church produces convincing proofs from Scripture, demonstrating the necessity of infant baptism for the maintenance of the covenantal theology running from Genesis to Revelation. *Intermediate.*

Packer, J. I. *Keep in Step with the Spirit* (Old Tappan, N.J.: Revell, 1984). *Intermediate.*

————. *A Quest for Godliness* (Wheaton, Ill.: Crossway, 1991). A collection of essays and addresses on Dr. Packer's favorite subject: Puritan spirituality. *Intermediate.*

Sartelle, John. *What Every Christian Parent Should Know about Infant Baptism* (Phillipsburg, N.J.: Presbyterian and Reformed, 1989). Even shorter, but very helpful. *Beginner.*

Last Things

Clouse, Robert, ed. *The Meaning of the Millennium: Four Views* (Downers Grove, Ill.: InterVarsity, 1977). This is what you want for a basic overview of the major eschatological positions, written by those who hold them. *Beginner.*

Davis, John Jefferson. *Christ's Victorious Kingdom: Postmillennialism Reconsidered* (Grand Rapids, Mich.: Baker, 1987). Davis defends the postmillennialism which reigned in American evangelicalism since the Puritans and distinguishes the position from the common distortions. If you think that postmillennialism equals theonomy or Christian Reconstruction, Davis will give you something to reconsider. *Intermediate.*

Erickson, Millard J. *Contemporary Options in Eschatology* (Grand Rapids, Mich.: Baker, 1983). For those who already have some background, this volume explains some of the more subtle nuances of the positions and the minds that have shaped modern eschatological studies. *Advanced.*

Hendriksen, William. *More Than Conquerors* (Grand Rapids, Mich.: Baker, 1940). If you're looking for a readable, sound commentary on the Revelation, look no further. *Beginner.*

Hoekema, Anthony. *The Bible and the Future* (Grand Rapids, Mich.: Eerdmans, 1979). The best introduction to amillennialism on the market. *Beginner.*

Ladd, George. *The Blessed Hope* (Grand Rapids, Mich.: Eerdmans, 1956). The dean of historic premillennialism presents his case cogently. *Intermediate.*

Ridderbos, Herman. *The Coming of the Kingdom* (Phillipsburg, N.J.: Presbyterian and Reformed, 1962). For the Reformation tradition, eschatology has more to do with the *history* of redemption than with speculation about the *future.* In this volume you will get a good feel for the depth and richness of Reformed eschatology. *Intermediate.*

Information on the Alliance
and the Cambridge Declaration

Alliance Information

The Alliance is a broad coalition of evangelical Christian leaders from a number of different denominations, including Baptist, Independent, Lutheran, Presbyterian, and Reformed. Our purpose is to call the church, amidst our dying culture, to repent of its worldliness, to recover and confess the truth of God's Word as did the Reformers, and to see that truth embodied in doctrine, worship, and life.

Cambridge Declaration

Evangelical churches today are increasingly dominated by the spirit of this age rather than by the Spirit of Christ. As evangelicals, we call ourselves to repent of this sin and to recover the historic Christian faith.

In the course of history words change. In our day this has happened to the word "evangelical." In the past it served as a bond of unity between Christians from a wide diversity of church traditions. Historic evangelicalism was confessional. It embraced the essential truths of Christianity as those were defined by the great ecumenical councils of the church. In addition, evangelicals also shared a common heritage in the "solas" of the sixteenth century Protestant Reformation.

Today the light of the Reformation has been significantly dimmed. The consequence is that the word "evangelical" has become so inclusive as to have lost its meaning. We face the peril of losing the unity it has taken centuries to achieve. Because of this crisis and because of our love of Christ, his gospel and his church, we endeavor to assert anew our commitment to the central truths of the Reformation and of historic evangelicalism. These truths we affirm not because of their role in our traditions, but because we believe that they are central to the Bible.

Sola Scriptura: The Erosion of Authority

Scripture alone is the inerrant rule of the church's life, but the evangelical church today has separated Scripture from its authoritative function. In practice, the church is guided, far too often, by the culture. Therapeutic technique, marketing strategies, and the beat of the entertainment world often have far more to say about what the church wants, how it functions and what it offers, than does the Word of God. Pastors have neglected their rightful oversight of worship, including the doctrinal content of the music. As biblical authority has been abandoned in practice, as its truths have faded from Christian consciousness, and as its doctrines have lost their saliency, the church has been increasingly emptied of its integrity, moral authority and direction.

Rather than adapting Christian faith to satisfy the felt needs of consumers, we must proclaim the law as the only measure of true righteousness and the gospel as the only announcement of saving truth. Biblical truth is indispensable to the church's understanding, nurture, and discipline.

Scripture must take us beyond our perceived needs to our real needs and liberate us from seeing ourselves through the seductive images, cliches, promises and priorities of mass culture. It is only in the light of God's truth that we understand ourselves aright and see God's provision for our need. The Bible, therefore, must be taught and preached in the church. Sermons must be expositions of the Bible and its teachings, not expressions of the preacher's opinions or the ideas of the age. We must settle for nothing less than what God has given.

The work of the Holy Spirit in personal experience cannot be disengaged from Scripture. The Spirit does not speak in ways that are independent of Scripture. Apart from Scripture we would never have known of God's grace in Christ. The biblical Word, rather than spiritual experience, is the test of truth.

Thesis One: Sola Scriptura

We reaffirm the inerrant Scripture to be the sole source of written divine revelation,which alone can bind the conscience. The Bible alone teaches all that is necessary for our salvation from sin and is the standard by which all Christian behavior must be measured.

We deny that any creed, council or individual may bind a Christian's conscience, that the Holy Spirit speaks independently of or contrary to what is set forth in the Bible, or that personal spiritual experience can ever be a vehicle of revelation.

Solus Christus: The Erosion of Christ-Centered Faith

As evangelical faith becomes secularized, its interests have been blurred with those of the culture. The result is a loss of absolute values, permissive individualism, and a substitution of wholeness for holiness, recovery for repentance, intuition for truth, feeling for belief, chance for providence, and immediate gratification for enduring hope. Christ and his cross have moved from the center of our vision.

Thesis Two: Solus Christus

We reaffirm that our salvation is accomplished by the mediatorial work of the historical Christ alone. His sinless life and substitutionary atonement alone are sufficient for our justification and reconciliation to the Father.

We deny that the gospel is preached if Christ's substitutionary work is not declared and faith in Christ and his work is not solicited.

Sola Gratia: The Erosion of The Gospel

Unwarranted confidence in human ability is a product of fallen human nature. This false confidence now fills the evangelical world; from the self-esteem gospel, to the health and wealth gospel, from those who have transformed the gospel into a product to be sold and sinners into consumers who want to buy, to others who treat Christian faith as being true simply because it works. This silences the doctrine of justification regardless of the official commitments of our churches.

God's grace in Christ is not merely necessary but is the sole efficient cause of salvation. We confess that human beings are born spiritually dead and are incapable even of cooperating with regenerating grace.

Thesis Three: Sola Gratia

We reaffirm that in salvation we are rescued from God's wrath by his grace alone. It is the supernatural work of the Holy Spirit that brings us to Christ by releasing us from our bondage to sin and raising us from spiritual death to spiritual life.

We deny that salvation is in any sense a human work. Human methods, techniques, or strategies by themselves cannot accomplish this transformation. Faith is not produced by our unregenerated human nature.

Sola Fide: The Erosion of The Chief Article

Justification is by grace alone through faith alone because of Christ alone. This is the article by which the church stands or falls. Today this article is often ignored, distorted, or sometimes even denied by leaders, scholars, and pastors who claim to be evangelical. Although fallen human nature has always recoiled from recognizing its need for Christ's imputed righteousness, modernity greatly fuels the fires of this discontent with the biblical Gospel. We have allowed this discontent to dictate the nature of our ministry and what it is we are preaching.

Many in the church growth movement believe that sociological understanding of those in the pew is as important to the success of the gospel as is the biblical truth which is proclaimed. As a result, theological convictions are frequently divorced from the work of the ministry. The marketing orientation in many churches takes this even further, erasing the distinction between the biblical Word and the world, robbing Christ's cross of its offense, and reducing Christian faith to the principles and methods which bring success to secular corporations.

While the theology of the cross may be believed, these movements are actually emptying it of its meaning. There is no gospel except that of Christ's substitution in our place whereby God imputed to him our sin and imputed to us his righteousness. Because he bore our judgment, we now walk in his grace as those who are forever pardoned, accepted and adopted as God's children. There is no basis for our acceptance before God except in Christ's saving work, not in our patriotism, churchly devotion, or moral decency. The gospel declares what God has done for us in Christ. It is not about what we can do to reach him.

Thesis Four: Sola Fide

We reaffirm that justification is by grace alone through faith alone because of Christ alone. In justification Christ's righteousness is imputed to us as the only possible satisfaction of God's perfect justice.

We deny that justification rests on any merit to be found in us, or upon the grounds of an infusion of Christ's righteousness in us, or that an institution claiming to be a church that denies or condemns sola fide can be recognized as a legitimate church.

Soli Deo Gloria: The Erosion of God-Centered Worship

Wherever in the church biblical authority has been lost, Christ has been displaced, the gospel has been distorted, or faith has been perverted, it has always been for one reason: Our interests have displaced God's and we are doing his work in our way. The loss of God's centrality in the life of today's church is common and lamentable. It is this loss that allows us to transform worship into entertainment, gospel preaching into marketing, believing into technique, being good into feeling good about ourselves, and faithfulness into being successful. As a result, God, Christ, and the Bible have come to mean too little to us and rest too inconsequentially upon us.

God does not exist to satisfy human ambitions, cravings, the appetite for consumption, or our own private spiritual interests. We must focus on God in our worship, rather than the satisfaction of our personal needs. God is sovereign in worship; we are not. Our concern must be for God's kingdom, not our own empires, popularity or success.

Thesis Five: Soli Deo Gloria

We reaffirm that because salvation is of God and has been accomplished by God, it is for God's glory and that we must glorify him always. We must live our entire lives before the face of God, under the authority of God and for his glory alone.

We deny that we can properly glorify God if our worship is confused with entertainment, if we neglect either Law or Gospel in our preaching, or if self-improvement, self-esteem, or self-fulfillment are allowed to become alternatives to the gospel.

A Call To Repentance & Reformation

The faithfulness of the evangelical church in the past contrasts sharply with its unfaithfulness in the present. Earlier in this century, evangelical churches sustained a remarkable missionary endeavor, and built many religious institutions to serve the cause of biblical truth and Christ's kingdom. That was a time when Christian behavior and expectations were markedly different from those in the culture. Today they often are not. The evangelical world today is losing its biblical fidelity, moral compass and missionary zeal.

We repent of our worldliness. We have been influenced by the "gospels" of our secular culture, which are no gospels. We have weakened the church by our own lack of serious repentance, our blindness to the sins in ourselves which we see so clearly in others, and our inexcusable failure to adequately tell others about God's saving work in Jesus Christ.

We also earnestly call back erring professing evangelicals who have deviated from God's Word in the matters discussed in this Declaration. This includes those who declare that there is hope of eternal life apart from explicit faith in Jesus Christ, who claim that those who reject Christ in this life will be annihilated rather than endure the just judgment of God through eternal suffering, or who claim that evangelicals and Roman Catholics are one in Jesus Christ even where the biblical doctrine of justification is not believed.

The Alliance of Confessing Evangelicals asks all Christians to give consideration to implementing this Declaration in the church's worship, ministry, policies, life, and evangelism.

For Christ's sake. Amen.

The Council of the Alliance of Confessing Evangelicals

Dr. Gerald Bray
Dr. Mark Dever
Dr. Ligon Duncan
Dr. Robert Godfrey
Dr. John Hannah
Dr. Michael Horton
Rev. John Nunes
Mrs. Rosemary Jensen
Rev. Ken Jones
Dr. J.A.O. Preus
Dr. Rod Rosenbladt
Dr. Philip Ryken
Dr. R.C. Sproul
Dr. Mark Talbot
Dr. Gene Edward Veith
Dr. Paul F.M. Zahl

Notes

Introduction: Welcome to the Reformation

1. Randall Balmer, *Mine Eyes Have Seen the Glory: A Journey into the Evangelical Subculture in America* (New York: Oxford University Press, 1989), 156.

Chapter 1: Jumping through Hoops Is for Circus Animals

1. Daniel Thrapp, *The Choice of Truth,* in *The Encyclopedia of Religious Quotations,* Frank S. Mead, ed. (Westwood, N.J.: Revell, 1976), 677.

2. Eugene F. Rice, Jr., *The Foundations of Early Modern Europe, 1460–1559* (New York: Norton, 1970), 136.

Chapter 2: Created with Class

1. John Calvin, *The Institutes of the Christian Religion* (Philadelphia: Westminster, 1960), 1.15.1.

2. Sir John Eccles, "Science Can't Explain," *U.S. News and World Report* (February 1985).

3. Calvin, *Institutes,* 1.14.20.

4. Ibid.

5. Rabbi Harold S. Kushner, *When Bad Things Happen to Good People* (New York: Avon, 1981), 42–43.

6. Henri Frederic Amiel, in *The Encyclopedia of Religious Quotations,* Frank S. Mead, ed. (Westwood, N.J.: Revell, 1976).

7. Philip James Bailey, ibid.

Chapter 3: Rebels without a Cause

1. Bernard Spilka et al., *The Psychology of Religion: An Empirical Approach* (Englewood Cliffs, N.J.: Prentice-Hall, 1985), 267–68.

2. Robert Rosenblatt, "What Really Matters?" *Time* (October 1983), 24–27.

3. Martin Luther, *The Bondage of the Will.* In Weimar edition of *Luther's Works,* 18.643—E op var arg 7, 156.

Chapter 4: Grace before Time

1. Martin Luther, *The Bondage of the Will* (Grand Rapids, Mich.: Baker, 1976), 113.

Chapter 5: So What?

1. James Daane, *The Freedom of God: A Study of Election and Pulpit* (Grand Rapids, Mich.: Eerdmans, 1973), 14.

2. Martin Luther, *The Bondage of the Will* (Philadelphia: Westminster, 1975), 117.

3. Ibid.

4. Martin Luther, *The Bondage of the Will* (Grand Rapids: Baker, 1976), 217.

5. John R. W. Stott, *God's New Society: The Message of Ephesians* (Downers Grove, Ill.: InterVarsity, 1982).

Chapter 6: Climbing Jacob's Ladder

1. John Boys, quoted in *The Golden Treasury of Puritan Quotations,* compiled by I. D. E. Thomas (Carlisle, Penn.: Banner of Truth, 1977), 47.

Chapter 7: Mission Accomplished

1. Lewis Sperry Chafer, "For Whom Did Christ Die?" reprinted in *Bibliotheca Sacra* (Oct.-Dec. 1980), 325.

2. Benjamin B. Warfield, *The Plan of Salvation* (Grand Rapids, Mich.: Eerdmans, 1942, reprinted 1980), 95.

3. Charles G. Finney, *Systematic Theology* (Minneapolis, Minn.: Bethany Fellowship, 1985), 217, 206.

4. Robert Lightner, "For Whom Did Christ Die?" in *Walvoord, a Tribute,* John F. Walvoord and Donald K. Campbell (Chicago: Moody, 1982), 162.

Chapter 8: Intoxicating Grace

1. J. B. Phillips, quoted in Norman Geisler, "God, Evil, and Dispensation," *Tribute to Walvoord,* John F. Walvoord and Donald K. Campbell (Chicago: Moody, 1982), 162.

2. A. W. Tozer, *The Best of A. W. Tozer* (Grand Rapids, Mich.: Baker, 1980), 175.

3. John R. W. Stott, *God's New Society* (Downers Grove, Ill.: InterVarsity, 1982).

4. Martin Luther, *The Bondage of the Will* (Grand Rapids: Baker, 1976), 36.

5. D. James Kennedy, *Truths That Transform* (Old Tappan, N.J.: Revell, 1974), 39–40.

6. Will Metzger, *Tell the Truth* (Downers Grove, Ill.: InterVarsity, 1981).

Chapter 9: Righteous Sinners

1. Donald Alexander, ed., *Christian Spirituality: Five Views of Sanctification* (Downers Grove, Ill.: InterVarsity, 1988), 84.

2. Russell P. Spittler.

3. William Law, *William Law on Christian Perfection* (Carol Stream, Ill.: Creation House, 1975), 137–38.

4. Outler, ed., *Wesley's Works* 2:127.

5. *Christian Spirituality,* 84.

6. John Dillenberger, ed., *Martin Luther* (New York: Doubleday, 1961), 18.

7. John Calvin, *Institutes,* 4.8.15.

8. C. H. Spurgeon, quoted in *The Presbyterian* (February 19, 1876), 9.

9. Benjamin B. Warfield, *Studies in Perfectionism* (Phillipsburg, N.J.: Presbyterian and Reformed, 1958), 376.

10. Ibid.

11. Ibid.

12. Calvin, *Institutes,* 2.16.19.

13. Ibid., 3.19.1.

14. Ibid., 3.19.7–9.

15. Ibid., 3.19.9.

Chapter 11: Two Keys to Spiritual Growth

1. Kenneth Collins, *Wesley on Salvation* (Grand Rapids, Mich.: Zondervan, 1989), 127.

2. Thomas Aquinas, *Summa Theologica,* Question 84, articles 6–10.

3. Randall Balmer, *Mine Eyes Have Seen the Glory* (New York: Oxford University Press, 1989), 106.

4. Richard Muller, *Dictionary of Latin and Greek Theological Terms* (Grand Rapids, Mich.: Baker, 1985), 267.

5. Henry Vaughan, "The Holy Communion," in *The Anchor Anthology of Seventeenth-Century Verse,* vol. 1 (New York: Doubleday, 1963), 384.

Chapter 12: A Kingdom of Priests

1. Lewis Sperry Chafer, *Basic Bible Doctrines* (Grand Rapids, Mich.: Zondervan), 127.

2. Ibid., 135.

3. Ibid., 136.

4. Ibid., 357.

5. Ibid., 128.

6. R. J. Rushdoony, *Institutes of Biblical Law* (Nutley, N.J.: Craig, 1973), 1:4.

7. Gary North, *Liberating Planet Earth* (Tyler, Tex.: Institute for Biblical Economics, 1987), 23–24.

8. Mark Noll, ed., *Confessions and Catechisms of the Reformation* (Grand Rapids, Mich.: Baker, 1991), 132.

9. Ibid., 53.

10. Quoted in Edward Plass, *What Luther Says* (St. Louis, Mo.: Concordia, 1959), 956.

11. Ibid.

12. Randall Balmer, *Mine Eyes Have Seen the Glory* (New York: Oxford University Press, 1989), 67.

13. John Calvin, *Institutes,* 3.11.6.

14. Thomas Watson, *A Body of Divinity* (Carlisle, Penn.: 1986, reprinted), 306.

15. Ibid.

The Rev. Dr. Michael S. Horton is Associate Professor of Apologetics and Historical Theology at Westminster Theological Seminary in California. In addition to his work at the seminary, Dr. Horton is the President and Chairman of the Council of the Alliance of Confessing Evangelicals. Dr. Horton also co-hosts the *White Horse Inn*, a nationally syndicated, weekly radio talk-show exploring issues of reformational theology in American Christianity. He received his Ph.D. from Wycliff Hall, Oxford, and the University of Coventry. He has also completed a Research Fellowship at Yale University Divinity School.

Dr. Horton is the author/editor of fourteen books. His latest are *A Confessing Theology for Postmodern Times* (Crossway) and *A Better Way: Rediscovering the Drama of God-Centered Worship* (Baker). Another yet to be released is *Covenant and Eschatology: The Divine Drama* (Westminster John Knox). He has written articles for *Modern Reformation, Pro Ecclesia, Christianity Today, The International Journal of Systematic Theology,* and *Books and Culture.* He is a member of the Oxford University Union Society, the Royal Institute of Philosophy, the American Academy of Religion, the American Theological Society, and the Calvin Studies Society.

Dr. Horton is a minister in the United Reformed Churches. He has served three churches in Southern California. Currently, Dr. Horton and his wife, Lisa, reside in Escondido, California.